Tradition

Exploring the Roots of Church Traditions

By Robert Cornuke

Koinonia House

Tradition
© Copyright 2018 Robert Cornuke.
Published by Koinonia House
P.O. Box D
Coeur d'Alene, ID 83816-0347
www.khouse.org

ISBN: 978-1-57821-759-5

All Rights Reserved.
No portion of this book may be reproduced in any form whatsoever without the written permission of the author.

Unless otherwise noted, all Scripture quotations are taken from the Holy Bible, New King James Version. Copyright © 1982 by Thomas Nelson, Inc. Used by permission.

PRINTED IN THE UNITED STATES OF AMERICA

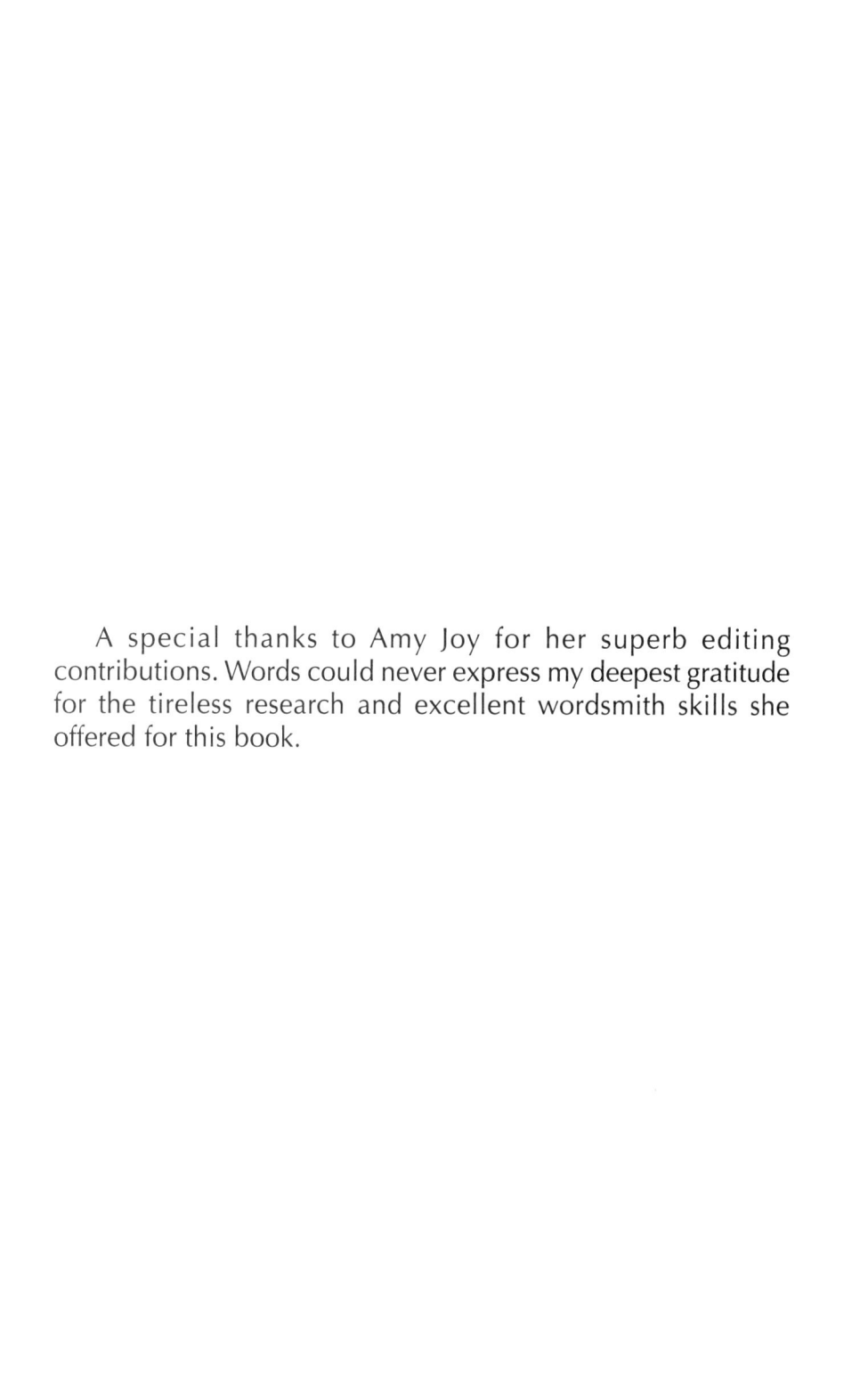

A special thanks to Amy Joy for her superb editing contributions. Words could never express my deepest gratitude for the tireless research and excellent wordsmith skills she offered for this book.

Table of Contents

Introduction 1
Ch. 1: Back in Time 5
Ch. 2: Handling Heretics 9
        The Inquisitions 11
        Church Authority 14
        The Stake 16
        Madame Boursier 16
        The Betrayal of Justice 17
        Robbers and Thieves 18
        Dead Men Tell No Tales 20
        Tradition vs. Christ 20
Ch. 3: Father George 23
        Father George 24
Ch. 4: Usurping Authority 27
        Professing God's Authority 30
        The Precious Word of God 33
        The Kiss of Peace 35
Ch. 5: Metanoia 39
Ch. 6: The Lightning Storm 43
Ch. 7: The Trouble with Tradition 47
        From Servants to Masters 49
        Cheated by Tradition 50
        It is Written 52
Ch. 8: Papal Authority 55
        The Church's Foundation 56
        The Bishop of Rome 58
        Infallibility 60
        Tyranny of the Powerful 63
        Pope Formosus 65
Ch. 9: Vatican I 69
        Vatican I 70
        Personal Responsibility 72

Ch. 10: Rotten Popes 73
Ch. 11: Protestants 77
    Martin Luther 79
Ch. 12: False Documents 81
    The False Decretals... 81
    Donation of Constantine 83
Ch. 13: Major Events: An Overview.................................... 91
Ch. 14: Purgatory 97
    Texts for Purgatory... 98
    History of Purgatory 99
    Gethsemane 102
    Fresh, Clean Clothes.. 104
    Cleansing by Fire.. 104
    Relief in Purgatory.. 105
    Brand New in Christ... 107
    The Fruits of a Tree 108
    Through the Flames... 109
Ch. 15: Treasures.. 111
    A Holy Building 112
    The Treasury of Merit 113
    Pope Sixtus IV 115
    God's Faulty Leaders.. 117
Ch. 16: Holiness and Marriage 119
    Celibacy.. 119
    Celibacy of the Priesthood:... 121
    Marriage.. 123
    Neglect of the Body... 124
    All the Single Ladies 125
Ch. 17: Mary Adulation.. 127
    The Queen of Heaven 130
    Idealism 133
Ch. 18: Saints and Angels 137
    Age-Old Veneration... 139
    Deceptive Spirits 141
    Veneration of Angels 141

- Ch. 19: The Latin Vulgate 143
  - The Apocrypha: 144
  - The Vulgate of Sixtus V 145
- Ch. 20: The Eucharist 149
  - The Elements 149
  - The Massacre at Béziers 150
  - In Remembrance 151
  - Figurative Language in the Bible 154
- Ch. 21: The "Angelic" Religions 157
  - Islam 158
  - In the Face of the Jews 159
  - The Islamic Messiah 160
  - Mormonism 162
- Ch. 22: Archeology and Calvary 169
  - The Garden Tomb 174
- Ch. 23: Galileo 179
- Ch. 24: Jim Irwin 185
- Ch. 25: The Early Church 189
  - Christmas 195
  - Outward v. Inward 196
  - Anti-Semitism: 198
  - State Religion 199
- Ch. 26: Martyrs and Relics 201
  - Relics 201
  - Empty Tombs 202
  - Miracles 204
  - The Pilgrims 206
  - Reliquary Income 207
  - Stumbling Stones 208
  - Fakes and Frauds 211
  - The True Cross 212
- Ch. 27: Charlemagne 215
- Ch. 28: The Crusades 219
  - At Antioch 222
  - At Jerusalem 223

ix

Ch. 29: The Third Crusade and After 227
    International Trade 228
Ch. 30: Torture 231
    Torture Devices 231
    The Witches 233
    No Confidence Vote 234
Ch. 31: The Black Plague 235
Ch. 32: John Wycliffe 239
Ch. 33: The Lollards 245
Ch. 34: Jan Hus 249
Ch. 35: Joan of Arc 253
Ch. 36: Opening the World 261
Ch. 37: St. Peter's Basilica 265
    The Naves in the Nave 266
Ch. 38: John Colet and Erasmus of Rotterdam 269
    Erasmus 270
Ch. 39: Martin Luther 273
Ch. 40: Luther and the Pope 277
Ch. 41: The Popular Response 281
    The Diet of Worms 283
Ch. 42: Final Thoughts 287
About the Author 291

INTRODUCTION

Ignorance. Mud. The plague. When Rome fell to barbarian tribes, the civilization that the caesars had created fell apart. The Mediterranean Sea had been transformed into a Roman Lake as the Empire stretched across the known world, but 500 years after Augustus took the throne, a feeble Rome wallowed in gluttony and laziness. Waves of invasions from Germanic tribes left the Western Roman Empire in disarray. Trade routes were disrupted, infrastructure fell into disrepair, and education was abandoned in the interest of mere survival. The once-mighty empire took its final gasps of dissipated greatness and succumbed to a dusty collapse. Thus, began the Dark Ages, a time known historically for warfare and misery as illiterate hoards overran Europe. During this time of uncertainty, the religious leadership of Rome stepped in to fill the enormous power vacuum.

In many ways, the Roman Church alone preserved the civilization of the dissolved Roman Empire, protecting ancient manuscripts and promoting clerical learning. Church leaders provided direction for fearful populations reeling from an undefined fate. Yet, as the power of the church increased, so did the draw of high church positions. Lingering corruption from pagan Rome seeped into the religious hierarchy, and while there were good popes and bishops devoted to morality and righteousness, there were some really corrupt ones as well. As time went on, the church of Christ looked less and less like Jesus and more like any other human institution. In all times of church history, there have been those who sincerely sought to follow God in Christ Jesus and this is true in the Roman Catholic Church. Conversely, there have been those who used the church to pursue their own self-aggrandizing agendas, to the harm of all.

Tradition

They were dark times. The Word of God was sucked into the religio-political whirlwind of the Middle Ages and copies of the Bible became scarce. Few people could read anyway, and they had to depend on church leaders to teach them God's Word. But, in the mountains and scattered villages of Europe, even the clerics lacked a Bible and most were not up to the task. It was in this medieval petri dish that many church traditions were cultured. Ideas that seemed very reasonable were adopted into law as if they had floated down from God on gossamer wings. But without testing them against the whole counsel of God, practices found nowhere in the Bible became commonplace. Slowly, slowly these traditions from the creative minds of men came to replace simple biblical teachings. Some of these have incited centuries of heated deliberation, raising the serious question: which church traditions are organic to God's intended purposes and which were promoted long ago by men with agendas? That's the primary question.

We have traditions in our churches, and nobody even knows where they came from! We find that a number of traditions crept into the church during the Middle Ages, during a time when people did not have the Bible readily available to read themselves. Confusing ideas crept in, ideas that pointed people in every direction except closer to Jesus Christ. People added their own ideas as additions to the Bible, and we find that's a very dangerous thing to do.

The warning we find in the last words of the Bible should ring alarm bells in the souls of each one of us:

> *For I testify to everyone who hears the words of the prophecy of this book: If anyone adds to these things, God will add to him the plagues that are written in this book; and if anyone takes away from the words of the book of this prophecy, God shall take away his part from the Book of Life, from the holy city, and from the things which are written in this book.*
>
> Revelation 22:18-19

We need to heed these words in Revelation and be careful not to put our own words in God's mouth.

*Beware lest anyone cheat you through philosophy
and empty deceit, according to the tradition of men,
according to the basic principles of the world, and not
according to Christ.*

Colossians 2:8

It is easy to find books that present a hyperbolic history of the Middle Ages with an end game of Catholic bashing. That is not my purpose here. The history of the Roman Catholic Church is the history of the Christian church in the West. It belongs to all of us. What's more, the situation today is light years from the times when popes sanctioned the mass killings of Christian minorities and Jews and any others considered heretics. No more fathers are being dragged from their homes to town squares to be burned alive in front of their children. The screams for mercy have been replaced with calls of "that was then and this is now."

Roman Catholic ministries today practice acts of love that stand across the universe from the abuse of those nefarious times. Roman Catholics perform countless charitable relief efforts in some of the most dangerous and inhospitable places on earth, and these men and women today deserve respect for their devotion to humanitarian acts of feeding the poor and relieving widows and orphans.

Our world looks completely different today than it did during the Spanish Inquisition or the Reformation. Protestants and Catholics have aligned together on many common areas of interest, on morality and family and faith in Christ. There are still profound disagreements and still stark divisions, but we also find a lot of common ground.

As Christian believers, we need to work together to honestly discern what is true. Too often, we find that the unbending faith of those around us is based on nothing more than what their parents told them, without question or biblical justification. We should all dare to be like the Bereans in Acts 17:11, who were called "noble" because they searched the Scriptures to see if the things Paul was teaching them were accurate. God pleads for us to test Him, because through testing comes ultimate truth. Remaining faithful to church dogmas is only commendable if those dogmas are based on the intentions of the Bible's writers.

I find it remarkable that some — not even active in their churches — will defend their particular denomination against challenges even though they may not have a remote clue what the Bible actually says on the matter. Many can quote one verse or another from the Bible, but they have no idea about the multitude of other verses that add perspective to the issue. This is a very thin and dangerous tightrope on which to walk into eternity. If a tradition is from God, we will be able to find it already lodged in the pages of God's Word. If not, we are letting a democracy of the dead guide us into the unknown.

> *Why do you also transgress the commandment of God because of your tradition?*
> Matthew 15:3

To get some answers to this most challenging subject, I determined to perform a historical autopsy on the medieval times for the purpose of finding the roots of common church traditions. These include both those within the Catholic and Protestant faiths. I wanted to know where these doctrines originated and how they came to be so tightly wedged in the public consciousness. I wanted to see if they were justified by the Bible or whether they contradict the words of Jesus Christ. It was a far more difficult task than anticipated as I hacked my way through the thick hide of historical misinformation and past gobs of distortions. I eventually ended up deep into the marrow of those moldering old bones of church tradition, and what I found there left me absolutely stunned.

Chapter 1

Back in Time

Figure 1: Medieval plowman and ox (c. 1300).

Let's say you are a man living in 13th century Europe. Fear is an ominous dark cloud following you for your entire life. Yes, you will love, have children, drink, dance, sing and pray, but lingering behind your every step will be the dread of detrimental mischief from God and the Devil.

Tradition

From as long as you can remember, you have been taught that cunning demons can occupy just about anything. Animals, spiders, dust, the trunk of a tree, or even a stranger, all might be the abode of the Devil himself. As a child, you listened to your grandfather tell scary stories in front of the embers of late night fire. In that flickering glow, you clung breathlessly to every word, imagining frightening things prowling just outside the mud walls of your humble dwelling. You sat, eyes wide open, as the old man told of *dracs* which could grab inattentive lads and drag them, screaming, into the maw of a nearby cave. Then there were the stories of *ghouls* walking along the village edge, creeping in and out of moonlight shadows in search of freshly dug graves.

Fear is everywhere; and sadly, the church seems to add to the problem. The common people know they will suffer God's vengeful wrath if they divert from the priest's words. They fear the church, purgatory, hell, mass, confessionals, torture, war, plagues, witches and all manner of superstitions. A woman might stand vigilant over a shrouded body until burial, fearing a black cat will scamper across the corpse, transforming the deceased into a vampire. To prevent a recently dead man from drowning in the afterlife, ladies hurriedly dump all the water from the flower vases, pots, and bowls in the home.

Despite these things, your small village has always been your home and you know nothing better than the cramped cottages separated by rain rutted lanes and weedy rock walls. Outside your front door, razor backed hogs grunt and wallow in the puddles. Geese and nervy chickens squawk and cluck about the streets. Your yard is piled high with corn cribs, pigeon pens, and a dung mound taller than your front door. Soot from a thousand fires blackens the rafters inside your home, where rats scamper about under the rustling thatch of your roof. The floor beneath your feet is moist from spilled beer and spit. Dried fish skin is stretched over a small window opening to keep out the rain while allowing a few light beams to penetrate the smoky haze.

The church is the most important building in town, although the parapets of the castle poke high above the canopy of trees.

Your neighbor serves as a scullery maid in the castle kitchen, and she tells your wife of bountiful feasts, where tables groan under the weight of pigs and mutton, pies and puddings. Lords and ladies gather around the massive fireplace while their meat roasts to perfection. You don't know whether to believe therse descriptions, but you don't envy the superiors who are granted such wonders. God has made you what you are. Who are you to question God?

You have seen snooping busybodies hanging about under the eaves of your roof, listening to your conversations in the evening. You know that a lonely neighbor woman was overheard talking to herself in her cottage. It was determined she had been communicating with an evil spirit, and she was summarily put on trial. They tortured her horribly until she confessed to being a witch. She was then burned alive at the stake while the other villagers cursed her wickedness. You fear that somebody will find evil in your wife or daughters, and you keep them quietly inside at night.

It's a world of constant anxiety, and there is little comfort from God the supreme Judge. It's not that God is absent. The whole village knows that God is watching and closely observing the daily village activities. When a gust of wind flings open a door, all those present hurriedly make the sign of the cross. The large timbered cross in the square reminds all that God casts His long shadow over their business dealings. God is He who shoots bolts of lightning from the rain gorged clouds, sending many to the church altar to shudder in teeth-grinding terror.

Sunday is a compulsory day for church. If you work in the field on Sunday you fear God will be irritated and perhaps kill you or make your next child malformed. There is no option to remain at home; you will attend church or spend Monday on a wooden cucking stool in the town square to face the jeering of all who pass by.

In the church, there are no pews — just straw scattered to lightly pad the hard ground. A neighbor has carried in a small, hollow metal sphere with a few smoldering coals to add some warmth to the cold, damp room. The village priest dutifully recites the Mass, but neither he nor those in the room can understand a single word of the strange, tortured Latin. It is an exercise in patience to sit silently until the prescribed words come to their end, a stream of little more than mumbled incantations.

Nobody in town owns a Bible. Bibles are rare, carefully copied out by monks in distant monasteries, and lay people aren't permitted to own them. They are especially not free to own Bibles in the common language. A Bible translated into the vernacular is considered contraband, and an unthinkable crime punishable by imprisonment or death.

This was the religious life of the common man in the 13th century. He was required to trust the church leaders for his religious instruction, but too many of the church leaders themselves were ignorant of the Bible's words. Today we question how innocent people were killed for their faith in the Middle Ages. How could such brutality take place in the Christian lands of Europe? To get our answers, let's go back to a time when the official church leadership decided to toss out the Bible as the basis for the Christian faith. It was in the maelstrom of isolation and fear that the light of God's Word was bent into an ethereal abyss and replaced by church traditions that favored those in control. It was also a time when heretics were hunted and killed.

Chapter 2

Handling Heretics

Nor do they light a lamp and put it under a basket, but on a lampstand, and it gives light to all who are in the house.

Matthew 5:15

With the Edict of Thessalonica in A.D. 380, Nicaean Christianity became the official religion of the Roman Empire. Heretical views had cropped up from nearly the very beginning, and Paul was already combatting some of these incorrect ideas in the first century. Church leaders did not resort to violence in those early years, even though some heretical traditions had serious unbiblical beliefs. Cathars, for instance, believed in reincarnation and the transmigration of the soul. Manichaeism and Catharism were both forms of Gnostic dualism, which taught the existence of both a good God and a bad God. They regarded the physical body as evil and the spirit alone as good, which meant their version of Jesus was evil while in His physical body. Gnostics taught that salvation was obtained by knowledge (*gnosis*) rather than the simple sacrifice of Christ. Other heresies were Priscillism and Donatism, which were dedicated to salvation by works. These focused on extreme asceticism or perfection — what Paul calls "will worship" in Colossians 2:23.

Certain church officials believed that the Old Testament gave permission to deal abruptly and physically with all those convicted of heretical beliefs. For instance, in the fourth century, Saint Optatus of Milevis used the golden calf incident in Exodus 32:18-28 and the Midianite incident in Numbers 25:6-9 to defend the right of the civil authorities to put such people to death. In his work *Against the Donatists*, he stated:

> But, say you, the State cannot punish in the name of God. Yet was it not in the name of God that Moses and Phineas consigned to death the worshippers of the Golden Calf and those who despised the true religion?[1]

In the early fifth century, the Bishop of Hippo, Saint Augustine, spoke against the death penalty by citing Jesus' admonition in Matthew 5:44 to love our enemies and pray for them. He wrote:

> It is not their death, but their deliverance from error, that we seek to accomplish by the help of the terror of judges and of laws, whereby they may be preserved from falling under the penalty of eternal judgment..."[2]

The culture of the Middle Ages was hardly gentle. From the beginning of the Medieval Church, cruel punishments were seen as just and necessary toward maintaining holiness. In A.D. 600, Saint Columban demanded six lashes to be laid on the bare back of a monk who had forgotten to say *Amen* after praying. In another case, six lashes were administered to a monk who *sang out of tune*.[3] Even children who simply expressed admiration for those accused as heretics might be taken from their families and thrust into prison.

Eventually the leadership of Europe rejected any merciful, laissez faire approach to heretics. In 1022, France's King Robert the Pious worried that the Manichaeans who had spread throughout Europe were a danger to the kingdom and their message a danger to the salvation of its citizens. A variety of clerics were gathered up and accused of denying the Trinity, the virginity of Mary, and the Bible's version of Creation. They were also indicted (whether justly or not) for taking part in orgies and worship of the Devil. After an eight-hour trial, they were sentenced to death by burning. It was a first for the West.

---
1 St. Optatus of Mileve, *De Schismate Donatistarum*, III, cc. 6-7 (A.D. 375).
2 Augustine of Hippo, *Epistle* 100, n. 1 (A.D. 409).
3 Morris Bishop, *The Middle Ages* (1965; reprint, New York: First Mariner Books, 2001), 12.

December 28, 1022 at least 13 condemned as heretics were burnt alive.[4]

Still, there was an ongoing debate over whether to use the death penalty for heretics. In the 12th century, the learned Petri Cantoris (Peter Canter) argued against executing Catharists, saying:

> Whether they be convicted of error, or freely confess their guilt, Catharists are not to be put to death, at least not when they refrain from armed assaults upon the Church. For although the Apostle said, 'A man that is a heretic after the third admonition, avoid', he certainly did not say, 'Kill him'. Throw them into prison, if you will, but do not put them to death.[5]

THE INQUISITIONS

After the centuries of back-and-forth arguments on the issue, the Old Testament justifications for destroying heretics won out over the New Testament's injunctions of prayer and avoidance. The Medieval Inquisition was established in 1184 to deal with heretics in southern France and northern Italy. When we think of the Inquisition, we think of horrific tortures and executions. In a generic sense, an inquisition is a tribunal court system. The heretical Cathars were the primary targets of this first Inquisition. However, the other principal victims were Waldensians, with whom most Protestants today would identify. The Waldensians affirmed the atoning sacrifice of Jesus Christ for salvation and rejected the idea of

Figure 2: The burning of Cathars at Montsegur.

---
4   Jim Bradbury, *The Capetians: Kings of France 987-1328* (Cornwall: MPG Books, 2007), 88.
5   Petri Cantoris, *Verbum Abbreviatum* c. lxxviii, in Jacques-Paul Migne, *Patrologia Latina* (1845), CCV, 231.

purgatory. The attack on these two groups lasted through the 1230s, but other persecutions followed.

In 1231, Pope Gregory IX instituted the Papal Inquisition to bring heretics to trial. His purpose was actually a good one; he wanted to keep mobs from lynching people who had been accused of heresy and to increase order in the trial process. Gregory did not authorize the use of torture, but the inquisitors often took things into their own hands. Gregory gave a chilling name to his inquisitors; he called them *inquisitor hereticae pravitatis* (inquisitor of heretical depravity). The goal of his Inquisition was to make an inquiry into the nature of the defendant's beliefs and, if necessary, to instruct the accused in the way of correct doctrine.

By 1252, it became clear that the inquisitors were using brutal methods to illicit confessions from accused persons. Pope Innocent IV issued a papal bull *Ad Extirpanda* of 1252, which laid out the circumstances in which torture might be used by the Inquisition. This was as much an effort to establish limits on torture as it was a justification of its use. Jews, Muslims, and Christian minorities were the focus of different waves of persecution, along with any nonbelievers or those suspected of witchcraft.

The Inquisition never reached as far as England, but the British religious authorities did their own part to force fidelity to the Roman Church. When King Henry IV rose to the throne, he cracked down on Christian minorities, particularly the Lollards who had followed John Wycliffe. In 1401, Henry IV legalized the burning of heretics, something his predecessor Richard II had been unwilling to do. A few days before Henry IV's 1401 law *De heretico comburendo* was pronounced, the first Lollard martyr, William Sawtrey, was burned at the stake for heresy. In 1408 Archbishop Thomas Arundel issued his *Constitutions against the Lollards*, making it clear that nobody was permitted to preach or teach from the Bible or produce new Bible translations without going through the official Catholic Church authorities.

Lollards were brave souls who sneaked into villages at night to avoid the attentive eyes of church officials, a vernacular Bible concealed under their cloaks. They read from the Bible in hushed words to those who dared listen. I am sure many hearts soared with hope as they heard and understood the words of Jesus spoken for the first time in a language they understood. Yet, Lollards had to do their work secretly, lest they be caught and face the most brutal punishments.

It wasn't until 1478 that Pope Sixtus IV authorized the infamous Spanish Inquisition, when he gave Ferdinand and Isabella of Spain the authority to name inquisitors. The purpose at that time was to investigate Marranos, Jews forced to convert to Christianity who continued to practice Judaism in secret. The Spanish monarchs used the Inquisition to establish complete dominance over Spain. Severe tactics were used and Pope Sixtus IV tried without success to put a damper on the cruelty. While heretics were investigated under various authorities across Europe, the official Inquisitions in Spain and Portugal were particularly vicious.

The Middle Ages took the teachings of an itinerant preacher named Jesus and manipulated it into a religion of power and wealth. Jesus claimed to be the Way, the Truth, and the Life, and He proved His identity as God's Son by healing multitudes of people, calming storms, and ultimately rising again from the dead. Yet, Jesus never beat or killed anybody who refused to follow Him. When people wanted to leave, He let them leave. Somehow, Christ's love toward human beings was cast aside in the Middle Ages, as those in charge justified the most horrific tortures and executions in His name.

A former Spanish secretary to the Inquisition named Juan Antonio Llorente (1756–1823) gives us one of our earliest histories of those times. Llorente numbered those burned at the stake during the Spanish Inquisition at nearly 32,000, while 300,000 were tried and required to perform various penances.[6] Modern scholars doubt these numbers and offer more conservative figures. However, even if just a few thousand were formally executed by the Spanish Inquisition like historian Henry Kamen suggests,[7] well over 100,000 are believed to have died by torture or languishing in filthy Spanish prisons. And that was

---
6   Cecil Roth, *The Spanish Inquisition* (1937; reprint, New York: W. W. Norton, 1996), 123.
7   Henry Kamen. *The Spanish Inquisition*, (1965; reprint, Yale University Press, 2014), 253.

just Spain. When the executions and persecutions across Europe are considered, those affected can easily number over a million.

CHURCH AUTHORITY

The concern of the Roman Catholic Church was, of course, that heretics would infect the population and bring confusion and schism to the Christian world. Those in charge trusted that the leadership in Rome had produced the purest form of Christian religion and had codified that pure religion into canon law. Therefore, anybody who dared to disagree with those teachings were rebels not only against Rome and the papacy, but against Jesus Christ. The church leadership felt a responsibility to protect Christendom from Satan's pernicious deceptions.

These are not petty concerns. We know that Satan is the father of liars[8] and he is constantly roaming about seeking those he can chew up and swallow.[9] Unbiblical views have infected different Christian groups over the years, some of them very dangerous. We find that cults pop up, and admirers of charismatic leaders might follow them anywhere. The devotees of Jim Jones followed him to Guyana where they ultimately committed mass suicide by drinking poisoned punch in 1978.

We can't forget that religious leadership itself can be corrupted. In other words, being in the position of leadership has never guaranteed that a person is righteous and close to God. In the Bible, there were righteous kings like Josiah and righteous priests like Jehoiada, and they led Israel to follow God faithfully. Walking in accordance with them was therefore walking in accordance with God. There were also corrupt kings like Zedekiah[10] and corrupt priests like Pashhur the son of Immer.[11] If the prophet Jeremiah had wanted to fall into lockstep with the likes of Zedekiah or Pashhur, he would have had to ignore God. Of course, Jeremiah prophesied what God told him to prophesy, and Pashhur had the prophet beaten and put into the stocks. Zedekiah left Jeremiah in prison until Nebuchadnezzar

---
[8] John 8:44
[9] 1 Peter 5:8
[10] Jeremiah 24:8
[11] Jeremiah 20:1-2

the Babylonian conquered Jerusalem.[12] Even in the Bible, those in charge often persecuted the religious minorities who were God's true followers.

In the Middle Ages and into the Renaissance, it became customary to execute those who defied the traditional teachings of the church. There were two big problems with this. First, Jesus never taught his disciples to abuse and kill people. Second, those who were executed were not necessarily defying the teachings of Jesus or the apostles. They were executed for stepping outside the authorized views of the Roman Catholic Church. *Foxe's Book of Martyrs* describes an incident in 1519 in which seven people were burned at the stake for teaching their children the Ten Commandments and the Lord's Prayer *in English* instead of in *Latin*.[13] It seems ludicrous to us today that seven villagers would be burned alive for saying the Lord's Prayer in the wrong language. Jesus didn't even teach the Lord's Prayer in Latin. Yet, the traditions of men, solidified by fear, had shoved the pure Word of God to the back of the line.

We are not burning people at the stake today, but we can still find church congregations with the same bizarre lack of perspective. Whether they are Baptist or Methodist or Pentecostal, we can find some church bodies today that are run by fear and intimidation, and the people within feel that if they leave, they risk giving up their salvation. I'm confident this type of tyranny is *not* the norm, but it's tragic wherever it takes place. The Bible gives us confidence that our salvation is by the blood of Jesus, and not by sitting in any particular pew or following any one particular set of man-made rules.

In the Middle Ages, multitudes were declared heretics simply because they dared to question a religious dictatorship. Of course, this led to abuses of power. Political enemies, those whose lands were coveted, and even those with pretty wives might be subjected to false accusations and unfair trials by men with ulterior motives.

---

12 Jeremiah 38:28
13 John Foxe, "The History of Seven Godly Martyrs Burnt at Coventry," in *Foxe's Book of Martyrs*, Book 8, no. 163 (1563).

The Stake

Burning people alive in Europe was officially legalized by the church in 1197. The civil authorities carried out the executions that the religious authorities had sanctioned. The holy leaders wanted no blood on their own hands.

Heretics were considered possessed by demons, and torture was seen as the means of forcing these unholy spirits from their victims' bodies. It was believed that the spirits would flee if enough pain was applied. The burning flames that produced deadly punishment were seen as a preemptive taste of hellfire, giving the accused a chance to recant before they were consumed.

It seems strange to us that church leaders did not consider torture or burning people as acts of cruelty. They saw these as good deeds that protected the people from spiritual pollution.

Madame Boursier

One sad story is that of Madame Boursier. On August 5, 1234, Dominican inquisitors Guillaume Pelhisson and Raymond de Fauga arrived unannounced at the front door of Madame Boursier's home in Toulouse, France. They had heard rumors of her unorthodox beliefs.

The men shoved the front door open and made their way past stunned family members, up creaking wooden steps to a room at the top of the stairs. The intruders stepped into the dimly lit room where an old woman lay quietly in her bed. Her blurry eyes turned in the direction of the commotion.

An unfamiliar man's voice came from under a woolen hood. "The fear of death should not make you confess anything other than that which you hold firmly and with your whole heart," he told her.

Ill and near delirium, the old woman exhaled a few words too soft to understand. The inquisitors leaned in close to the woman's mouth. She whispered again, but only God and the men knew exactly what she said. Those words would be Madame Boursier's last. The intruders glanced at each other knowingly; they had enough evidence to condemn her as a heretic.

The men wasted no time. They used ropes to tie her tightly against her bedstead. They then carried the bed down the stairway and into the street. Curious onlookers stared at the scene of an old woman lashed to her bed with taut ropes. The crowd followed to a field at the edge of town where a raging bonfire waited. In the dancing glow of flames, the inquisitors flung the accused, bed and all, into the face of the fire.[14]

What thought processes, what reasoning would motivate men to burn a dying old woman in her bed?

When people in Samaria refused to receive Jesus, the disciples suggested they call down fire like Elijah and consume them. Jesus immediately corrected their thinking:

> *But He turned and rebuked them, and said, "You do not know what manner of spirit you are of. For the Son of Man did not come to destroy men's lives but to save them...*
>
> Luke 9:55-56a

This is a serious statement by Jesus. The cruel torture and slaughter of people in Christian Europe did not originate in the heart of Christ. Jesus came to save us, yet the religious leaders of the Middle Ages took it upon themselves to murder anybody they chose. The people then had no option but to follow.

THE BETRAYAL OF JUSTICE

Like Madame Boursier, a large number of alleged heretics suffered under a dysfunctional system. It became possible to accuse a neighbor with no solid evidence. A jealous townsperson might condemn another simply by declaring, "She is a witch! I saw a spider riding happily upon her shoulder."

We are used to a legal system that protects the accused, in which the burden of proof is on the prosecution. The Sixth Amendment guarantees Americans the right to a fair and

---
[14] Based on events from Brenda R. Lewis, *A Dark History: The Popes* (New York: Metro Books, 2009), 68.

speedy trial. We have the right to a jury of our peers and the right to remain silent. We take these rights for granted, but they were developed from unjust practices over the course of many centuries of cruel legal history. We need to be thankful they are offered to us, because they did not protect victims in the past, back when it was possible to be convicted of cavorting with the Devil based on nothing more than the accusation of a scary arachnid perched upon a shoulder.

There were trials and inquiries in those days, but guilt was often assumed. Defense at the trial could be futile, especially since any who dared come to the aid of the accused could be suspected as a confederate in the Devil's cause. Those accused of heresy were tortured to solicit confession, but any stalwart souls who refused to admit guilt, might spend decades in a dungeon. Not confessing meant horrifying torture chambers and squalid prison conditions. Confessions often came — whether in truth or not.

Once convicted, the accused was hanged, or worse, bound to a pike erected in the middle of the town square. Straw was piled at the victim's feet. The fortunate were mercifully garroted before the pyre was lit, but others were left alive to face the flames. When the fire erupted, bystanders cheered wildly.

We might expect fellow townspeople to feel sorrow or compassion, but in those days of hardened ignorance, an execution offered a source of entertainment. Any tender souls would have hidden in their homes or watched from the back, fearing to express their sympathy. The rest of the townspeople shouted and laughed at the condemned in the name of justice. Few were moved by doomed individuals yanking frantically on their sooty chains, pleading. The screams would eventually fade amidst the swirling black smoke.

Robbers and Thieves

Conveniently, church officials and the inquisitors themselves divided up the land holdings and money left behind by those executed. What irony! Was not Jesus Christ killed as a heretic and blasphemer, and didn't soldiers divide up His garments?[15]

Bernard Délicieux (c. 1265–1320) was a Franciscan monk who boldly opposed the Inquisition in Carcassonne, France, accusing the inquisitors of corruption and of abusing their power. He churned up trouble both among religious and political leaders, and in April of 1304, Pope Benedict XI ordered the arrest of Délicieux for "saying such things as we must not."[16] It wasn't until 1317 under Pope John XXII that Délicieux was finally arrested and tortured. After eventually confessing to the charge of obstructing the Inquisition and found guilty of treason, the weakened Délicieux was sentenced to life in solitary confinement. He lived in chains, surviving on bread and water until he died in 1320.

Figure 3: "The Agitator of Languedoc" depicting the trial of Bernard Délicieux before the Inquisition, by Jean-Paul Laurens (1838–1921, Musée des Augustins in Toulouse).

---
15 Psalm 22:18; Matthew 27:35; Luke 23:34; John 19:24
16 O'Shea, Stephen, The Friar Of Carcassonne. Vancouver, BC, Canada: Douglas & McIntyre (2011).

Not all inquisitors escaped justice. In 1560, an official was seen openly consorting with the wife of a man he'd put to death as a heretic. The inquisitor was promptly tried and executed for his opportunistic dalliance.[17]

DEAD MEN TELL NO TALES

As time went by, the numbers of those killed by the church rose to staggering numbers. In their mania, inquisitors even sought out the dead. The call went out far and wide for the names of heretics who had died before they could be officially punished. I imagine interrogators tramping over cemeteries with a shovel in one hand and a list of dead heretics in the other. They dug up corpses in every condition and carted them to their postmortem executions. As the wagon wobbled through town, piled high with decadent bodies, priests followed behind chanting, *"Qui a tal fara, atai pendra"* (Whoever does the same, will suffer a similar fate).[18] When the macabre procession reached the place of execution, the rotted corpses were tied to posts and burned to ash.

TRADITION VS. CHRIST

As we consider these things, it's important to remember that Jesus saved and healed people, eating with tax collectors and prostitutes. People repented of their sins wherever Christ went because of His *love*.[19] Those judged by God in the New Testament, like Ananias and Sapphira in Acts 5 or Herod in Acts 12, are dealt with by God Himself. Yet, the popes ignored the teachings of Jesus and authorized brutal tactics, depending on the traditions of those who had gone before them rather than on the sayings of Jesus, the Lord himself.

Traditions can be good when they help us remember important religious truths, but they can be dangerous when they take the place of dedication to the Word and Spirit of

---
17 Michael Kerrigan, *Dark History of the Catholic Church* (London: Amber Books Limited, Kindle, 2014), 1322.
18 Louis Tanon, *Histoire des Tribunaux de l'Inquisition en France* (Paris: L. Larose & Forcel, 1893), 63.
19 Matthew 9:10-13; Luke 9:54-56, 19:1-10; John 8:1-11

God. Traditions can blind hearts and bend thoughts. Even those dedicated to "obedience" can follow their leaders into evil, because their obedience and devotion are given first to a faulty human being rather than to God.

Ultimately, we have to be careful to take ownership of what we believe. We should never blindly follow the guy in front of us without knowing where he's going. Of course, we also can't go off on our own, creating our own religions based on personal beliefs or feelings. Each of us will stand before God and give account of ourselves, and the Bible must be the authority for every person who desires to be a follower of Christ. That's where we find the trustworthy words of the prophets and apostles. That's where we find the words of Jesus himself.

Chapter 3

Father George

During the Sermon on the Mount, Jesus offered a set of principles, including the following:

But I say to you, love your enemies, bless those who curse you, do good to those who hate you, and pray for those who spitefully use you and persecute you;

Matthew 5:44

When Jesus told one young man to sell everything and follow Him, the young man walked away sad because he was rich.[1] Notice that Jesus didn't chase down the fellow and torment him into changing his mind. The Lord didn't interrogate or torture him. He let the man go.

On the night He was betrayed, Jesus wrapped a towel around himself, took a bowl of water, and went to each of His own disciples and washed their feet. Do you remember what He then said?

So when He had washed their feet, taken His garments, and sat down again, He said to them, "Do you know what I have done to you? You call Me Teacher and Lord, and you say well, for so I am. If I then, your Lord and Teacher, have washed your feet, you also ought to wash one another's feet. For I have given you an example, that you should do as I have done to you."

John 13:12-15

How unlike Christ was church in the Middle Ages!

---
[1] Mark 10:21-24

Father George

Just as I began to write this chapter, right on this page, I received an email from a good friend informing me that another dear friend of mine had died. I feel I now must stop with my intended flow and write about this man. It seems most appropriate and relevant that I do so. I'm changing the chapter title as well, dedicating it to him.

Father George was a Catholic Priest. I am a born again Christian and we obviously shared differing opinions on theological issues of importance. But I came to love Father George as a brother in the cause of Christ's commandment to love orphans and widows. In that we were as one in Christ. My heart is weighed down by the news of his death, and I want to honor this excellent man. Please allow me to insert here a memory of Father George Grima.

Father Grima was born on the tiny island of Gozo in Malta. He was without a doubt, the most humble and giving man I have ever met. His extreme kindness reflects that offered by many in the Catholic Church today.

I once attended an event in Pennsylvania to raise money for African orphans living in abject poverty. I had the pleasure of spending a few days with Father George. We were both guests on a large farm, and we immediately hit it off. We had both spent extensive time in Ethiopia, and both of us had worked to bring aid to the orphans in that country. We talked all day about matters of life and faith, but mostly about the poorest of the world's suffering children.

Father George's kindly face was weathered rough from baking so many years under the African sun. It was mantled by silver hair that guarded his head from those unforgiving rays. He had worked tirelessly in Ethiopia and Kenya to provide food and shelter resources for the impoverished natives while living in the same conditions they did. I learned later that Father George had started hundreds of schools and given care to forty-thousand orphans.

I happened to notice that Father George kept two curled photos in his shirt pocket. Being a bit nosey, I asked him about them, and he willingly slid out the images and showed them to me. One photo was of him standing with Mother Teresa, and the other showed a lonely blue plastic shoe resting alongside the trickle of a once muddy river. He explained that water levels recede during the drought seasons in Africa, and the shoe belonged to a small boy. The child had gone to get some water for his mother and was never seen again — except for this lonely plastic shoe. It was suspected a crocodile had snatched him.

Father George held the image in his hand a long while. His eyes glistened in the afternoon sun as he slowly slid the photo back into his shirt pocket. No words were said after that; none were needed. We sat a long while, staring at the field of tall Pennsylvanian grasses as they swayed back and forth in a humid breeze.

That evening featured a well-catered, sumptuous dinner. Father George seemed unaccustomed to so much food. His eyes scanned the fundraiser's extravagant fare with a look of lingering amazement. He had a quiet demeanor, and he smiled throughout the evening presentations while others made their donation appeals.

The big house sat quiet that night as the guests retired for bed. I was heading off to my own room when a faint light and a rustling in the kitchen caught my attention. I pushed open the door to investigate, and I watched Father George take a loaf of bread from its perch on a full can of garbage. The bread had been left over and thrown out. He tucked the loaf gently under his arm and, offering no explanation, bid me goodnight. I stopped him and asked, "Are you hungry?" I was sure we could provide him fresh food from the well-stocked refrigerator.

"Oh no," he said softly. "I have had more than enough to eat from dinner, and the food in the refrigerator will be eaten by someone soon. This bread has been thrown away needlessly and will be wasted." He tapped the loaf with his strumming fingers and smiled, "I will have this bread for breakfast and will have enough for lunch tomorrow. It is all I need, and it should not go to waste." He said kindly, "I have learned that even old bread is a great and valuable blessing from God and should never go unused."

I learned more about love and humility from a Catholic Priest on a farm in Pennsylvania than anyone else in my life. Here was the humblest of men, who could not let even a single scrap of bread go to waste.

This book will be about God's intended Word. I believe every word in the Bible has authority from above without any need of man's alterations and amendments added from below. In my writing of this book, I will be frank about the trouble with certain traditions, because I cannot let a single scrap of God's grace go to waste. Jesus said in Matthew 4:4, *"It is written, 'Man shall not live by bread alone, but by every word that proceeds from the mouth of God."* If we live our lives by God's Word, then we cannot allow it to be thrown away. However, as I proceed, I do so with a tenderness toward all who are devoted to God, whether or not they embrace the same traditions that I do.

Chapter 4

Usurping Authority

When Pope Nicholas I came to power in A.D. 858, ecumenical councils of the church were still held in the Greek language near Constantinople. There was rampant immorality among the bishops and Charlemagne's empire had disintegrated. Into this general chaos, Nicholas I entered and notably promoted marriage over the wanton adultery and lasciviousness of various church leaders. He excommunicated the eastern patriarch Photius I, who excommunicated Nicholas right back. Most importantly, Nicholas got busy promoting the Roman primacy of the church and his own position as its leader.

Nicholas was an ascetic and respected in Rome, and after his death he was named a saint. However, he is also believed to be the first pope to wear a princely crown with the white linen papal cap, and he fostered the idea that the Roman popes were the highest authority in Christendom. Seeking to solidify the authority of the Roman Catholic Church over Europe, he declared:

> Fear, then, our wrath and the thunders of our vengeance; for Jesus Christ has appointed us [the popes] with his own mouth absolute judges of all men; and kings themselves are submitted to our authority.[1]

This was the toxic soup which was fed to all in the medieval world, and it was boiled from the venomous renderings of fear. Barbarians, wolves, thieves, and demons were all sources of

---
[1] As cited in Richard W. Thompson, *The Papacy and the Civil Power* (New York: Harper & Brothers 1876), 369.

terror, but the church was not a place of refuge, because the church itself nurtured fear. Sadly, this was the platform from which many church traditions were launched.

The Roman Catholic Church prides itself today (and rightly so) for easing much pain, defending human rights, fighting moral injustices, and soothing the deepest of despair around the world. At the same time, the foundations of many church traditions have remained obscure to the faithful, and the veil needs to be pulled back. To this day, the church leadership will defend its traditions, even when those traditions depart from the plain meaning of God's Word.

In the beginning, the early church was instructed by the apostles, who were filled with the Holy Spirit. They traveled the known world, spreading the Gospel and raising up bodies of believers in city after city. The members of the early church were often poor and hungry and cold, persecuted and publicly abused. They taught from the Hebrew Scriptures, and the epistles of leaders like Paul and Peter and John were copied and passed between the churches.

Emperor Constantine legalized Christianity in the fourth century, and under Emperor Theodosius it became the religion of the realm. This started to change everything. Christianity suddenly had the honor of respectability, and its offices of leadership became positions of political as well as religious power. Traditions emerged slowly at first, step-by-step, and those traditions were backed by all the authority of Rome.

Many traditions were said to have originated with the apostles as oral teachings that weren't recorded in the Gospels. Whether this is true is unfortunately impossible to prove. By its very nature, oral "tradition" can be ephemeral; it can appear and disappear at the will of those who require it. The apostles wrote the Gospels and epistles decades after Christ's death, but there were people still *alive* who were able to verify the events they described. In 1 Corinthians 15:6, Paul tells us that 500 people at one time saw Jesus alive after his death, and most of those people were still alive when Paul wrote the epistle. They were still available for interviews if needed. After the deaths of those first-generation Christians, there was nobody left to say, "No. I didn't say that."

People can also misinterpret oral communications. Something small can be built up into a full doctrine that has nothing to do with its original intended meaning.

It's dangerous to treat tradition as though God has ordained it. While teaching about the Pharisees, the 19th century English minister J.C. Ryle related the same problem with traditions to the Church of England under the Stuarts. The official church persecuted the Puritans while ignoring those who were openly sinning. It was outrageous. Obvious and blatant sins were passed over while the Puritans face systematic condemnation. Ryle states:

> Experience supplies painful proof, that traditions once called into being are first called *useful*. Then they become *necessary*. At last they are too often made idols, and all must bow down to them, or be punished.[2]

Minister Ryle's closing line is chilling. We find that once a tradition became solidly beneficial to the official church's accumulation of power and wealth, that tradition itself became an idol. It doesn't matter whether it's the Church of England or the local village church, traditions can get solidified when they favor those in power. The early Christians were often required to bow down to the Roman emperors or face punishment, but under the Church of Rome, it became no different.

At the beginning, the Roman Catholic Church was ruled by men who sought to bring Christ to the world. The adage that "power corrupts" is found too true in history. As time went on, holding onto power became more important to certain church leaders than following in the footsteps of Jesus. There are times in history when the popes looked much like the emperors, because the choice hadn't changed much; it was still either "bow" or "be punished." As the church pushed its way into the Middle Ages, the problem grew worse and not better. History hands us

---

[2] John C. Ryle, *Expository Thoughts on the Gospels: St. Mark, Vol 2* (New York: Robert Carter & Brothers, 1874), 138. Italics are in the original.

a gruesome picture; more Christians were slaughtered under the vicars of Christ than were ever killed under the Roman emperors.

Professing God's Authority

Pope Nicholas I, honored for his dedication to marriage, his opposition to immorality, was also overtaken by powerful lust. Whether he promoted his authority for his own benefit or from a genuine concern for the good of the church, his self-aggrandizement was at best exceedingly foolish. According to Gratian, Nicholas I claimed absolute authority backed by God, decreeing:

> It is evident that the popes can neither be bound nor unbound by any earthly power, nor even by that of the apostle, if he should return upon the earth, since Constantine the Great has recognized that the pontiffs hold the place of God upon earth, the divinity not being able to be judged by any living man. We are, then, infallible, and whatever may be our acts, we are not accountable for them but to ourselves.[3]

Notice that his claim to authority came from Constantine and not from the Bible.

The Bible never treats human leaders as though they are infallible and beyond judgment. Abraham, Moses, and David all erred, and the Bible openly tells us this.[4] In Romans 3:23, Paul tells us that *"all have sinned and fall short of the glory of God."* As John warned us in 1 John 1:8, *"If we say that we have no sin, we deceive ourselves, and the truth is not in us."* Jesus, the Son of God, God in the flesh, is the only person in the Bible declared to have no sin.[5] Yet Nicholas I claimed that the pope was infallible and could be judged by no other human being. This is how abuse of power begins.

Nicholas I was certainly zealous for his faith, but so was Saul of Tarsus before his Damascus road experience. Like Saul,

---
3   As cited in Richard W. Thompson, *The Papacy and the Civil Power* (New York: Harper & Brothers 1876), 369.
4   Genesis 12:10-20, 20:1-18; Numbers 20:7-12; Deuteronomy 34:4-5; 2 Samuel 11:1-12:14
5   1 John 3:5; 2 Corinthians 5:21; 1 Peter 2:22

Nicholas used his alleged authority from God to vindicate barbarous behavior. He notably wrote a letter praising the King of Bulgaria for the brutal slaughter of those who resisted him:

> I glorify you for having maintained your authority by putting to death those wandering sheep who refuse to enter the fold…A king need not fear to *command massacres*, when these will retain his subjects in obedience, or cause them to submit to the faith of Christ…[6]

Nicholas also wrote to Charles the Bald to attack the lands of the King of Lorraine, saying:

> We order you, in the name of religion, to invade his states, burn his cities, and massacre his people, whom we render responsible for the resistance of their bad prince.[7]

Today's popes are viewed as kind, holy, and benevolent. However, in the centuries after Rome took over the church leadership, there were little or no checks on their cruelty. They not only held temporal power, they declared they had the authority of God to do whatever they chose. The popes of those years were sometimes vile, depraved, and pitiless. They felt free to exterminate all those they considered heretics — that is, any and all who opposed their will.

Jesus loved us and gave His life for us. Satan is the accuser of the brethren.[8] We should never confuse the destruction caused by the evil one for the work of the Lord. No matter how dedicated the leaders of the Inquisition were, it is clear that they did not follow Christ in their methods.

> *But God demonstrates His own love toward us, in that while we were still sinners, Christ died for us.*
>
> Romans 5:8

We cannot reverse time and watch the cruelty of those days ourselves. We cannot watch the slow starvation of families

---
6 Thompson, *Papacy and the Civil Power*, 369. Italics are in the original.
7 *Ibid*, p. 368.
8 Revelation 12:10

whose fathers and husbands were arrested on the whim of some accuser. We do not see the little children torn from their mother's arms. We can imagine their dirty faces, streaked with tears as they were tied to stakes in the town square, but they weren't our neighbors, our families, our children. We can only try to conceive of their desperation, their terror, their grief. There is no jolt of moral outrage when we read of the multitudes that were murdered during the Inquisitions, because we cannot see the faces of the people who were killed. We are insulated by time and distance.

Yet, in that day, men under the authority of the church dragged whole families through the streets, starved and beat and tortured them and put them to death in horrific ways, all in the name of Christ. All we have left are benign numbers printed on paper, tally amounts of the dead, without the smell of human smoke to torment our memories.

Figure 4: Figure 4 "Two hundred and twenty-four Waldensians burned near Toulon, AD 1243" by Jan Luiken, in Martyr's Mirror (1685).

Church traditions permitted and encouraged this brutality. Not the words or example of Jesus Christ, but church traditions. We can use our flexible human logic to justify any position or behavior, but the Word of God cuts through the joints and marrow and exposes church traditions to the light of truth.

For the word of God is living and powerful, and sharper than any two-edged sword, piercing even to the division of soul and spirit, and of joints and marrow….

Hebrews 4:12a

The Precious Word of God

In 1 Samuel 3:1 we read, *"…And the word of the LORD was precious in those days…"* Samuel tells us that when he was a child the word of the LORD was rare (and therefore precious) because there were no prophets; there was no "open vision." The Word of the LORD was also precious during the Middle Ages, but for a different reason. There were few copies of the Scriptures, and few people could read those copies that existed. God had already spoken by Moses and His prophets and by the apostles of Jesus Christ, but those words were not readily available to the common man.

In the days before the printing press, all Bibles were carefully and tediously copied by hand in the Latin language. This worked decently as long as Latin was in common use by the people, but as Rome deteriorated, the world no longer spoke the language of Rome — not even as the trade language. After the collapse of the western Roman Empire in the fifth century, the Vulgar Latin used by soldiers and slaves and the common people began to evolve and diverge into the distinct languages of Europe. Unique French and Spanish and Portuguese dialects developed in their separate lands. The people bantered in the Germanic and British and Frankish tongues instead of outdated vocabulary from Italy; and only highly educated folks learned Latin to read the Bible.

Even those who could read rarely had access to God's Word — and certainly they were not permitted to translate it into the languages of the people. Then it got worse. The church leadership didn't trust people to read the Bible on their own. It took several centuries for this to transpire, but it did. In 1229, the Council of Valencia in Spain declared:

> ...We prohibit also the permitting of the laity to have the books of the Old and New Testament, unless any one should wish, from a feeling of devotion, to have a Psalter or breviary for divine service, or the hours of the blessed Mary. But, we strictly forbid them to have the above books in the vulgar tongue.[9]

Thus, the European church forbade the distribution of Bibles to common people, and even the psalter had to be in Latin. The Council of Trent, held in Italy for nearly two decades from 1545 to 1563, solidified this law at its Fourth Session in 1546. The Synod made it clear that nobody was to read the Bible outside the Latin Vulgate, and nobody was to interpret the Bible on their own. It was declared:

> [T]hat the said old and vulgate edition, which, by the lengthened usage of so many years, has been approved of in the Church, be... held as authentic; and that no one is to dare, or presume to reject it under any pretext whatever.
>
> Furthermore, in order to restrain petulant spirits, It decrees, that no one, relying on his own skill, shall, –in matters of faith, and of morals pertaining to the edification of Christian doctrine, –wresting the sacred Scripture to his own senses, presume to interpret the said sacred Scripture contrary to that sense which holy mother Church,–whose it is to judge of the true sense and interpretation of the holy Scripture.[10]

What happened to Acts 17:11? Paul trusted the people of Berea to double check his words against the Scriptures, but in

---

9 Tom Streeter, *The Church and Western Culture: An Introduction to Church History.* (2006; reprint, Bloomington, IL: Booktango, 2012), 262.
10 The Council of Trent, Session 4, Second Decree.

the Middle Ages, the church did not encourage people to think for themselves. While the church leadership claimed service to Jesus, many of those leaders also used His authority as the means to solidify their own power.

Real heretics have existed throughout all ages — those who reject biblical morality or deny the basic teachings of Christianity. However, during both the Middle Ages and the Reformation, those punished as heretics were not necessarily those who disobeyed the clear doctrines of the Bible. "Heretics" might be any innocent person who dared contradict the ruling religious leadership. The church leadership claimed to stand in God's place, and they stood so tall that they blocked the people's view of God himself.

The insidious allure of power and control in the name of God moved spiritual leaders to choose man's way of handling problems over the love of God provided in the example of Jesus Christ.

THE KISS OF PEACE

In the Middle Ages, punishment was the usual solution to almost any offense, no matter how seemingly insignificant. We find the story of a hungry woman who followed a praying priest on a Lenten procession through a Brenton village. The woman quietly slipped away from the trailing crowd to get something to eat. In her home, she started a fire under a pot to heat up mutton and ham. An inquisitive passer-by caught a whiff of the savory aroma, and the woman was reported, seized, and taken before the local bishop. She was convicted of breaking Lent and sentenced to walk the streets all day for a month carrying a quarter of mutton on a metal spit. A ham hock was also slung around her neck dangling by a rope. Of course, the spirit of the time is revealed not simply in the punishment, but in the fact that a jeering mob followed her around on her cross-town walks.

Petty crimes were taken seriously, as when a baron made the mistake of getting drunk and running off with the chalice from a local church. He was thoroughly cursed by the church and rejected by the local people. To return to good standing in the community, he was required to forfeit his entire fortune to the bishop. For a day and night, he had to lie on his stomach on the floor of the church and pray for forgiveness. He was then pulled to his knees as sixty priests and monks beat him in cadence with sticks. As the baron was being clobbered, he had to call out with each blow, "Just are thy judgements O Lord." At the end of this ordeal, the bishop gave him a kiss of peace.

As strange as this sounds, the baron likely accepted his punishment with willingness in order to receive the bishop's kiss. He believed he was thus absolved from sin, and he feared his soul otherwise teetered precariously over the fires of hell. A person could eventually escape from purgatory after his sins had burned away, but hell was an eternal place of torment which reverberated with the endless shrieks of demons. A mere beating hardly compared to an eternity of unquenchable heat, where swarms of flies bit the skin of the damned and worms feasted upon their organs. There was no hope in hell, and its victims could only wail and gnash their teeth. Under the era's teachings, the baron believed his bishop's kiss provided the key to his salvation.

Of course, while real crimes were punished by the local clergy, people were also punished and killed for faults that had little to do with disrespecting God. One of the saddest cases, is the story of an Anabaptist woman named Janneken Munstdorp, who was burned at the stake on October 5, 1573, for the crime of reading the Bible. In late September, she wrote a long and touching letter to her infant daughter, commending her into the care and protection of God. Janneken's young husband had already been executed, but the authorities waited until Janneken gave birth to complete her sentence. The baby girl was taken away soon after birth, and the grieving mother wrote to her newborn, urging her to trust and fear God and seek the narrow way to salvation.

The letter in its entirety has been preserved, and it will break your heart to read it. Janneken clearly trusts that God will care for the newborn little girl, but she is in grief for her child: "… you who are yet so young, and whom I must leave here in this wicked, evil, perverse world."[11] She does everything she knows to do for her child: she prays for her and places her into God's care — and writes this letter.

Was Janneken a terrible heretic? Was she a witch casting spells? Had she attempted to spread the plague? No. She simply trusted in Jesus Christ alone for salvation, contrary to the teachings of the official church. A century had passed since the printing press made Bibles more readily available, and it is easy to see that Janneken had been reading the Bible of her own accord. In her letter, she directly quotes 1 Corinthians 3:11, *"For other foundation can no man lay than that is laid, which is Jesus Christ."* She then alludes to Isaiah 53:5, 1 Peter 2:24, and 1 Peter 1:18-19 in declaring to her infant, "…by whose stripes we are healed, and through whose blood we have been dearly purchased; for we have not been bought with gold or silver, but through His bitter death, and His precious blood which He shed for us."[12]

Janneken Munstdorp was executed for worshiping Jesus as an Anabaptist. That's all. The Catholic Inquisition in Holland burned thousands of innocent people just like Janneken. I want to end this young mother's story with her own precious words:

> …And now that I have abided the time and borne you under my heart with great sorrow for nine months, and given birth to you here in prison in great pain, they have taken you from me. Here I lie, expecting death every morning, and shall now soon follow your dear father…
>
> Since I am now delivered up to death and must leave you here alone, I must through these lines cause you to remember, that when you have attained your understanding, you endeavor to fear God and see and examine why and for whose name we both died; and be not ashamed to confess us before the world, for you must know that it is not for the sake of any evil. Hence be not ashamed of us; it is the way which the prophets

---
[11] Janneken Munstdorp, "Letter to Her Daughter" (1573) as found in Denis Janz, ed., *Reformation Reader*, 2nd Ed. (Minneapolis: Fortress Press, 2008), 231-236.
[12] *Ibid.*

and apostles went, and the narrow way which leads into eternal life, for there shall no other way be found by which to be saved.

Hence, my young lamb, for whose sake I still have, and have had, great sorrow, seek, when you have attained your understanding, this narrow way, though there is sometimes much danger in it according to the flesh...[13]

If we can imagine the grief of a mother whose young husband has been murdered, whose newborn child has been taken to be raised by strangers, who is facing death for loving and trusting in Jesus, we can begin to grasp the gross injustices perpetrated by those who claimed the authority of Christ.

---

[13] *Ibid.*

CHAPTER 5

METANOIA

Metanoia. It's hard to believe that one word out of the thousands tossed about so indifferently can rattle a religious empire. In the fourth century, the Greek word *metanoia* was mistranslated, and that mistranslation has monumentally affected church history. It's a mistake that might affect the destiny of souls. As amazing as it sounds, few know of this mistranslation today, but this one razor-sharp word changed Christendom's view on how to get to heaven and helped to spark the Reformation.

In the original Greek, *metanoia* means "repentance" or a "change of the mind." It indicates that the inner man has changed and turned away from sin. Unfortunately, when Saint Jerome (A.D. 322-420) translated the Hebrew and Greek texts into the Latin Vulgate, he translated the word *metanoia* as the Latin word *pænitentia*, from which we get both our words "penitence" and "penance." Penitence is sorrow for sin, which can lead to repentance if it turns the sinner away from sin. However, penance is something a bit different. Penance is a form of discipline meant to show the reality of sorrow for sin by doing works. The church thus started using the mistaken interpretation of *metanoia* back in the fourth century, and it is still used today.

According to the Bible, the only "penance" we need to perform is turning away from the sin itself. That's it. No amount of good deeds or self-punishments can make up for our sins. All we are required to do is seek God's forgiveness, turn from our sin (repentance) and go on in our walk with our Lord. Of course, if we are truly repentant it will be obvious from our behavior, but it's Christ's blood that saves us, not the works we do.

The word that Jerome chose in the Latin Vulgate has sadly affected Christendom in a biblically unfamiliar way. According to the Roman Catholic Church, the Sacrament of Penance reconciles us with God. According to the CCC, no. 1468: "The whole power of the sacrament of Penance consists in restoring us to God's grace and joining us with him in an intimate friendship."

After baptism, Catholics believe sin is forgiven after confession to a priest and then doing an act of penance as prescribed by the priest. We might be required to recite the Our Father a prescribed number of times or – in the Middle Ages — crawl up and down stairs on raw, bloody knees. Jesus required no such things; He simply said, "Go and sin no more." The Bible teaches us to reject our sin and depend on God's mercy through faith in Christ Jesus.

Figure 5: Portrait of Erasmus of Rotterdam by Hans Holbein the Younger (1530), Royal Collection.

When the famed 16th century scholar Erasmus of Rotterdam began his translations of the Greek New Testament, he translated John the Baptist's words in Matthew 3:2 as "repent" rather than "do penance," and that has made a world of difference. "To repent" is to turn away from sin, rather than trying to earn enough merit for salvation by adding good works to what Christ has already done on the cross.

This one glaring difference completely changes the issue of salvation. In one case, we are earning our salvation and we're burdened by constant guilt because of endless *doing*. In the other case, Christ gets all the glory for being the One who set us free from our sin and guilt. Do we see the distinction? In one case, we wait for the kiss of a bishop who has decided we have recognized our failing. In the other case, we enjoy the touch of God Himself, who looks upon our innermost man.

Professor Norm Samworth once told me the phrase "to justify" in the book of Romans was also mistranslated to express a moral change inside the person. That is, many people think a person is "made righteous" by making a change within himself. This is not simply a Roman Catholic issue — many Protestants hold to it as well. It's a misunderstanding throughout Christendom and throughout the world. Humans often feel that they must fix themselves before they come to the Lord, that they must do enough good works to make up for their sins before God will accept them. This is not what the Bible teaches.

When the term "to justify" is used in the Greek New Testament, it is always used in a legal sense to "declare righteous." Justification is something that God Himself gives a person. This is important. Humans are not justified by working hard to "be good" enough so that they can come to God. When they fail and fail again, they feel they have no hope, and they give up trying. That's precisely why Christ died, though. He died so that God could justify us. That's why we can come boldly to the throne of God's grace. He wants us clean and whole in His sight. We can't be good enough to do it ourselves. It has to be the covering of Christ that justifies us. Then, forgiven and restored, we can continue doing the good work God has called us to do.

If you get nothing more out of this book, I want you to appreciate this principle: we cannot justify ourselves by doing penance. We can't pay for our sins through some sort of act or payment to the church. The original Greek teaches us that God justifies us through repentance. Jesus on the cross made the payment with His blood attornment for our sins. He paid for our sins, and our devotion to Him is a response to that great love and sacrifice on our behalf.

Evangelicals and Catholics alike have a misunderstanding about "works." The Bible speaks of good works, but it is always in the context of our *first* being saved by grace through faith. If we have a genuine conversion, we will inevitably produce a life of good works. Branches grafted into a living tree will naturally produce fruit. If we are grafted into Christ, we will produce good works. We don't have to work our way to God first by doing. Instead, once we are born again, the byproduct of that will be our striving to do good works because we are new creatures in Christ, and His Spirit works through us. Jesus said, "If you love me, you will obey my commandments." We serve Christ from love and not to earn our salvation.

Our goal should always be to free ourselves of any tradition that is invented by humans and to cling only to the Word of God. Even reasonable statements by righteous men can be confused, and we have to make sure everything is balanced against the words of Christ and His apostles.

Saint Cyprian stated, "Nulla salus extra ecclesiam." That is, "Outside the Church there is no salvation." The spiritual Church is the Body of Christ, those believers who are saved by Him. All those who are saved in our time are a part of God's Church. However, Jesus was not nailed to a particular church denomination; He was nailed to a cross!

Our salvation, according to the Bible, does not come by belonging to a particular church group. No religious organization, no matter how massive, no matter how opulent or wealthy, can get us one toe into heaven. Salvation cannot come by way of any church, ritual, mosque, synagogue, prophet, angel, pastor, priest, bishop, cardinal, human deed, cleric, mullah, rabbi, payment, shaman, chieftain, Billy Graham, Gandhi, Joseph Smith, or even the pope himself. Salvation comes only from the shed atoning blood of Jesus Christ. If we believe in Christ as our savior, confess we are sinners and ask Christ into our hearts, then a transformation of the inner person occurs and we then become recipients of God's unmerited grace. We are literally saved by grace through faith in Jesus and not by our good deeds.

Not by works of righteousness which we have done, but according to His mercy He saved us, through the washing of regeneration and renewing of the Holy Spirit...

Titus 3:5

CHAPTER 6

THE LIGHTNING STORM

Almost every one of the ten books I've previously published are about biblical archaeology. During the past 30 years, I have participated in about 70 expeditions doing research and exploration around the world. Before I started doing biblical research, I worked as a FBI-trained homicide investigator and a CSI police investigator. I am not an expert on medieval history. How did I decide to write about church tradition and fear in the Middle Ages?

It started when I was on a layover in Dallas. The airport had closed due to lightning, and I lounged in the gate area for hours, bored out of my mind. As I waited for the torrential storm to pass, I watched two nuns seated across from me. One was younger and one was older, and they sat patiently in their traditional black and white habits, their hands folded in their laps.

Eventually, I stood to stretch and ended up engaging them in a conversation. They looked up at me and smiled warmly, so I felt encouraged to solicit information from them. Curious, I asked, "From your Catholic perspective, how does one get eternal salvation and go to heaven?" As soon as I asked my question, the young nun dropped her eyes. Her demeanor had been so gentle, and now she stiffened and offered no answer. I don't know whether she was just timid or if she was embarrassed by a stranger's direct question.

The older nun looked at me with a contemplative expression, clearly deep in thought. She nodded slowly after a long pause, as though she had come upon the appropriate response, and she looked up at me with kind eyes. This was a vital matter, and I assumed she would offer me a holy dissertation from a

43

lifetime of learning and leaning on the Lord. Instead, she simply said, "To get to heaven, you need to think good thoughts and do good deeds."

I didn't know how to answer her, so I respectfully thanked her. She said nothing further. She simply turned her head to gaze outside at the brooding storm clouds and watch for the occasional slash of lightning. I sensed that our impromptu theological discussion was over.

The nun's response had surprised me. These two women were clearly devout and sincere in their faith. They appeared to me to be patient and kind, and I was puzzled by the answer I had received. For all they knew, I was a simple lost soul standing on the fulcrum between heaven and hell. I was told my heavenly reward was predicated on my *thinking good thoughts and doing good deeds?* The older nun said nothing about faith in Jesus, or even faith in God. She said nothing about confession of my sins or seeking God's forgiveness. This amazed me.

Roman Catholics have great reverence for the apostles Peter and Paul. Saint Paul was one of the first Christian missionaries and the author of much of the New Testament. Saint Peter is regarded as the first bishop of Rome and the precursor to all the popes. Yet these primary Christian leaders, Peter and Paul, both taught something entirely different than what the nun told me. They taught that we must repent and turn from our sins, and that salvation and eternal life are by faith in Jesus Christ who died for our sins:

> *For by grace you have been saved through faith, and that not of yourselves; it is the gift of God, not of works, lest anyone should boast.*
>
> Ephesians 2:8-9

> *Then Peter said to them, "Repent, and let every one of you be baptized in the name of Jesus Christ for the remission of sins; and you shall receive the gift of the Holy Spirit."*
>
> Acts 2:38

> *... that by the name of Jesus Christ of Nazareth, whom you crucified, whom God raised from the dead, by Him this man stands here before you whole.... Nor is there salvation in any other, for there is no other name under heaven given among men by which we must be saved.*
>
> Acts 4:10b,12

Of course, Jesus Christ, the Lord Himself, taught that we are saved through His death. This is a very familiar passage:

> *For God so loved the world that He gave His only begotten Son, that whoever believes in Him should not perish but have everlasting life. For God did not send His Son into the world to condemn the world, but that the world through Him might be saved.*
>
> John 3:16-17

Why, then, did the nun *not* tell me to trust in Jesus? The vows a nun makes are all about living like Jesus — living faithfully without worldly possessions, chaste, and obedient. Why did she tell me to "be good" and that's it?

I think the answer lies in certain traditional teachings that focus on good works rather than on the saving blood of Jesus. In being obedient, gentle souls, the nuns didn't question the things they had been taught. This is a common human habit, especially for those who are dedicated to humility and duty. We obey those who are our teachers, who pass down to us the information that was handed to them. This is excellent when *what* we are taught is straight from the heart of God. When it's not, however, trouble is the beneficiary of our choices.

The nun's answer led me to begin this study. I started doing research into traditional church beliefs, and I discovered something. I discovered that there are many places where Christians are taught according to traditions that part ways with the Word of God itself. This has been true both in the historical Roman Catholic Church and in the churches that sprouted from the Reformation. Our church traditions don't always coincide with the very words of Jesus, and that should be of concern to every person dedicated to the Christian faith.

CHAPTER 7

THE TROUBLE WITH TRADITION

The 1971 movie *Fiddler on the Roof* famously describes the Jews' dependence on tradition to maintain their cultural and religious identity — and to find stability in a hostile world. Traditions can offer many blessings. For the Jews, the tradition of celebrating Passover reminds them every year of God's provision and His power in rescuing their ancestors from Egypt. It's a good tradition.

At the same time, Jesus rebuked the Pharisees for their dependence on tradition above all else.

Figure 6: "The Fiddler" by Marc Chagall (1912–1913).

Jesus was not pleased with those who followed traditions above the revealed Word of God in the Scriptures. The Lord had come to fulfill the Old Testament prophecies — to fulfill God's Word through Moses and the Prophets. However, Jesus found that the Jewish leaders often honored their oral traditions ahead of the Old Testament. In fact, they obeyed their traditions even when the traditions directly contradicted the Bible, and Jesus roundly reprimanded them for this:

> He answered and said to them, "Why do you also transgress the commandment of God because of your tradition?"
>
> Matthew 15:3

> ... Thus you have made the commandment of God of no effect by your tradition.
>
> Matthew 15:6b

He accused them of teaching the commandments of men as though they were the commandments of God, and this was wrong.

When we obey church leaders, why do we do so? We do it out of respect and obedience to God. That's why we obey them. The faithfulness to God must of course come first. That means that if the menu of religious food our fathers handed us contradicts what God Himself says about the Bread of Life, then we're in big trouble. We have to be like the early apostles! They were forced to choose between obeying the religious hierarchy and obeying God Himself.

When Christ's disciples were brought before the High Priest and the council, they boldly declared their allegiance to God first:

> But Peter and the other apostles answered and said: "We ought to obey God rather than men. The God of our fathers raised up Jesus whom you murdered by hanging on a tree. Him God has exalted to His right hand to be Prince and Savior, to give repentance to Israel and forgiveness of sins."
>
> Acts 5:29-31

The apostles were publicly beaten for taking this position, and they were told not to keep preaching in the name of Jesus. However, they went away rejoicing that they were able to suffer for Christ, and they continued to preach in His name.

Saint Thomas Aquinas agreed when writing about abusive rulers:

> ...[F]or instance if he dictates vices contrary to the virtues authority is supposed to promote and sustain. In that event, not merely is a man not bound to obey, he is also bound not to obey, following the martyrs, who suffered death, rather than carry out the wicked decrees of tyrants.[1]

We all have to be careful that what we hand down to our children are the teachings of God and not doctrines that men concocted out of their own heads; which are destructive if they are in error — even if they were developed with good intentions. If any church leaders in any denomination develop sets of doctrines, all who serve Christ must hold up those doctrines to the light of God's Word.

From Servants to Masters

Jesus came as a servant and to be the ultimate Passover Lamb for us, and in the beginning, Christianity was all about sacrifice. During the first 300 years after Christ's ascension, it was generally dangerous to be a Christian. Then, the Roman Emperor Constantine converted, and suddenly government posts opened up to Christians. Power and prestige were to be had in church leadership positions. When the previously pagan government of a primarily pagan world took over the church, a variety of rooms were opened up in a house of trouble.

Emperor Theodosius focused on eradicating the outward pagan establishment of the day, but the people were still steeped in pagan traditions. Bits and pieces of other religions crept in, and human ideas came to compete with the Word of God as the source of guidance. This is why we have to carefully examine our own church traditions and ruthlessly edit what we believe to conform to the Bible.

---

[1] St. Thomas Aquinas, Commentary *II Sentences*, XLIV, ii. 2 (Translated by Thomas Gilby).

CHEATED BY TRADITION

A pastor friend once said to me that church traditions are the only thing on earth that can nullify the Word of God. I was a bit stunned at that statement, but he then pointed to Mark 7:13: *"… making the word of God of no effect through your tradition which you have handed down. And many such things you do."*

Jesus repeatedly warns his followers against man-made traditions. In fact, the words of Christ and the apostles make it clear that we can be *cheated* through trusting too much in human ideas:

Figure 7: Dispute of Jesus and the Pharisees over tribute money by Gustave Doré (1866).

> *Beware lest anyone cheat you through philosophy and empty deceit, according to the tradition of men, according to the basic principles of the world, and not according to Christ.*
>
> Colossians 2:8

Do traditions really make the Word of God of no effect? Yes. When people embrace the tradition *instead* of the Word of God, then yes, they are treating the Word of God as nothing. The Word of God will still stand true, but the understanding of our minds is darkened when we choose our traditions over the plain words of the Scriptures.

While Protestants claim *sola scriptura* — that the Bible is their only authority — they can get caught in their own traditions just the same. Faithful church members can get dedicated to their favorite doctrines, even if those doctrines are based on just a verse or two taken out of the context of what the whole Bible says. In time, man-made ideas become laws to be followed as strictly as if they were floated down on the wings of angels. That is the problem. How can we discern between traditions that were just somebody's "good idea" and those that are truly from the Lord?

This might surprise some people, but the Five Points of Calvinism are not written in any chapter of the Bible. They were gleaned from somebody's interpretation of Scripture. There are verses that can support those five points, but there are other verses that offer balance. Some Calvinists preach the doctrine of "limited atonement" as though Jesus himself wrote it out, and He didn't. The issue of God's predestination versus God's foreknowledge is complex, but a host of verses indicate that God desires all people to be saved.[2] We have to be careful about using human logic to fill in the blanks.

I recognize that I am stepping on toes throughout this book, but we need to know the whole Word of God. We need to make sure our beliefs are in full compliance with what Jesus and the apostles taught. Catholics or Methodists or Primitive Baptists or Seventh Day Adventists — or members of any other denomination — must take care that they don't depend on their own church traditions above an open reading of the Scriptures. At the same time, good Roman Catholics are often *expected* to choose traditions in the place of Scriptures. That's not what the catechism says, but that is the reality in practical application.

A Roman Catholic Monsignor wrote recently:

> Even when a Catholic considers the source of his own personal Catholic belief he has to admit that his instruction in the Faith basically all came from the Tradition of the Church...and that relatively little to none of what was originally taught came directly from Scripture.[3]

In 1546, the Council of Trent declared that the Word of God is contained both in the Bible and tradition, the two being "equal in authority."

Yet, Paul warned in Galatians 1:8 that, *"But though we, or an angel from heaven, preach any other gospel unto you than that which we have preached unto you, let him be accursed."*

---

[2] Cf. Ezekiel 18:31-32, 33:11; Matthew 18:13-14; John 3:16-17; 1 Timothy 2:4; and 2 Peter 3:9.
[3] From the publishers preface, George Agius, *Tradition and the Church* (1928; reprint, Rockford, IL: Tan Books and Publishers, 2005).

Which means that anything additional that contradicts the basic Gospel the apostles gave, as explicitly written down, is to be rejected. Paul explained justification through faith in great detail. It's difficult to find any room for indulgences there.

Jesus knew how man's traditions could foul-up his clear message, so the apostles wrote it all down for us. We do a good enough job of confusing the plain words of Jesus and Peter and Paul all by ourselves without adding to it oral tradition that can't be verified. The written words themselves aren't moving, and that's incredibly important for the strength of our faith.

It is Written

Christ quoted from the Hebrew Scriptures and He never relied on traditions. He depended on the words that Moses, Samuel, David, Daniel and others wrote as God gave them inspiration through His Spirit. Jesus says over and over "it is written." He never quoted the Jewish rabbis from the Talmud. He condemned oral traditions that were put forth by the rabbis and accused them of polluting the Word of God.

The Greek word translated "tradition" in the New Testament is *paradosis* (παράδοσις). It signifies something that is transmitted or delivered, generally by teaching. Connotatively, it is used for the Jewish rabbinical traditions, but it can also be used for any teaching or ordinance. Thus, *paradosis* is always used in a negative light, except in the following three verses when Paul is talking about the lessons he and the apostles had directly given:

> *Now I praise you, brethren, that you remember me in all things and keep the traditions just as I delivered them to you.*
>
> 1 Corinthians 11:2

> *Therefore, brethren, stand fast and hold the traditions which you were taught, whether by word or our epistle.*
>
> 2 Thessalonians 2:15

But we command you, brethren, in the name of our Lord Jesus Christ, that you withdraw from every brother who walks disorderly and not according to the tradition which he received from us.
                                              2 Thessalonians 3:6

These verses explain that the brethren should stand fast only to the conduct and teachings that were given them directly by the apostles or by way of epistle. Unfortunately, the only words from the apostles we can now trust are those in the Gospels and the epistles, since the apostles aren't here to verify any others for us.

These three verses all show quite clearly that traditions should be unswervingly based upon apostolic and biblical revelation. Traditions are forbidden to be manufactured as any amendment to the Bible.

In Galatians 6:7, Paul warns *"Do not be deceived, God is not mocked; for whatever a man sows, that he will also reap."*

We are all responsible for seeking out the truth, and we are all responsible for what we do with the truth we've been given. We are all ultimately going to stand before God, the righteous Judge, and He will judge us according to His great wisdom. The truth may come as a bolt of lightning or it may come as silently as a blade of grass sprouting through a crack in the concrete slab. The truth will eventually find us all, whether we like it or not.

Chapter 8

Papal Authority

And I also say to you that you are Peter, and on this rock I will build My church, and the gates of Hades shall not prevail against it. And I will give you the keys of the kingdom of heaven, and whatever you bind on earth will be bound in heaven, and whatever you loose on earth will be loosed in heaven.

Matthew 16:16-19

Jesus anointed Peter as the chief shepherd and pastor of the early church. We read in John 21:15-17 three times Jesus asks Peter to feed His sheep and feed His lambs. Peter repeatedly affirms that he loves Jesus, and in response Jesus tells Peter, "Feed my sheep."

The Roman Catholic Church has historically treated the passage in Matthew 16 as a justification for the succession of the popes. Peter is declared to have been the first pope, and the popes who followed are seen as chosen by God to fill Peter's shoes.

In his *Catechism for Adults*, William Cogan states:

6. When did Jesus actually make Peter the first Pope?
Shortly before He ascended into Heaven, Jesus gave Peter complete authority over the whole Church...

7. Did Peter's authority die with him?
No, it was handed down to a man named Linus, and after he died (A.D. 78), it was handed down to Cletus (A.D. 90), and then to Clement (A.D. 100), and after that to another, and so on, during the past nearly 2,000 years...

8. Do all Catholics have to obey the Pope?
Yes, because he speaks with the authority of Christ…

9. Can the Pope make an error when teaching religion?
No, not when he speaks as head of the whole Church…[1]

There is something in the Greek here, however, that we miss in the English and even in the Latin. The passage in Matthew 16 is often misunderstood. It's interesting that in the Greek, the name Peter is *petros,* which is a masculine name and means a *chunk* of a rock — a piece of a larger rock. When Jesus says, "upon this rock I will build my church," he is making a play on words with Peter's name, but he's not referring to Peter. The word for "rock" is *petra,* a slightly different form that indicates a large *mass* of rock. The mass of rock is Jesus. Peter has just made a declaration of faith in Christ, and Jesus says he will build his church on himself and the truth of his identity, which Peter has just declared by the Holy Spirit.

There is a reason we have to be careful here; this is the only place in the Bible where it sounds like the church will be built on Peter, the rock. We need to interpret this passage with reference to the rest of Scripture. According to the rest of the Bible, the church is built on the Lord. Paul tells us in 1 Corinthians 3:11, *"For no other foundation can anyone lay than that which is laid, which is Jesus Christ."* Paul had just explained in verse nine that we (the church) are God's building, and Jesus Christ is the foundation of that building.

THE CHURCH'S FOUNDATION

We do see here in Matthew 16 that God gave Peter the power to loose and bind. The word "you" here is singular. Jesus is speaking specifically to Peter when he says he's giving him the keys to the kingdom of heaven — that he's giving him the power to loose and bind. This is a powerful moment between Jesus and Peter, and Peter is being given great responsibility.

---
[1] William Cogan, ed., *A Catechism for Adults* (Washington D.C.: U.S. Conference of Catholic Bishops, 1975), 55-56.

However, we find two chapters later that Jesus is also giving the power to loose and bind to all the disciples (connotatively including those beyond the inner twelve). Jesus speaks this time using a plural "you" — speaking to all of them when he says:

Assuredly, I say to you, whatever you bind on earth will be bound in heaven, and whatever you loose on earth will be loosed in heaven. Again I say to you that if two of you agree on earth concerning anything that they ask, it will be done for them by My Father in heaven. For where two or three are gathered together in My name, I am there in the midst of them.

Matthew 18:18-20

That's important. Jesus was speaking to those who would be the original church leaders, the apostles who spread the Gospel of Jesus Christ to all the known world. They taught from the Hebrew Scriptures, showing that Jesus was a fulfillment of the Law and the Prophets, and they performed miracles by the Holy Spirit as they traversed the Middle East and southern Europe.

Peter and Paul were both vastly important teachers in the early church. They were instrumental in spreading the Gospel and starting churches. The disciples were sent out to all the known world to tell the good news of Christ's death and resurrection. They were given great power and authority to do the work God had called them to do.[2]

We know God used Peter mightily in the beginning as a leader of the early church, giving wisdom from God. He was a pillar and a source of encouragement, guidance and great miracles. However, the Bible always treats God as the rock, and Jesus as the foundation for the church and its chief cornerstone.

No one is holy like the LORD, For there is none besides You, Nor is there any rock like our God.

1 Samuel 2:2

---

[2] There is a question about whether we are given a similar authority, along with the power to bind and loose, as the spiritual descendants of the disciples. The work they started hasn't been completed, and there is a lost world yet to reach. We trust that when two or more of us are gathered in Christ's name, he is in the midst of us. That's a topic for several Bible studies.

> *For who is God, except the LORD? And who is a rock, except our God?*
>
> Psalm 18:31

> *...You are My witnesses. Is there a God besides Me? Indeed there is no other Rock; I know not one.*
>
> Isaiah 44:8b

> *But why do you call Me 'Lord, Lord,' and not do the things which I say? Whoever comes to Me, and hears My sayings and does them, I will show you whom he is like: He is like a man building a house, who dug deep and laid the foundation on the rock. And when the flood arose, the stream beat vehemently against that house, and could not shake it, for it was founded on the rock.*
>
> Luke 6:46-48

Paul goes into great detail in 1 Corinthians 13-15 about the spiritual gifts that God will use among His people. Pay attention to this: Paul describes offices and spiritual gifts, but he describes no disciple of Christ as the head of all the church. Ephesians 5:23 tells us that Christ is the head of the church, and we are not given any indication that a human being on earth can stand in Christ's place as his ultimate representative.

In Matthew 16:16-19, Jesus offers great responsibilities to Peter, but it's a huge leap for any one man to claim to hold the keys to the kingdom as Peter's successor — even the Bishop of Rome.

THE BISHOP OF ROME

In the beginning, the church was simply the collection of believers in this or that town. As the apostles spread the Gospel, they established churches along the way, which met in the homes of prominent Christians in each city.

> *The churches of Asia greet you. Aquila and Priscilla greet you heartily in the Lord, with the church that is in their house.*
>
> 1 Corinthians 16:19

> *Greet the brethren who are in Laodicea, and Nymphas and the church that is in his house.*
>
> Colossians 4:15

To guide the churches after they left, the apostles established bishops. We see in Acts 15:13 and 21:17-18 and elsewhere, James the brother of Jesus was made the leader of the church in Jerusalem, an appointment confirmed by other sources.[3] Paul spends chapter 3 of his first letter to Timothy describing which sort of men to choose as church leaders, including both bishops and deacons. Timothy himself is often considered the first Bishop of Ephesus. Titus is considered the first Bishop of Crete. Eusebius says that Mark was the first Bishop of Alexandria.[4] Each city had its bishop, and Rome was just one city.

Who was the first Bishop of Rome? We are told that Peter eventually arrived in Rome, but did he ever serve as its bishop? Paul declares that he was sent to the gentiles, just as Peter was sent to the Jews,[5] but the Bible suggests neither of them as Rome's bishop. Romans 16 greets a long list of people by name, but it does not even mention Peter.

According to the fourth century church historian Eusebius (A.D. 260-341), Peter did arrive in Rome and was preaching there, but he and Paul were both martyred about the same time.[6] Eusebius continues, saying of Peter, "And at last, having come to Rome, he was crucified head-downwards; for he had requested that he might suffer in this way."[7]

While bishops oversaw all the house churches in their cities, the churches were led by apostles, evangelists, pastors, prophets, teachers, and deacons. The first bishop of Rome that Eusebius mentions absolutely is Linus. Paul mentions Linus when writing

---
3   *Ibid*, II.23.1.
4   *Ibid*, II.24.1.
5   Galatians 2:8
6   Eusebius, *Church History*: II.17.1; II.25.5-8 (A.D. 314).
7   *Ibid*.

to Timothy from Rome in the salutation at the end of the epistle.[8] Linus was followed by Clement, who had been Paul's coworker in Rome.[9] Early church writer Tertullian (A.D. 155-240) tells us that Clement was ordained by Peter as the Bishop of Rome, and Polycarp was ordained as the Bishop of Smyrna by the apostle John.[10]

Pope Marcellinus (296-304) was the first Bishop of Rome documented to have the actual title "pope." The word comes from the Latin *papa*, for "father," and it became a general term for the bishops of all the cities. It wasn't until about A.D. 500 that it started being used solely for the Bishop of Rome.

While Peter is traditionally referred to as the first pope, there is no evidence that he ever served as Rome's bishop. He taught in Rome at the end of his life, and he died there, but he did not appear to have served in an official capacity. Peter would never have accepted the title "Papa" at any rate, because Jesus had specifically told His disciples not to let themselves be called Rabbi or Master or Father.[11]

INFALLIBILITY

The pope is said to be the successor to Saint Peter, but even if that were true, the Bible never treats Peter as though he's faultless. In Galatians 2:11, Paul describes Peter's bad behavior in Antioch: "*Now when Peter had come to Antioch, I withstood him to his face, because he was to be blamed...*" We know that Peter was filled with the Spirit on Pentecost after having walked with our Savior for three years. If any human leader should have been given the gift of never-failing faith, made incapable of committing sins, it would have been Peter! Yet the Bible never treats Peter as a leader who is beyond reproach. Today, the Vatican's Code of Canon Law teaches that nobody can question the pope. An *ex cathedra* ("from the chair") pronouncement by a pope is said to come directly from the Holy Spirit, which enables him to proclaim the Bible's true intent. That's what the Vatican

---
8 *Ibid*, III.2.1, in reference to 2 Timothy 4:21
9 *Ibid*, III.iv.10.
10 Tertullian, *Prescription Against Heretics*, XXXII (A.D. 197).
11 Matthew 23:8-10

PAPAL AUTHORITY

tells us. The pope is regarded as Christ's representative on earth and as such has been empowered to legislate for additional pronouncements as new situations have arisen.

As Roman Catholic theologian and Bible translator Ronald L. Conte Jr. wrote in 2015:

> The Pope ... does not teach from his own mind, but from the mind of Christ... Can the Pope be excommunicated by violating a law of the Church, whose penalty is automatic excommunication? No, he cannot. He is above the law. The sins of apostasy, heresy, and schism teach [sic] carry the penalty of automatic excommunication under the eternal moral law as well as Canon law. But the Pope can never commit any of these sins, because the prevenient grace of God gives him the gift of a never-failing faith.[12]

Is that true? Does the prevenient grace of God give the pope the gift of never-failing faith, or is that just wishful thinking? It would be a wonderful thing if the pope always spoke from the heart of Christ on important matters. I am absolutely serious. The whole world would benefit from a powerful voice speaking from God's own Spirit through the centuries.

It's clear that Conte is not just giving his opinion. The view he gives here is supported by canon law. According to Canon 1404, "The First See is judged by no one." Instead, Canon 1405 dictates that, "It is solely the right of the Roman Pontiff himself to judge-" in cases related to spiritual matters and ecclesiastical law, as well as to:

1. those who hold the highest civil office of a state;
2. cardinals;
3. legates of the Apostolic See and, in penal cases, bishops;
4. other cases which he has called to his own judgment.

---

[12] Conte, Ronald L. "Can a Pope be Excommunicated? Is he above Canon Law?" The Reproach of Christ. October 09, 2015. Accessed February 13, 2018. https://ronconte.wordpress.com/2015/10/09/can-a-pope-be-excommunicated-is-he-above-canon-law.

Canon 1405 goes on to say that, "A judge cannot review an act or instrument confirmed specifically (in *forma specifica*) by the Roman Pontiff without his prior mandate." In other words, the pope's word is final. Canon 749 teaches:

> By virtue of his office, the Supreme Pontiff possesses infallibility in teaching when as the supreme pastor and teacher of all the Christian faithful, who strengthens his brothers and sisters in the faith, he proclaims by definitive act that a doctrine of faith or morals is to be held.

There it is. Black and white. But is it true? Does God actually *want* us to trust something just because the pope said it? Do we have to trust something because a council decided it? I am picking on the papacy, because the pope is still the most powerful spiritual leader in the world today, followed by millions. However, the same question should be asked about any church leader or any church council that claims infallibility.

It is frighteningly easy to find pastors today who insist that *their* church is the only way to salvation. There are pastors who demand loyalty and allegiance to their particular faith body. That attitude alone should flap red flags in our faces. Any time a minister says, "I'm it! Listen to me!" we need to be extremely wary. We always have to go back to the Bible to see what it says, and if any church teaches things that directly contradict the words of Jesus, that church is out of line.

Christians might not realize that the pope's infallibility is actually a relatively new idea in canon law, one that goes back just over a century to Vatican I. I'll explain more about Vatican I in a later chapter. Many popes have *tried* to claim infallibility, but it was not universally accepted. In fact, a number of popes willingly agreed that the supreme pontiff could make mistakes.

In Pope Innocent IV's (1243–1254) *Commentary on the Decalogue*, he wrote:

> Of course, a pope can err in matters of faith. Therefore, no one ought to say, 'I believe that because the Pope believes it', but because the Church believes it. If he follows the Church he will not err.

He's not alone. Many popes offered the same sentiments, including Vigilius, Innocent III, Clement IV, Gregory XI, Adrian VI and Paul IV.

I wish it *were* the case that the pope always spoke from the heart of Christ. I really do. The history of Europe would have been much different if all the popes were men who served God faithfully, who truly depended on the Holy Spirit for guidance. Sadly, we cannot trust any man simply because he holds a particular position. Sitting in the Chair of Saint Peter doesn't guarantee that a man will love God the way Peter did.

TYRANNY OF THE POWERFUL

Sadly, in both the New and the Old Testaments, we find that those in charge repeatedly punished and killed the prophets who *did* speak from the heart of God. At the climax of history, the High Priest of Judaism — the holy man who entered into the Holy of Holies on Yom Kippur, was the same High Priest who accused Jesus Christ of blasphemy and assented to His death.[13] We should not assume that Christian leaders are any better than the Jewish leaders who went before them; because we gentiles are merely grafted into the vine that *is* Israel.[14]

The Israelites were the chosen people of God, the apple of God's eye. They were the children of Abraham, the friend of God. God had performed massive miracles among them over and over again, but throughout the Bible we watch Israel led into idolatry over and over by the very men who were supposed to be leading them to love the LORD with all their hearts.

Human beings fail. They fail constantly, and it's foolish to assume infallibility of any man, even if it's his job to faithfully speak by the Spirit of Christ.

Church historian Michael Walsh notes:

> Papal authority as it is now exercised, with its accompanying doctrine of papal infallibility, cannot be found in theories about the papal role expressed by early

---
13 Matthew 26:65
14 Romans 11:18-21

Popes and other Christians during the first 500 years of Christianity.[15]

What does Jesus say? Does He tell us to unquestionably obey those who came after Him? No, Jesus said no such thing! In fact, He warns us:

> *Beware of false prophets, who come to you in sheep's clothing, but inwardly they are ravenous wolves. You will know them by their fruits. Do men gather grapes from thornbushes or figs from thistles? Even so, every good tree bears good fruit, but a bad tree bears bad fruit.*
> Matthew 7:15-17

What else does Jesus tell us? He tells us to be innocent but wise.

> *Behold, I send you out as sheep in the midst of wolves. Therefore be wise as serpents and harmless as doves.*
> Matthew 10:16

We always have to be on the lookout for deceptive philosophies. Paul warned the Colossians to keep Christ as supreme, reminding them that it is in Him alone that we are complete:

> *As you therefore have received Christ Jesus the Lord, so walk in Him, rooted and built up in Him and established in the faith, as you have been taught, abounding in it with thanksgiving. Beware lest anyone cheat you through philosophy and empty deceit, according to the tradition of men, according to the basic principles of the world, and not according to Christ. For in Him dwells all the fullness of the Godhead bodily; and you are complete in Him, who is the head of all principality and power.*
> Colossians 2:6-10

---

15 From Introduction of Michael Walsh, *An Illustrated History of the Popes* (New York: St. Martin's Press, 1980).

All Christians can agree on this. We can all agree that Christ has all primacy. His word is preeminent. However, many faithful church goers do not realize that the traditions they have been taught actually contradict the words of Christ. They have believed things taught "after the traditions of men, and after the rudiments of the world." And that's why I'm writing this book.

Church leaders are important, and the Bible makes this clear. Teachers and pastors and evangelists are listed as spiritually gifted positions. However, the Bible also makes it clear that no human being has ever been sinless but Jesus Christ. Therefore, when we want to know what is true, we have to go to His words first. If any religious teacher denies the plain teachings of Christ, then we don't have to listen to that teacher. We do not want Jesus to say of us what He said of the people of His day:

These people draw near to Me with their mouth, And honor Me with their lips, But their heart is far from Me. And in vain they worship Me, Teaching as doctrines the commandments of men..

Matthew 15:8-9

We do not want Jesus to say that of us. We want him to say of us, "these are people who worship God in spirit and in truth."[16]

So, are the popes infallible? It is clear from history that they are not.

Pope Formosus

We see a bizarre possibility arise in church history. Popes not only were able to disagree with each other, but one pope might seek punishment for a preceding pope that had already died. Even a one-time Holy See was not immune to being punished after death, as in the case of Pope Formosus. A trial for this pope was held in the tomb of St. John Lateran in Rome in January of A.D. 897.

I envision a row of flickering candles descending into the consuming darkness. The yellow lights glimmer, illuminating the way for monks dressed in frayed robes. The holy men stop before

---
[16] Cf. John 4:23-24

Figure 8: "Pope Formosus and Stephen VI" by Jean-Paul Laurens (1870), Musée des Beaux-Arts de Nantes.

the crypt of Pope Formosus and strain at the heavy slab of marble until it slides back, exposing the sarcophagus contents.

At the time of this event, Pope Formosus has lain buried undisturbed for nine months, and his body is only partially decomposed in the stone coffin. As the lid slides back, a putrid stench emanates from the rotting remains wrapped in a penitential hair shirt. The monks step back from the foul smell and cover their noses. They then slowly raise curled fingers to their foreheads and crossed their chests. The sunken face of Pope Formosus stares up at them from vacant eye sockets. Gray, matted hair sprouts in tufts from the pope's brown skull.

The monks gently lift the corpse from the crypt, along with trailing strands of spider webs. They dress the corpse in pontifical vestments, using great care not to tear the sinew holding each bone in place.

It is a matter of history that Pope Formosus was carried to a large, stone-arched chamber courtroom and propped up in an ornately-carved chair. The skull of the dead pope was positioned to stare directly at his accuser; the presiding judge Pope Stephen VI. A teenage deacon stood beside the cadaver, quavering. It was his unpleasant task to offer a defense for the mute defendant.

Stephen VI reigned (quite briefly) as Supreme Pontiff at the time of this gruesome trial. He wasted no time reading aloud a stream of charges. A group of clergy stood at one side of the room, and the corpse sat in wilting silence at the other. Pope Stephen VI unleashed a long tirade of accusations, and I imagine his eyes bulging with passion. The jawbone of the defendant merely dangled, offering no defense and no distinct expressions of fear or concern.

Those in the courtroom watched in stunned silence as Stephen shouted vindictive criticisms and insults. No one had ever witnessed such a scene. The young deacon had an occasional opportunity to speak in defense of his mute client, but he only managed a few hushed comments. It was unwise to make a great effort.

When this pretense of a trial reached its predetermined finale, Pope Formosus was found guilty. Immediately Pope Stephen VI ordered the three fingers of Formosus' right hand hacked off — the three fingers that had been used to give the papal blessing. Any ordinations Formosus had made were formally rescinded, and his body was stripped of its vestments and returned to the ground — this time in a pauper's grave.

From this point, the story has a variety of endings. Whatever else was done to the body of Pope Formosus, his remains were eventually reinterred in St. Peter's Basilica — according to basilica records.

Things didn't end well for Pope Steven VI. Not long after the trial of Formosus, Stephen was taken prisoner following a palace revolt. He was stripped of his pontifical attire, clothed in rags, and locked in a dank cell. He was later found cold, stiff, and blue on the floor, having been strangled to death.

A struggle for power followed the death of Stephen VI. In the span of only six years, seven popes and anti-popes came and went.[17]

We would hope and pray that the person holding the judgment seat at the Vatican would be a true man of God — just and wise, following Jesus Christ with all his heart. That would be a blessing to faithful believers everywhere. However, in this cruel and wicked world, we find that having worldly power says nothing about a man's position with the Lord. The Son of God was born in a stable. He took the role of the Lamb of God, who came to take away the sins of the world. During the time of Christ, the Pharisees held wealth, power and religious

---
17 Chamberlin, E.R. (1969). Bad Popes. New York: Dial Press, page 21.

position; but they did not please the Father. The popes — just like the Pharisees — have sadly held the highest positions of worldly power, but their fruits have often resembled those of the very enemy of our souls.[18]

---

[18] Cf. Isaiah 14:12-14; Revelation 12:10. In John 8:31-59, Jesus speaks in the Temple to Jews who believed on him and also to those who were planning to kill him. Pharisees were there. They were the most righteous-looking men in their day, but their hearts were far from God. In all ages we have seen this. God often chooses the young, the weak, the poor to represent Him. According to 1 Corinthians 1:26-29, He will not have men glorifying themselves in His presence.

CHAPTER 9

VATICAN I

Many popes had claimed infallibility in the past, but it was only at Vatican I in 1869-1870 that Pope Pius IX was formally declared infallible as a virtue of his office.

Before Vatican I, several popes willingly recognized their own failures and the failures of those who had gone before them. In 1523, Pope Adrian VI grieved over the extent of the Black Plague, and in humility acknowledged that the Holy See had not always conducted himself in a holy manner. The Reformation was sweeping through the Germanic states, and Adrian openly recognized that the church needed reforming. He wrote a *Self-Accusation of the Papacy* to give to the Nuremberg Diet as an effort to acknowledge the church's faults.

Figure 9: Pope Pius IX by George Peter Alexander Healy (1871).

Adrian VI also told the Consistory:

If by the Roman church you mean its head or pontiff, it is beyond question that he can err even in the matters touching the faith. He does this when he teaches heresy by his own judgement or decretal. In truth, many Roman Pontiffs were heretics...[1]

Adrian VI died of an illness later that year, and schism between the Reformers and the Roman Curia grew ever deeper. The violence between Catholics and Protestants that followed is a time of European history that should shame all of Christendom. Unspeakable crimes were committed by both sides, and Christ's called to "love your enemies" appeared to have gone unheeded. In March of 2000, Pope John Paul II made an official apology for wrongs done by the Roman Catholic Church over the centuries, and it was well-received by the world.

Yet, popes who recognize their own failings are few and far between. The Vatican has long held onto power by insisting its decisions are above reproach, and any debate about the pope's infallibility was silenced in 1869-1870 during Vatican I.

Vatican I

All of those in attendance at the council knew what Pope Pius IX wanted. In his effort to counteract the rationalism and liberalism in Europe, he wanted to push through the proposition that the pope was infallible. Opposition was stiff, because the church had repeatedly squashed this notion in the past, and support for infallibility existed only amongst a small minority of voting members. They knew full-well church support was against such preposterous notion, but Pope Pius IX wanted his way in the matter, and he eventually got it.

One of those in attendance was the German theologian J.H. Ignaz von Dollinger, a devoted Catholic who had taught theology for 47 years. He stood firmly against the pope's claim for infallibility, insisting there were no criteria for it to be found

---

[1] James C. Bouffard, *A Quest for Absolute Power*, 2nd ed (Pomona, California: Lynn Paulo Foundation, 2009), 28.

in the Bible. No one in the church could pressure Dollinger to change his mind on the matter, so Catholic leadership unceremoniously excommunicated him on April 17, 1871. When he was urged to return to the church, he responded in a letter, "Ought I to appear before the Eternal Judge, my conscience burdened with a double perjury?"[2]

The Swiss historian August Bernhard Hasler was the Vatican Secretariat for Christian Unity for five years, and thus had access to Vatican archives. He researched the issue and died in an untimely manner after penning his manuscript *How the Pope Became Infallible*.[3] Vatican I voted for an unpopular position, but only after a great deal of manipulation in the council.

According to Hasler, the majority of bishops at Vatican I were against the issue on the table. A list of embarrassing résumés by bad popes had plagued the papacy down the long road of church history. In fact, it was well known by those in attendance that many popes had sinned egregiously and made unbiblical statements. Because of that, several voting members left before the final vote was taken. Many were forced to return under personal threat. Bishop Francois Le Courtier was so disgusted with the whole affair; he threw his conciliar document into the river and then headed off for Rome. He was later removed from his bishopric.

Intimidations and threats boiled over, forcing most of the others into line. Travel visas were cancelled to keep bishops from fleeing the vote. In his diary about the troubling events, Archbishop Georges Darboy's wrote "the elections are dishonest." Another bishop criticized the "utter worthlessness of these elections." Bishop John Stephanian refused to support the vote for infallibility of the pope; he was later arrested on the street by the papal police.

On July 17, 1870, the day before the final vote was to be taken, 55 bishops in opposition declared they did not want or wish to take part. When the vote was finally taken, there were only 535 "aye" votes out of the 1084 original members entitled to vote.

---

2 *The Catholic Encyclopedia* entry on Johann Joseph Ignaz von Döllinger.
3 August B. Hasler, *How the Pope Became Infallible: Pius IX and the Politics of Persuasion* (Garden City, NY: Doubleday, 1981). The statements that follow about Vatican I are gleaned from his book.

Of course, popes are fallible. The manipulated council of Vatican I didn't change the reality; it just changed what good Catholics are "supposed" to believe.

Personal Responsibility

The model we have in the Bible is always of personal responsibility. Even if every single pope and bishop and every other Christian leader demonstrated the fruit of the Spirit according to Galatians 5, and even if all manner of miracles took place wherever they went, we would still be responsible for double checking everything they taught against the Bible itself. The pope has the job of representing Jesus Christ, but the fact is that every one of us has the job of representing Jesus Christ to the world. No matter who our teachers are, we should never give up our own right to exercise discernment.

When the popes declared that they had the same authority as Christ and that their words were as the words of God himself, they were in grave and shameful error. The early church leaders should have withstood them, because they had begun to trust in their own self-righteousness.

Beloved, believe not every spirit, but try the spirits whether they are of God: because many false prophets are gone out into the world.

1 John 4:1

This tradition of the Pope's infallibility is not based in the Bible. It just isn't. It's a usurpation of authority that belongs only to God. When papal infallibility was pronounced in 1870 by the Vatican Council, all democratic processes within the church were forever placed on the slippery slope of totalitarianism.

Chapter 10

Rotten Popes

Pope Pius II (1458-1464) is said to have declared that Rome was "the only city run by bastards." Whether he really said this, there are a wide variety of popes and cardinals known to have sired illegitimate children. Other popes were violent, murderous, and cruel.

It's important to remember how many church traditions are based on the guidance of the popes — not just in their official capacity to offer papal bulls, but also in their leadership of councils. I'm coming against church traditions that contradict the Bible. I want to establish that it's dangerous to depend on the church leadership of the Middle Ages for anything trustworthy. It's important to recognize how many ungodly men held the sacred office.

Rodrigo de Borgia openly acknowledged the many children he had produced by his mistresses, yet the College of Cardinals still voted him in as Pope Alexander VI in 1492. Several movies and television shows have been based on the Borgia family for the intrigue, nepotism and violence that surrounded them. Machiavelli's philosophical treatise *The Prince* took a lot of lessons from Alexander VI's son Casare Borgia. Machiavelli practically worshiped the young man for murdering his opponents and crushing people to maintain power.

Pope Julius II "the Terrible" (1503-1513) followed shortly after Alexander VI. He is notorious as the "warrior pope" who used warfare to advance his purposes. He was also a patron of the arts, like his successor Leo X, but Leo really took papal spending to a new level.

Leo X (1513-1521) was the son of the famous Medici ruler of Florence, Lorenzo the Magnificent, and he was just 37 when he became pope. Leo loved all things beautiful, and within two years he had spent up all the money that Julius II had saved. He raised money for the new St. Peter's Basilica through the sale of indulgences, but his extravagance and excesses likely encouraged the violent confrontations of the Reformation even among those who cared nothing for theology.

It is well recognized that Leo X had a spending problem. However, historians of Leo's day also insinuated that he had a variety of male lovers. Bishop and historian Paolo Giovio noted that Leo X showed his handsome male chamberlains far more playful attention than looked good. A few short years after Leo's death, the 16th century historian Francesco Guicciardini wrote:

> At the beginning of his pontificate most people deemed him very chaste; however, he was afterwards discovered to be exceedingly devoted – and every day with less and less shame – to that kind of pleasure that for honour's sake may not be named.

As bad as they were, these popes who reigned on the cusp of the Reformation could hardly compete with the popes of the 9th through 11th[th] centuries, who initiated a time in history known as the "Midnight of the Dark Ages." Of the twenty-five popes between 955 and 1057, thirteen were appointed by the local aristocracy. The other twelve popes were appointed by German emperors. Obviously, there was a conflict of interests here. For two hundred years, things were rotten in Rome, until the reforming pope Gregory VII (1073-1085) took the papal throne.

Pope John XII (955-964) was one of the most vile, heinous popes ever. The Catholic Encyclopedia openly declares that John XII was:

> ...a coarse, immoral man, whose life was such that the Lateran was spoken of as a brothel, and the moral corruption in Rome became the subject of general odium. War and the chase were more congenial to this pope than church government.

Holy Roman Emperor Otto I wrote a damning letter to the young man, stating:

> Everyone, clergy as well as laity accuses you, Holiness, of homicide, perjury, sacrilege, incest with your relatives, including two of your sisters, and with having, like a pagan, invoked Jupiter, Venus, and other demons.[1]

This was a dangerous letter to write, because John XII had flayed the skin off a bishop and decapitated 63 members of the clergy and nobility in Rome. He was a violent man who had gouged out the eyes of a cardinal who displeased him, as well as having two of the unfortunate man's fingers removed along with his nose and tongue. Still, the word was that John gambled incessantly and called upon pagan gods and goddesses to give him favor with throws of the dice. He'd slept with his father's mistress and reportedly his own mother. He was finally forced from the papacy, but he did not live long afterward. As the story goes, John was caught in the act of adultery with a married woman, and her enraged husband bashed in the pope's head with a hammer.

Pope Benedict IX (1032-1048) acted as pope three different times. He was elected for the first time at the age of 20 through a campaign of bribery by his father, Count Alberic III of the Tusculum family. This young man was such a debauched pope, so violent and depraved, the populace of Rome couldn't stand him. In 1045, Benedict was chased out of the city and replaced by Silvester III. Benedict was not a person to sit by idly while being kicked off the throne, so he financed a private army and forcibly made his way back into the papacy. His second reign didn't last long. Six months later he decided to sell his position to one John Gratianus (Gregory VI) for a large amount of money, and he abdicated — possibly to get married. Benedict was back for a third stint two years later, but in 1048, he was driven out of Rome for good.

It is outrageous to suggest that any of these men were ever infallible simply because they had fought, bought, connived their

---
1 Brian Moynahan, *The Faith: A History of Christianity* (New York: Image Books, 2003), 215.

way into the papacy. I don't want to suggest there weren't good popes. Some incredible, dedicated men have held the papacy. However, there were plenty of rotten eggs in the basket, and they all underline the problem of depending on one single man to be the worldwide Vicar of Christ.

Chapter 11

Protestants

Protestants should also be careful. There have been great evangelists and preachers of the Gospel throughout the years who have said things the Bible does not support. Even if Charles Wesley or Charles Spurgeon or Charles Swindoll preaches something, we are still under obligation to hold up those teachings to the light of the Bible.

All human beings are fallible, and during the Reformation, both Catholics and Protestants were guilty of violence. Bloody and brutal punishments were not exclusive to the Roman Catholic Church. In the early years of the Reformation, Protestants watered their own sprouting roots with blood.

The renowned Reformation leader John Calvin (1500-1564) served in Geneva, Switzerland, both preaching and proposing reforms. While Calvin preached a separation of church and civil government, the council of Geneva supported many of his proposals. The city council created a Consistory, an ecclesiastical court for non-civil matters, which kept strict discipline in the city. Most punishments were minor — they involved going to sermons or catechism classes. After 1543, the civil government took charge of all punishments for those convicted by the Consistory.

Calvin's Geneva had very strict rules of morality. Bawdy singing and dancing were forbidden. There were those in town who called themselves "patriots" but were labeled "libertines" by Calvin. They were basically unsaved people who didn't want civil or religious authorities telling them what to do. They were pantheists who rejected the idea of sin in any practical sense, and they treated Christ's crucifixion as merely symbolic with no historic reality.

The libertines strongly opposed Calvin and the council. On June 27, 1547, a placard was attached to Calvin's pulpit in St. Peter's Church, stating:

> Gross hypocrite...if you do not save yourselves by flight, nobody shall prevent your overthrow, and you will curse the hour when you left your monkery. Warning has been already given that the devil and his renegade priests were come hither to ruin everything. But after people have suffered long they avenge themselves...[1]

Church officials rounded up one Jacques Gruet, whose house was searched and allegedly blasphemous writings were found, as well as verbal criticisms of Calvin. The handwriting on the placard was openly known not to be Gruet's, but he was accused of attaching it to the pulpit. He was summarily tortured for a month to elicit a confession. The victim finally confessed to his "crime" and was subsequently lashed to a wooden stake with his feet nailed through. He was beheaded on July 26, 1547.[2]

There was also the famous case of Michael Servetus, notable for his denial of the Trinity. He denounced Calvin and his theology, called for his removal from the ministry and even his death. The Council, along with the other Swiss churches, all condemned Servetus and voted to have him burned. Calvin sought to have him beheaded as a more compassionate execution, but his position was rejected and Servetus was burned at the stake on October 27, 1553. Thank you Council and Swiss churches for your warmth and love. The Catholic Inquisition in France burned Servetus in effigy some months later — but the Protestants had burned him in real life.

The Roman Catholic Church was not alone in choosing brutal punishments to deal with those they opposed.

---

[1] Opera, XII. 546, note 8.
[2] Jean M.V. Audin. *History of the Life, Works, and Doctrines of John Calvin*, trans. John McGill (Louisville: B.J. Webb & Brother, 1850), 397.

Martin Luther

Like all men, the Reformation leader Martin Luther had strengths and he had weaknesses. We know from his life that Luther went to the extreme in everything he did.

Early in his ministry, Luther disapproved of the poor treatment of Jews and sought to have them converted by kindness. In 1523, he wrote against treating them poorly, saying:

> I would request and advise that one deal gently with them [the Jews] ... If we really want to help them, we must be guided in our dealings with them not by papal law but by the law of Christian love. We must receive them cordially, and permit them to trade and work with us, hear our Christian teaching, and witness our Christian life. If some of them should prove stiff-necked, what of it? After all, we ourselves are not all good Christians either.[3]

As the years drew on, however, Luther came to abhor the Jews. By 1543, he had become utterly frustrated with their refusal to convert to Christianity, and he wrote a massive treatise entitled *On the Jews and Their Lies*. He said, "A Jewish heart is as hard as a stick, a stone, as iron, as a devil."[4] In this treatise, he urged the German princes to implement a variety of serious penalties against all Jews:

- Burn their schools and synagogues.
- Transfer Jews to community settlements.
- Confiscate all Jewish literature, which was blasphemous.
- Prohibit rabbis to teach, on pain of death.
- Deny Jews safe-conduct, so as to prevent the spread of Judaism.
- Appropriate their wealth and use it to support converts and to prevent the lewd practice of usury.
- Assign Jews to manual labor as a form of penance.

---

[3] As quoted in Gritsch, Eric W., "Was Martin Luther Anti-Semitic?" *Christianity Today*, No. 39 (1993).
[4] Martin Brecht, *Martin Luther: The Preservation of the Church*, 1532-1546, Volume 3, trans. James Schaff (Minneapolis: Fortress Press, 1999), 346.

Luther's friends and enemies alike censured him for offering such dark-hearted measures and pleaded with him to halt such rantings. He did not. Just before his death, Martin Luther declared, "*We are at fault for not slaying them.*"[5] Sadly, the Nazis used Luther's polemics against the Jews as a justification for their brutal treatment during the Holocaust.

Martin Luther was enraged against the Jews for many reasons, but one can be traced to German literature, which spread false rumors condemning Jews for spreading the disastrous plague. It was said Jews had poisoned Christian water wells with the horrific disease. Fabrications like these had led to a series of terrifying massacres against major Jewish communities in the years 1348-1350, and few Christians seemed to care because Jews were generally hated in Europe.[6]

It is my opinion that Martin Luther and John Calvin's church in Geneva fell into the same dark pit as the medieval Roman Catholic Church. These men are revered by Protestants for wanting to return to a rule by God with their Reformation cry of *sola scriptura*. However, all groups were influenced by a cultural residue in which harsh punishments were acceptable and in which religion and politics were hardly separated. No religious leaders can be held up as perfect. We can only take advantage of the valuable contributions of each teacher. Neither Calvin, nor Luther, nor any pope is the author and finisher of our faith. That job belongs to Jesus Christ alone.[7] That is why it is so very vital we adhere to His teachings and not constantly retool the Bible to create religious empires of our own.

---

5   Ibid.
6   Tzafrir Barzilay, *Well Poisoning Accusations in Medieval Europe*: 1250-1500 (Columbia University Academic Commons, 2016).
7   Hebrews 12:2

Chapter 12

False Documents

During the Counter Reformation at the Council of Trent, the Roman Catholic Church affirmed that the traditions of the church were equal to the Bible in inspiration and therefore had equal weight. One of the biggest troubles with this view is a variety of fraudulent documents had leaked into the church. Centuries often passed before these documents were determined to be forgeries, and by that time the ideas in those documents had worked their way into the minds of the people. While the fakes were finally discovered, the ideas they produced weren't dispelled as easily as their false provenances.

This is a serious issue. Our ability to trust many church traditions depends on whether the popes and church councils actually obeyed the Spirit of Christ or whether they were following their own logic and the political atmosphere of their day. If those edicts contradicted the Word of God, they should never have been embraced; and yet we find that traditions were accepted as equal to God's Word, and so there was no check on the traditions at all. The fact that fraudulent documents survived without excoriation for *centuries* should give us grave concern.

The False Decretals

For instance, documents known as the Isidorian Decretals — or Pseudo-Isidorian Decretals — have long been known to be complete forgeries. *The Catholic Encyclopedia* calls them the "False Decretals" that were included in the Collection of Isidore. These were obvious forgeries, about 100 letters credited to a variety of popes from the first to the eighth centuries. However, the letters appeared out of nowhere in the ninth century and are replete with anachronisms — quotes and allusions to events that took place during centuries *after* they were supposed to have been written.

Though known to be forgeries now, the False Decretals were taken at face value for at least six centuries before suspicions about them began to grow. It took another three centuries for the extent of the forgeries to be realized. In the meanwhile, they accomplished their goal in fraudulently establishing the authority of the church hierarchy over any secular powers, and thus provided a legal foundation for the ascendancy of the popes' unquestioned power in Western Christendom.

What were they exactly? An author (or authors) who used the pseudonym of Isidore Mercator of Seville was very clever when he invented the letters. He placed his forgeries in a collection of actual records of the Council of Nicaea, with a few other genuine decretals (very few).

It was recognized by the late 1800s that most of the Isidorian Decretals were faked. Yet, while the church knew these documents were forgeries, they were used in Vatican I to defend the vote in favor of the pope's infallibility. They were used to show that there was an old precedent, or tradition, granting the early popes full and complete authority in all matters. It was reasoned that if the early bishops of Rome had exercised full authority, then later popes also had that authority, and nobody should be free to question their judgment.

Yet, these papal letters were "all rot." They weren't based on reality at all. In fact, there wasn't even a proper "pope" that claimed to lead all of Christendom until the very end of the fourth century. Church historian Dollinger explained the situation in blunt terms in 1869, saying:

> It would be difficult to find in all history a second instance of so successful, and yet so clumsy a forgery. For three centuries past it has been exposed, yet the principles it introduced and brought into practice have taken such deep root in the soil of the Church, and have so grown

into her life, that the exposure of the fraud has produced no result in shaking the dominant system.[1]

Pope Pious IX knew full well these letters were forgeries, but nonetheless he used them in Vatican I to pressure council members to declare infallibility of all popes as an official dogma of the Roman Catholic Church. The Decretals were also the Pope's justification for the unlimited power to excommunicate church members. They were a lethal weapon of incalculable effect upon many unsuspecting church patrons, because those forged letters became one basis for theology and canon laws that last until today.

It doesn't matter whether it's the Roman Catholic Church or the Reformed churches or the Evangelical churches, once tradition gets rooted in, it likes to stay put. Thomas Torrance stated it well:

> It is high time we asked again whether the Word of God really does have free course amongst us and whether it is not after all bound and fettered by the traditions of men. The tragedy, apparently, is that the very structures of our Churches represent the fossilization of traditions that have grown up by practice and procedure, have become so hardened in self-justification that even the Word of God can hardly crack them open.[2]

DONATION OF CONSTANTINE

The Pseudo-Isidorian Decretals were not alone. One particular document can be considered the biggest real estate con-job in all history, and it provided the Roman Catholic Church with wealth beyond anything we can imagine. Much of that wealth is still enjoyed today.

In A.D. 753, after just one year as Supreme Pontiff, Stephen II made an arduous trek north in the dead of an icy winter. He went

---
1 Ignaz von Dollinger, et al. *The Pope and the Council, 2nd ed.* (London: Rivingtons, 1869), 94-95.
2 Torrance, Thomas F., "The Radical Consequences of Justification," *The Scottish Journal of Theology* 13, no 3 (1960): 237-246.

to see the King of the Franks, and with him may have travelled certain dusty documents dated to March 30, 315. He likely had no clue these documents, the "Donation of Constantine," were recently invented. They were credited to the great emperor, and they gave Stephen II some leverage.

The Frank's King Pépin III — "Pépin the Short" — had a son that history would remember as Charlemagne. The lad was just 11-years-old when he met Pope Stephen II and led the entourage to his father. As Stephen II stood before King Pépin, his hair was full of ashes, and his black robe was sullied and weathered from a long, muddy journey. The pope knelt at the king's feet and begged for his military assistance. The Lombards had conquered Ravenna, one of the last Roman Empire cities in northern Italy, and the pope was desperate for help.

We cannot be sure, but it's possible that Pope Stephen II handed over the faked Donation of Constantine documents to the king at this meeting. This decree claimed that four centuries earlier, Emperor Constantine had donated vast amounts of land to Pope Sylvester. The donation was a reward for Sylvester's

Figure 10: A fresco of Constantine the Great presenting his Donation to Sylvester (13th century) in the Santi Quattro Coronati, Rome.

education of Constantine in Christianity, as well as the baptism by Sylvester which healed Constantine of leprosy. Those lands included Rome itself, the Lateran palace, and "the provinces, districts, and towns of Italy and all the Western regions."[3] The Donation decreed the pope's right to wear a crown and use imperial signs, and it gave him authority over the patriarchs of Antioch, Alexandria, Constantinople, and Jerusalem. These gifts and honors were to be transferred to each and every succeeding Roman pope into perpetuity.

The amount of land that Constantine allegedly gave to Sylvester was vast. It would be as if a US president today held a document claiming George Washington had granted the presidents perpetual dominion over all lands west of the Mississippi. Of course, the presidents are only elected to four-year terms. Once elected, the popes remain in office for the rest of their lives. It is possible that Pépin was provided with these documents, and they encouraged him to hand over the cities of northern Italy to the pope.

The Donation of Constantine was a fraud, and a very obvious one to those who bothered to check it out. At the very least, Constantine's donation to Sylvester would not have continued after Constantine's death, because the empire is much greater than any one emperor. However, there were also a number of internal hints the document was a fraud. Its authenticity began to be questioned within a few hundred years, but it took many more centuries for the Donation of Constantine to be proven a forgery.

In 1440, a Roman Catholic priest named Lorenzo Valla showed indisputably that it was a fraudulent document, written between 750 and 850.[4] Nobody knows who penned the Donation of Constantine, but its language and its use of materials written long after Constantine demonstrated that it had been forged.

We do know that Pope Stephen II managed to convince King Pépin the Short to come to his aid against the Lombards, with

---

[3] "Donation of Constantine," *The Catholic Encyclopedia*.
[4] *Ibid*.

whom the Franks had previously been at peace. The Lombards were forced to give up their conquests, and King Pépin gave Ravenna and an array of other cities in northern Italy to the papacy. This was the beginning of the Papal States, and the pope no longer merely held religious authority over the Roman Empire; he now held temporal power as well.

As long as the medieval world believed that Constantine had given extravagant holdings to Pope Sylvester, it offered precedence for the Holy See to hold worldly power, to wear a crown, and to rule over the other patriarchs and bishops around the world. The Donation of Constantine was used extensively by Pope Leo IX in 1054 in a letter to the Patriarch of Constantinople, and his arguments for the supremacy of the Bishop of Rome led to greater schism between the East and West. The Donation was used in the papacy's claims for political authority and in its constant power struggles with the kings of Europe.

Lorenzo Valla openly declared the Donation a fake. He stated that the church had been corrupted by temporal power, which had caused wars in Italy and perpetrated the "overbearing, barbarous, tyrannical priestly domination."[5] He recognized the failure of the papacy to seek the care and spiritual health of the people, instead, used the people to build the wealth of those in control. He mourned, "So far from giving food and bread to the household of God. ...they have devoured us as food."[6]

While the individual popes did not possess these land holdings, the Chair of the Pope did, which made it convenient to pass a Titanic's worth of power and wealth down the line of succession. This meant that political authorities worked to put men on the papal throne who would benefit them, and it meant that men were willing to do anything to be placed on that throne.

Of course, the influence of the Donation permitted policies that remained ever after, even after it was deemed a fake. The pope's foot is still kissed, a holdout from a Byzantine ritual known as *proskynesis* which is to offer total adoration to an emperor. The Vatican still has incredible wealth, and the jewel-

---
5 Prosser, Peter. "Church History's biggest hoax: Renaissance scholarship proved fatal for one of the medieval papacy's favorite claims," *Christian History* no. 72 (2001): 35.
6 Christopher B. Coleman, ed., *The Treatise of Lorenzo Valla on the Donation of Constantine* (New Haven: Yale University Press, 1922), 166.

encrusted crown, the papal tiara, was last worn by Pope Paul VI in 1963.

Martin Luther himself managed to get hold of a copy of the Donation of Constantine in 1517, the very year he unleashed his criticism of the Roman Church for the lucrative sales of indulgences. Droves of German citizens protested against the leadership in Rome due to the darkening shadow of scandals. The forgery of the Donation offered the reformers more ammunition against a church hierarchy seen as corrupt; one focused more on riches and power than on providing the people with the Word of God.

With that, let's look at a few traditions that have plagued Christendom…

Part II

Troubling Traditions

Chapter 13

Major Events: An Overview

Year (A.D)	Event
30/33	Death and Resurrection of Christ
34	Martyrdom of Stephen
44	Martrydom of James, son of Zebedee
64	Great fire burns Rome. Emperor Nero blames Christians.
70	Jerusalem and Temple burned by Romans
41-305	Time of Persecution under Roman Emperors, during the reigns of:

- 41-54   Claudius
- 54-68   Nero
- 81-96   Domitian
- 98-117   Trajan
- 161-180   Marcus Aurelius
- 193-211   Septimius Severus
- 235-238   Maximinus Thrax
- 249-251   Decius
- 253-260   Valerian
- 284-305   Diocletian

135	Last Jewish forces in Bar Kochba Revolt defeated at Betar.
312	Battle at Milvian Bridge. Constantine Converts to Christianity.
313	Emperors Constantine and Licinius sign the Edict of Milan, which proclaimed religious toleration in the Roman Empire.
324	Constantine founds Constantinople on site of ancient Byzantium.
325	First ecumenical council held at Nicaea. Nicene Creed produced.
380	Edict of Thessalonica institutes Christianity as state religion of Roman Empire.
393	The Council of Hippo sanctions 27 books for the New Testament.
397	The Council of Cartage confirms the same 27 books as Scripture.
405	Jerome completes the Latin Vulgate translation of the Bible.
410	Visigoths led by King Alaric sack Rome.
419	In *The City of God*, Saint Augustine suggests purification of souls after death.
431	The Council of Ephesus gives Mary the title "Mother of God."
529	Eastern Roman Emperor Justinian publishes his legal code.
593	Pope Gregory the Great makes case for purgatory in his *Dialogues*.
606	Emperor Phocus declares Boniface III the "Universal Bishop" of the church, placing the Bishop of Rome over all other bishops as the first empire-wide pope.
632	Mohammed completes the Quran.

Major Events: An Overview

800	Charlemagne is crowned emperor of the Romans.
852	Pseudo-Isidorian Decretals (or False Decretals) first quoted by Archbishop Hincmar of Reims.
993	Ulrich of Augsburg is the first saint canonized by a pope (Pope John XV).
1054	East-West Schism permanently splits Roman Catholic and Eastern Orthodox Churches.
1079	Pope Gregory VII mandates celibacy for the priesthood.
1095	At the Council of Clermont, Pope Urban II calls for the First Crusade to free the Holy Land from the Moors.
1184	The Medieval Inquisition was established in northern Italy and southern France.
1192	King Richard the Lionheart and Saladin sign the Treaty of Ramla, ending the Third Crusade and making way for Christian pilgrimages to Muslim-dominated Jerusalem.
1209	Sixty thousand citizens, Cathars heretics and faithful Catholics alike, are massacred in the sack of Béziers, France.
1215	Pope Innocent III holds Fourth Lateran Council. The Council issues 70 decrees and officially sanctions the doctrine of transubstantiation.
1229	Council of Toulouse forbids the laity to possess the Bible, especially in the vernacular.
1231	Pope Gregory IX institutes the Papal Inquisition to investigate heretics.
1234	The *Decretals of Gregory IX* is printed as an update of canon law.
1234	The Council of Tarragona rules that vernacular translations of the Bible must be turned over and burned.

1347	The Black Death hits Europe and wipes out 40-60% of the population.
1395	John Wycliffe completes an English translation of the whole Bible.
1401	The first Lollard martyr, William Sawtrey, is burned at the stake.
1401	Burning heretics legalized in England under King Henry IV's *De Heretico Comburendo*.
1408	Archbishop of Canterbury Thomas Arundel issued his *Constitutions Against the Lollards*.
1415	Ecumenical Council of Constance ends Western Schism and condemns the teachings of John Wycliffe and Jan Hus.
1415	Jan Hus is burned at the stake as a heretic for criticizing the Catholic Church.
1431	Joan of Arc is burned at the stake.
1439	Gutenberg first uses movable type.
1455	Gutenberg completes 42-line Gutenberg Bible.
1476	Pope Sixtus IV offers sales of indulgences to spare those in purgatory.
1478	Pope Sixtus IV authorizes Ferdinand and Isabella to found the Spanish Inquisition.
1492	Ferdinand and Isabella evict the Jews from Spain on the 9th of Av.
1516	The Greek New Testament of Erasmus of Rotterdam is published.
1517	Martin Luther nails his 95 Theses to the Castle Church door in Wittenberg.
1533	Henry VIII divorces Catherine of Aragon.
1534	Act of Supremacy makes the king the head of the Church of England.

Major Events: An Overview

1546	Roman Catholic tradition is declared equal in authority to the Bible, and apocryphal books affirmed as part of Roman Catholic canon at Council of Trent 4th session.
1555	Ridley and Latimer are burned at the stake by Queen "Bloody Mary."
1563	Official decree on purgatory is affirmed at Council of Trent, 25th session.
1563	William Tyndale is burned at the stake for translating the Bible into English.
1572	Tens of thousands of French Huguenots are murdered in the Saint Bartholomew's Day Massacre.
1555	The Peace of Augsburg gives princes freedom to choose the religion of their realms.
1692	Twenty people are executed during the Salem Witch Trials in Salem, Massachusetts.
1854	Pope Pius IX issues papal bull *Ineffabilis Deus*, declaring that Mary, the mother of Jesus, was conceived without original sin.
1870	Vatican I proclaims the pope infallible when he is speaking *ex cathedra*.
1883	Charles Gordon declares that he discovered the true location of Calvary.
1950	Pope Pius XII declares by *Munificentissimus Deus* the doctrine of the Assumption of Mary.
1971	Jim Irwin trudges through the mantle of dust that blankets the moon.

Chapter 14

Purgatory

We've established that we are permitted to think for ourselves — and are *responsible* to think for ourselves. We now must start examining certain traditions that arose in the church centuries after the deaths of the apostles. I've already stepped on some toes, and I'm going to step on more, because it's vital we consider these traditions and brutally compare them to the Word of God.

I want to start with the doctrine of purgatory, because many Christians do not realize that a place called "purgatory" isn't found in the Bible. In fact, the very idea of purgatory undermines everything the Bible teaches about salvation. That might come as a surprise, but it's vitally important we inspect this fundamental idea and assess it next to what the Bible actually says.

Figure 11: Souls in Purgatory in the nave dome of the Catholic parish church of St. Martin in Gabelbach, Bavaria.

What is purgatory? According to the *Catholic Encyclopedia*, it is:

Purgatory (Lat., *"purgare"*, to make clean, to purify) in accordance with Catholic teaching is a place or condition of temporal punishment for those who, departing this life in God's grace, are, not entirely free from venial faults, or have not fully paid the satisfaction due to their transgressions.

Official Catholic Church catechism states:

All who die in God's grace and friendship, but still imperfectly purified, are indeed assured of their eternal salvation; but after death they undergo purification, so as to achieve the holiness necessary to enter the joy of heaven. The Church gives the name purgatory to this final purification of the elect, which is entirely different from the punishment of the damned.[1]

In Catholic theology, purgatory is a place where the souls of Christians go after death to be cleansed of sins which were not fully paid for during their lifetime. Even popes once a year offer Mass for their predecessor popes who may be languishing in purgatory like everyone else.[2]

Official Catholic doctrine doesn't specify precisely where purgatory is. It's described simply as a place of cleansing fire and pain, where sins are burned away leaving only the pureness of our souls to enter heaven. Nobody knows how long any individual must remain there — whether a few years or ten million years. No priest knows how long this process takes, only that the cleansing procedure is necessary.

TEXTS FOR PURGATORY

The Roman Catholic Church does cite biblical sources for the idea of purgatory. For instance, 1 Corinthians 3:11-15, Matthew 5:25-26, and Matthew 12:31-32 are given as proof texts.

1 *Catechism of the Catholic Church*, 1030-1.
2 McCarthy, J. (1995). *The Gospels According to Rome*. Eugene, Oregon: Harvest House, pp. 113-114.

If we read these, however, we find that 1 Corinthians 3:11-15 is about our service to the Lord. The works we do in the Lord's service — whatever we do in our lives — building on the foundation of Jesus Christ's sacrifice — those *works* are put through a fire to see what's left. The wood, hay, and stubble of our lives are burned away, but the precious things we've done — portrayed as gold and gems — those are what remain after it's over. If we have anything left, we receive a reward. If we don't have anything left, we're still saved, but as though we just escaped a fire and lost all our stuff. This has nothing to do with purification for sins. It's about whether we'll receive additional rewards for our service to the Lord.

Matthew 5:25-26 is about wise behavior in this world, in accordance with the rest of the chapter. We want to avoid harsh punishments in this life — like jail — by dealing with problems quickly.

Matthew 12:31-32 is about blaspheming the Holy Spirit, the meaning of which is a matter of debate. We'll touch more on this passage in a moment.

We also find something else worth noting: people in the Bible still face the consequences of their sins, even after God has forgiven them. In 2 Samuel 12:13-20, David repented and God forgave him for his affair with Bathsheba, but because he had caused the God's enemies to blaspheme, his newborn son died. When Moses disobeyed God and struck the rock rather than speaking to it, God forgave him, but he was still forbidden to enter the Promised Land in Numbers 20:12.

These things are in the Bible, certainly. However, there is nothing in the Bible about a place of purification after death for those who are saved. That belief is an invention.

HISTORY OF PURGATORY

The idea of purgatory was an old one by the time it was adopted by the church in the Middle Ages. It was a concept rooted in the religious systems of ancient India and Persia. In Hinduism, for examples, Naraka is the place of torment after death, but it is considered a temporary place of punishment like purgatory. In Book X of Plato's *Republic*, Socrates tells Glaucon a story about "Er the son of Armenius, a Pamphylian by birth," who died in battle, but 12 days later awoke from the dead on the funeral pile and related what he had seen in the afterlife.[3] He described holy beings who judged the dead. Those considered righteous were sent to the beauty and glory of the heavenly realm and the unjust were sent into suffering. Those who had done wrongs suffered ten times over for the wrongs they had committed — before they could attain Elysium after 1000 years. Those who were too evil never entered Elysium, but were thrown into hell.

In Virgil's *Aeneid*, Book VI, the father Anchises says of the dead:

> Therefore are they schooled with punishments, and pay penance for bygone sins. Some are hung stretched out to the empty winds; from others the stain of guilt is washed away under swirling floods or burned out by fire till length of days, when time's cycle is complete, has removed the inbred taint and leaves unsoiled the ethereal sense and pure flame of spirit: each of us undergoes his own purgatory. Then we are sent to spacious Elysium, a few of us to possess the blissful fields.[4]

The main source of the current doctrine of purgatory is the concept of caring for and praying for the dead, which is found in many cultures. In the apocryphal book of 2 Maccabees 12:41-45, we find mention of praying for the dead.[5] The logic is that there is no reason to pray for the dead unless they can be freed from their suffering and escape more quickly to heaven through the intervention of our prayers on their behalf.

A variety of early church writings refer to making prayers for the dead. In the fifth century, Saint Augustine first dabbled

---
3   Written about 360 B.C.,
4   Virgil, *Aeneid*, VI:724. Written between 29 and 19 B,C. As translated by H. R. Fairclough.
5   In 1 Corinthians 15:29, we find that Paul makes an obscure remark about baptism for the dead while he's explaining the final resurrection. He doesn't say, "Why do we baptize for the dead?" He says, "Why then are they baptized for the dead?" The verse is as vague in Greek as it is in English, but he is also speaking to the people of Corinth and makes several allusions to Greek culture in the passage. It's possible Paul was referring to the practice of the cult of Demeter and Persephone at Eleusis, a city northeast of Corinth. As part of the rites leading up to celebration of Persephone's mythical return from the dead, the people of Eleusis would bathe - "be immersed" - in the sea.

with the idea of purgatory, describing the prayers and salvific sacrifices for the dead as something handed down from the church fathers to help sufferers gain more mercy than their sins deserved.[6]

In *The City of God* in A.D. 419, Saint Augustine offered an idea of purgatory as the purification of souls after their death, saying:

> Temporal punishments are suffered by some in this life only, by some after death, by some both here and hereafter, but all of them before that last and strictest judgment. But not all who suffer temporal punishments after death will come to eternal punishments, which are to follow after that judgment.[7]

Pope Gregory the Great (590-604) gave the idea of purgatory more formal credence through his interpretation of Matthew 12:31-32. Gregory the Great was one of the purest popes in all of Christian history. He graciously gave most of the church's money to the poor and had nothing to do with opulence and grandeur. Under disheartening circumstances, he managed the affairs of the church effectively. He promoted celibacy and morality and was a genuine lover of righteousness. However, Pope Gregory also offered confirmation to the existence of purgatory, which had been suggested by Augustine as a simple conjecture. Making an argument based on the passage about blasphemy of the Holy Spirit mentioned below, he said:

> As for certain lesser faults, we must believe that, before the Final Judgment, there is a purifying fire. He who is truth says that whoever utters blasphemy against the Holy Spirit will be pardoned neither in this age nor in the age to come. From this sentence we understand that certain offenses can be forgiven in this age, but certain others in the age to come.[8]

---

6   Augustine, *Sermons*, 159:1, 172:2 (A.D. 411) and Augustine, The City of God, 21:13 (A.D. 419).
7   Augustine, *The City of God*, 21:13.
8   Gregory the Great, *Dialogues* 4, 39: PL 77, 396 (A.D. 593).

Gregory's motives were certainly pure, but he still read into the Bible an idea that wasn't necessarily justified. Views like this, paved the way for the development of the doctrine of purgatory as an actual location, like heaven or hell.

An official position on purgatory was provided in the Decree of the Union produced by the Council of Florence (1438-1443),[9] but it was at the Council of Trent in 1548 that the doctrine of purgatory was officially affirmed. Purgatory took church fathers 600 years to develop and another 1,000 years to confirm.

It's easy to see how purgatory *seems* like a good idea. People die in their sins all the time. They certainly die with sins for which they have never fully repented, and we know that God must punish sin. Certainly, it seems better to go to purgatory for a little while to be cleansed so that we can enter heaven, rather than end up in hell for all eternity.

There are a number of problems with this doctrine, however, and we need to examine them.

GETHSEMANE

Remember how Jesus sought God the Father in the Garden of Gethsemane the night He was betrayed? Luke the doctor tells us that Jesus sweat blood because of His anguish.[10] Jesus repeatedly begged His Father to release Him from the terrible ordeal He was about to suffer. Yet, Jesus relented and said, *"O My Father, if it is possible, let this cup pass from Me; nevertheless, not as I will, but as You will."*[11]

Despite Jesus Christ's grievous prayer, God the Father did not spare His Son. Our Lord suffered and died in great anguish, in fulfillment of the Scriptures. If that was the *only* way — why do we think that we can pay for our sins through the burning fires of purgatory? If God required this terrible extreme to save us, why do we insist we still have to pay for our own sins? We are rescued from our sins through the blood of Christ. Isaiah prophesied in advance about the sacrifice of the Lord's perfect Servant:

---
9 Mansi, XXXI, 1031.
10 Luke 22:44
11 Matthew 26:39

Figure 12: "An angel comforting Jesus before his arrest in the Garden of Gethsemane" by Carl Bloch (1873), Museum of Natural History.

> *But He was wounded for our transgressions, He was bruised for our iniquities; The chastisement for our peace was upon Him, And by His stripes we are healed. All we like sheep have gone astray; We have turned, every one, to his own way; And the LORD has laid on Him the iniquity of us all.*
>
> Isaiah 53:5-6

That's one reason this is such a huge issue for me to tackle here. So many Christians — from all manner of backgrounds — believe we get to heaven by following "the rules." That's not what the Bible teaches. The New Testament writers repeatedly insist that we are saved by grace through faith in the work that Christ finished on the cross on our behalf. The sacrificial system of the Old Testament was fulfilled in the sacrifice of Jesus Christ, the Lamb of God who takes away the sins of the world.[12]

---

[12] Cf. John 1:29 and Hebrews

Fresh, Clean Clothes

In Zechariah, we see an interesting picture of a sinner before God's throne. Joshua the High Priest is brought before the Angel of the LORD, and Satan is there to oppose him. Joshua is dressed in filthy clothes, but the Lord does not incinerate Joshua to purify him. He merely gives him clean clothes to wear:

> *Then He answered and spoke to those who stood before Him, saying, "Take away the filthy garments from him." And to him He said, "See, I have removed your iniquity from you, and I will clothe you with rich robes."*
>
> Zechariah 3:4

Cleansing by Fire

In Isaiah 6, we find the prophet Isaiah before the throne of God, and in God's presence he feels the sinfulness of his own humanity. He cries out that he is a man of unclean lips from a people of unclean lips. He is cleansed by fire, but the process lasts just a second. One of the seraphim takes a live coal from the altar and flies to Isaiah. In verse 6:7, Isaiah explains:

> *And he touched my mouth with it, and said: "Behold, this has touched your lips; Your iniquity is taken away, And your sin purged."*

That was it. There were no years of painful suffering to purify him. Isaiah lived before Jesus Christ died on the cross, but his sins were paid for — because the blood of Jesus covers our sins for all time. We forget that God looks at us from outside of time. He is the Alpha and the Omega,[13] and He knew who would be His from the foundation of the world.[14] When we are born again according to John 3:16, all of our sins are paid for. All of them.

Paul explains to the Romans:

---

[13] Revelation 21:6, 22:13
[14] Hebrews 4:3; Revelation 13:8; 17:8

Now to him who works, the wages are not counted as grace but as debt. But to him who does not work but believes on Him who justifies the ungodly, his faith is accounted for righteousness...

Romans 4:4-5

Relief in Purgatory

What does that mean for indulgences? The Roman Catholic Church has long accepted payments toward relieving the time of our beloved ones suffering in purgatory.

Let's say for a moment that purgatory is real after all. If people are sent to purgatory to be purified, then how can that purification take place faster because we are praying for them or making payments on their behalf? If purification requires fire, it makes no sense to suggest we can *pay* for them to go through a purification process any faster than their sins require.

Nowhere in the Bible do we find that we can buy our way out of punishment. Moses describes the sacrificial system in in Leviticus, but that was set up only to give us an understanding of Christ's death. Hebrews 10:4-9 tells us God has no pleasure in our sacrifices; He prepared a body (Jesus) to be *the* sacrifice.

I once saw a Catholic woman who had just lost her beloved husband. She spent substantial money for Mass cards so that many ongoing Masses would be spoken on his behalf — not just one Mass, but one after another. She did this, believing her effort would shorten her husband's time in the refining fires of purgatory. She continues to offer money to this day, in the hope that she can buy him a small amount of refreshment and temporal repose during his time in purgatory's flames.

The very belief in paying or praying people out of purgatory suggests that we think that purgatory is a time of punishment for sins, and those sins can be paid for through prayer or alms. This is a terrible idea. The idea of purgatory all by itself devalues the sacrifice that Jesus made on the cross. Either Jesus' blood pays for our sins, or we pay for our sins. Peter reminds us,

> *...knowing that you were not redeemed with corruptible things, like silver or gold, from your aimless conduct received by tradition from your fathers, but with the precious blood of Christ, as of a lamb without blemish and without spot.*
>
> 1 Peter 1:18-29

In other words, any prayers for the dead must have nothing to do with helping people out of purgatory, because the price for sin requires a much higher payment than mere prayers or money. It is a tragedy that people pay for Masses for the dead — to *pay* to get people through purgatory faster.

Catholic author Susan Tassone has a passion is to get people out of purgatory. In 1993, she founded Holy Souls Mass Apostolate to raise money to free people from purgatory, and she has raised millions of dollars for this purpose. She asks people to make the Roman Catholic Church the beneficiaries of their wills to get people out of the burning fires.

Jessica Hartogs of CBS reported in 2013 the most bizarre idea yet: the Roman Catholic Church was offering indulgences to those who followed the Twitter feed of Pope Francis.[15]

Really? Following the pope on Twitter will shorten somebody's time in purgatory?

If we want to pray to save souls, let's pray for people *alive right now* to repent of their sins and turn to the Lord for forgiveness. Let's send our money to fund missionaries who proclaim the Gospel of Jesus Christ, to rescue people who are still alive. Let us focus our prayers on our next-door neighbors and the people in our communities, while they still have time to live for Him. We can pray for the blood of Jesus to cover the sins of our beloved dead friends and family, but we have a multitude of living people who need the covering of Christ's blood even now.

Here's a quick question. If the pope can keep a soul out of torture in purgatory by merely sending tweets, then why doesn't the pope just free everybody right now? In theory, the pope could

---

[15] Hartogs, Jessica. "Vatican: Get time off in purgatory by following Pope on Twitter." CBS News (July 17, 2013). https://www.cbsnews.com/news/vatican-get-time-off-in-purgatory-by-following-pope-on-twitter/ (accessed November 3, 2017).

sit down this very hour and stop all the dead souls languishing in the tormenting fires. He could do this under his authority as Christ's vicar. He doesn't, though. Why? Does he want people to burn for awhile, when Christ has already died for their sins? Or does he fear it would shut off the valve of money flowing 24-7 into church bank accounts?

We clearly do not appreciate the seriousness of the matter. We do not understand how shamefully this kind of thinking cheapens the blood of Jesus Christ, the Son of God. Is there anything less than the blood of Jesus that *can* pay for our sins? We need to read what Paul says in Romans, and we need to take it to heart:

> *But God demonstrates His own love toward us, in that while we were still sinners, Christ died for us. Much more then, having now been justified by His blood, we shall be saved from wrath through Him. For if when we were enemies we were reconciled to God through the death of His Son, much more, having been reconciled, we shall be saved by His life. And not only that, but we also rejoice in God through our Lord Jesus Christ, through whom we have now received the reconciliation.*
>
> Romans 5:8-11

That, dear friends, is the Gospel. That is the Good News. We do not have to hand over our children's inheritance to pay for Masses on behalf of dead relatives. Joining a Twitter account has no power to give grace, as though grace is something that can be bought and sold.

Brand New in Christ

The key to all of us is our rebirth in Christ. The Bible does not say we are mostly freed from our sins through Christ. It says we are made *brand new* in Jesus Christ. Jesus tells Nicodemus in John 3 that we must be born again, born brand new of the Spirit.[16] 1 Peter 1:23 explains that we are born again as something

---
16 John 3:3-7

incorruptible: *"having been born again, not of corruptible seed but incorruptible, through the word of God which lives and abides forever."* And this is the word by which the Gospel was given us, he says, in Jesus Christ we are dead to sin and alive under His grace.[17]

THE FRUITS OF A TREE

But wait. Doesn't the Bible say that we will be judged according to our works? It says so in several places!

And I saw the dead, small and great, standing before God, and books were opened. And another book was opened, which is the Book of Life. And the dead were judged according to their works, by the things which were written in the books.

Revelation 20:12

What about James? He tells us that faith without works is dead!

But do you want to know, O foolish man, that faith without works is dead? Was not Abraham our father justified by works when he offered Isaac his son on the altar?

James 2:20-21

In Matthew 25:31-46, Jesus separated the sheep from the goats by the things that they *did*. These are all in the Bible as well. There appears to be a contradiction, doesn't there? But, there's not of course. Jesus explains the situation to us in Matthew 7:

You will know them by their fruits. Do men gather grapes from thornbushes or figs from thistles? Even so, every good tree bears good fruit, but a bad tree bears bad fruit. A good tree cannot bear bad fruit, nor can a bad tree bear good fruit. Every tree that does not bear good fruit is cut down and thrown into the fire. Therefore by their fruits you will know them.

Matthew 7:16-20

---

17 Romans 6:5-14

And that is why we have to be born again of the Spirit. If we belong to Christ, then we will do the things that please Him. As we grow in the Lord, we will begin to bud and flower and in time we will bear the fruit of love and goodness and justice, simply because we are connected to Him. If we are living trees, growing by streams of water as Psalm 1 describes, we will bear our fruit in season. In John 15:5, Jesus says, "*I am the vine, you are the branches. He who abides in Me, and I in him, bears much fruit; for without Me you can do nothing.*" In other words, the proof is in the pudding.

Of course, we still do foolish things, sometimes every day. Proverbs 24:16 says, "*For a righteous man may fall seven times and rise again....*" We do fall and fail, but we just get back up and keep going. We have to daily hand our will into our Lord's hands. We have to "abide" in Him. But if we have Christ in our hearts, we will seek Him quickly when we mess up.

What's more, we won't just "do good works" — we will fulfill God's purposes for us,[18] and that's what really matters. When we sin, we will run to His throne — "*boldly to the throne of grace*" as Hebrews 4:16 tells us, and we will move on. Our good works aren't what save us. However, if we are abiding in Him, we will do good works, and they will be evidence that we belong to Him.[19]

Through the Flames

There are absolutely fiery processes we go through while we are alive. Jerusalem was judged on this earth to purge out her dross — which meant cleansing her of all those evil elements in her midst.[20] 1 Peter 4:12 talks about times when we have to face fiery trials as servants of Christ. These have nothing to do with fire after death, though.

Former Roman Catholic priest Dr. Joseph Zacchello explains the trouble, stating:

> ...even if all sins of a Roman Catholic are forgiven in confession by a priest and he does not perform enough of

---
[18] Matthew 7:15-20; Ephesians 2:10; Galatians 5:16-18
[19] James 2:18
[20] Isaiah 1:25

these "good works," he will go to purgatory and remain there in torture until his soul is completely purified.[21]

This (this issue right here) is why I believe the kindly nun at the Dallas airport told me to think good thoughts and do good deeds. She believed fully I was never going to heaven without first making a layover in the horrible purifying fires. Doing good deeds was my only way of shortening my inevitable stay.

The Bible makes it crystal clear there is no act we perform that can remove sin apart from putting our trust in the shed blood of Jesus. The doctrine of purgatory sounds reasonable, but if we could pay for our own sins, Jesus would never have had to die. It's wrong to insist we might go to an interim waiting room raging with fire to receive *additional* cleansing before we run into Christ's arms. This idea makes Christ's own suffering void and unnecessary. We might as well have paid for our own sins in the first place.

---

[21] Joseph Zacchello, *Secrets of Romanism* (Neptune, NJ: Loizeaux Brothers, 1988), 101.

Chapter 15

Treasures

Human logic is a wonderful thing. We are able to use our mental faculties to build bridges and produce large crops and move water to create bounty out of desert lands. Our reasoning skills can help us bring order to chaos, but they can also get us into trouble; we sometimes come up with reasonable-sounding ideas that have nothing to do with the truth.

In the Middle Ages, human logic produced some really bad ideas. From the obscure concept of praying for the dead came the doctrine of purgatory. From the idea of rewards for good works came the idea of buying and selling those good works to get family members through purgatory faster.

We know that Christ will reward those things we do in his name and for his sake. He promises it to us multiple times in Scripture.[1] The Catechism of the Catholic Church (CCC) teaches that the merits of Christ are stored in a spiritual "treasury of the Church" which benefits the whole community of saints in the Body of Christ. The prayers and good works of Mary are in this treasury of merit. According to the CCC:

> In the treasury, too, are the prayers and good works of all the saints, all those who have followed in the footsteps of Christ the Lord and by his grace have made their lives holy and carried out the mission in the unity of the Mystical Body.[2]

---
[1] Matthew 6:6, 16:27; Mark 9:41; Luke 6:23, 35.
[2] *Catechism of the Catholic Church*, 1476-1477.

A Holy Building

The Bible does not tell us there is a spiritual treasury of merit, like a giant good karma bank in the heavenlies. The reality in the Bible is much more than that. Our works are building the spiritual Church, through the work of the Holy Spirit in us, and that Church is exceptionally important because it is made of *people*. The Apostle Paul explains in 1 Corinthians 3 that we all have a different part to play, and we will all be rewarded for the work we do.

The people in Corinth had started to divide themselves into groups. Some saying they belonged to Paul and others saying they belonged to Apollos, and Paul rebukes them. He explains that he planted the seed of the Gospel, and Apollos is watering it — but God is the one that makes the plants grow and produce fruit. In this sense, Paul treats the holy Church like a field of plants — and those plants are *us*.

Later in 1 Corinthians 12-14, Paul explains the gifts of the Spirit, treating us all as parts of one interconnected Body. Some of us are evangelists, and some pastors, or teachers, or workers of miracles, or we have gifts of wisdom or knowledge — yet we are all working together for God's purposes. Paul is saying the same thing in different ways in different places.

In 1 Corinthians 3, after describing the work of Christ as cultivating a field, Paul goes on to use a different metaphor. He describes the Church as God's building, and those who do the Lord's work are adding to that building. The foundation of the building is Jesus Christ — it's the Gospel that Paul taught them. As we do work for the Lord, we build on that building. Paul likens the pure works we do as gold and silver and fine gems. He likens impure or useless work as wood, hay, and stubble. One day, all of our works will be judged, and only those pure works will be rewarded. The rest will burn up.

Paul makes it clear that these works are not what bring us salvation — because salvation is the gift of God through the work of Jesus Christ. That's why Jesus is the foundation. However, while we escape the fire, our works can burn up. Paul doesn't mean the fire of purgatory. He means it's like a house fire, when you escape, but all your stuff is destroyed.

We are building a living building on the foundation of Christ, and we will be rewarded for the work we do for the Kingdom of God.[3]

Paul is an excellent writer, and he is skilled at using metaphors in his descriptions. This picture he's painting for us, of "gold, silver, and precious gems" is not a literal description of treasures. We know this, because gold and gems are merely the construction materials of the New Jerusalem as described in Revelation 21. They're the bricks and mortar. Paul is just explaining that when we claim to be doing work for the Lord, we need to be careful how we're doing that work. Are we laboring for the Lord from pure motives and love, or are we doing it for selfish reasons like the Pharisees? We can interpret what Paul is saying based on the words of Jesus himself. As Jesus told his disciples:

> *Take heed that you do not do your charitable deeds before men, to be seen by them. Otherwise you have no reward from your Father in heaven… But when you do a charitable deed, do not let your left hand know what your right hand is doing, that your charitable deed may be in secret; and your Father who sees in secret will Himself reward you openly.*
>
> Matthew 6;1,3-4

Jesus tells us always to store up our treasures — our rewards — in heaven, where they can't be corrupted or destroyed: *"For where your treasure is, there will your heart be also."*[4]

THE TREASURY OF MERIT

Unfortunately, this simple idea was twisted in the Middle Ages. Christ promised to reward those who faithfully served Him, but this got bent over backwards when the medieval church took the position that the popes stood in the position and authority

---

[3] 1 Corinthians 3:8-15
[4] Matthew 6:21.

of Jesus Christ. Rather than encouraging good works, they took advantage of the doctrine of purgatory to procure money for the Roman Catholic Church, and they included the treasury of merit as part of this scheme.

Here's what happened. The people were told that the reigning pope held charge of the good merits within the spiritual treasury of the Church. The pope was seen as a sort of executor who could dispense or sell the good deeds that had accumulated in the treasury of merits. These deeds were at his disposal. In fact, the pope had the authority to *sell* these merits. Essentially, if some wealthy individual had done limited good deeds in his lifetime and had earned very few merits, he could buy good merits from the pope for money. We can easily see how quickly this could get out of hand. Since the pope held rule over in the bountiful treasury of merits, some dreadful, sinful person with few or no good works could buy some "good deeds" from the church — which would then allegedly save him time in the refining fires.

If we step back from this idea, we can see how foolish it is. It's not just foolish, it's outrageous. The reward for one person's good deeds can never be bought by another person for money. Remember in Acts 8:20 how badly Peter responded to the man who thought he could buy the Holy Spirit? Peter told him, *"Your money perish with you, because you thought that the gift of God could be purchased with money!"*

Human beings think money and wealth mean something. God is never impressed by it. Jesus was more astounded by the widow who gave her last mites — trusting God for her provision — than he ever was by the wealth of the Pharisees.[5] Imagine going straight to God and offering money for the reward somebody *else* earned through their good works. What do you think He would say? I don't think that exchange would end well.

It's despicable that people were told God's grace could be bought, as though God's grace is something so cheap. God's grace is a gift, but it is worth more than anything we could ever pay to receive.

---

[5] Mark 12:41-44

Pope Sixtus IV

When we walk through the Sistine Chapel in Vatican City, we can marvel at the amazing ceiling art of Michelangelo, painted carefully and painfully between 1508 and 1512. It was Pope Sixtus IV (1471-1484) who started the three-year project to restore the chapel in 1477. We can remember him as that pope — the pope who restored the Sistine Chapel. Michelangelo did his work of painting the ceiling a quarter of a century later under Pope Julius II, the nephew of Sixtus IV.

There are a variety of other things for which we can remember Sixtus IV. His role in kicking off the Spanish Inquisition was mentioned in chapter 2. We can also remember him as the pontiff who licensed brothels and taxed priests who kept their mistresses. He brought in 30,000 gold ducats each year in this manner, providing visiting ladies with golden chamber pots.[6]

It is possible that Sixtus IV was involved in even more shameful activities. In his diary, Stefano Infessura (1435 – 1500) accused Sixtus IV of being "a lover of boys and sodomites" who gave cardinal positions to good looking men,[7] but Infessura may have just been recording the gossip of his day.

Pope Sixtus IV was a busy pope. I bring him up here because he was the first pope to apply indulgences to getting the dead out of purgatory. In his efforts to collect money for the repair of the Saintes cathedral in France, he declared in 1476 that family members could contribute toward the repair effort (and thus toward the treasury of merit) on behalf of their loved ones in purgatory, saying:

> It is our desire to use the Church's treasury of merit to assist those souls in purgatory who would have gained this indulgence had they been alive. We therefor concede that parents, friends, or any others may secure the release of souls from the fires of purgatory by donating a sum

---
[6] Peter De Rosa, *Vicars of Christ, the Dark Side of the Papac* (1988; reprint, Dublin: Poolberg Press, 2000), 101.
[7] Stefano Infessura, *Diario della città di Roma di Stefano Infessura scribasenato. Nuova edizione a cura di Oreste Tommasini* (Roma: Forzani e c, 1890), 155-156.

to be assessed by the canons for the repair of the Saints cathedral.[8]

This was one of the first official sales of indulges by a pope. Twenty years earlier, Calixtus III had offered release from purgatory for anybody who donated 200 maravedis toward battling the Moors, but these were groundbreaking efforts to use purgatory as a source of church financing.[9]

Sixtus IV claimed power over the regions of the dead and declared that he could grant souls in torment immediate release. The bereaved believing gave vast amounts of money to the church on behalf of dead relatives.

This sort of thinking might shock any of us today, but in the world of medieval superstition it was seen as perfectly reasonable to pay down time in purgatory. Who wouldn't give all they had toward buying a loved one a shorter stay in the flames?

Thus, medieval Christianity came to be about *doing* things. Praying, going to Mass, paying for Masses, buying indulgences toward the popes' causes — these were all believed to contribute toward the treasury of merit and thus toward less time in the cleansing fires. The emphasis on loving and enjoying God, serving Him in peace and joy, those aspects of faith seem to have been neglected.

This is why it's wise to reexamine traditions. The common man was unable to read the Bible in those medieval centuries, and the people only knew what they were taught. Traditions became the central focus of the Catholic faith. By them, the bishops and cardinals and popes received their wealth and held on to their power, and thus without them the whole system would have imploded. If the people had been free to hold the traditions against the light of the Scripture, false ideas would never have taken hold.

---

[8] Jonathan Sumption, *The Age of Pilgrimage: The Medieval Journey to God*. (Hidden Spring, 2003), 432.
[9] *Ibid*, 431.

God's Faulty Leaders

Nowhere does the Bible promote blind devotion to religious authorities. Nowhere does the Bible say that being in a position of authority makes a leader faultless. God *gave* Jeroboam I the throne of Israel, but Jeroboam chose to lead Israel into idolatry, and for this God punished him.[10] The Pharisees were the religious authorities in Jerusalem, and Jesus spends Matthew 23 pronouncing woes against them. The Bible constantly warns us against the world's wolves prancing about in sheep's garb:

> *But there were false prophets also among the people, even as there shall be false teachers among you, who privily shall bring in damnable heresies, even denying the Lord that bought them, and bring upon themselves swift destruction. And many shall follow their pernicious ways; by reason of whom the way of truth shall be evil spoken of. And through covetousness shall they with feigned words make merchandise of you: whose judgment now of a long time lingereth not, and their damnation slumbereth not.*
>
> 2 Peter 2:1

Because the Roman Church had the temporal authority in the Middle Ages, it was able to use fear to convince the multitudes of Europe to pinch their pennies into church coffers. To their shame, bishops and cardinals could feast every day while the children of the common man cried in bed at night from hunger.

Today we find televangelists who make millions upon millions of dollars from trusting souls who watch them preach on the TV. Television is a wonderful way to spread the Gospel, but shame on those con artists who clearly care more about money than about the lost and dying of the world. While television and radio have reached multitudes with the truth of God's Word, they also have been used to fleece the flock.

This is why we must remain vigilant and wise even in our innocence.

---
[10] 1 Kings 11:28-38, 12:26-33; 4:7-10

Chapter 16

Holiness and Marriage

In 1519, Martin Luther started praising marriage, making the case that sexual desires remained in most humans, whether they had made vows of celibacy or not. To avoid sin, he argued most monks and nuns should marry, because the gift of celibacy was given to precious few humans.

In 1523, a nun named Katherine Von Bora left a convent and in 1525, like many other former nuns and monks who were marrying, she joined herself in holy matrimony to Martin Luther. Martin and "Katie" (as he called her) had six children and they both labored on the farm. Luther adored his wife. They had their squabbles and troubles, but Luther admired and enjoyed his wife, and he saw her as a huge blessing and a gift of God in his life.

The Church of Rome holds that marriage is one of the seven sacraments, holy and sacred. Yet the church requires that those who enter the priesthood be celibate.

What does the Bible actually say about celibacy and marriage?

Celibacy

First, there is a place for celibacy in the Scriptures, but it is treated as a specific calling. In Matthew, Jesus explains that God never intended men and women to get divorced and to remarry, and that this practice is actually a form of adultery. The disciples are surprised by this and suggest that it's better never to marry at all. Jesus says something interesting:

> *But he said unto them, All men cannot receive this saying, save they to whom it is given. For there are some eunuchs, which were so born from their mother's womb: and there are some eunuchs, which were made eunuchs of men: and there be eunuchs, which have made themselves eunuchs for the kingdom of heaven's sake. He that is able to receive it, let him receive it.*
>
> Matthew 19:11-12

We see two things here. First, Jesus said that only those "to whom it is given" can accept this idea. Next, he indicates that those who are to live in celibacy are those who have been physically altered to handle it. A eunuch was, quite literally, somebody who had been castrated. Some people are born malformed in their sexual body parts, but others were purposely castrated, whether to be made trustworthy to guard a king's harem or to preserve a youth's singing voice.

Yet, of course not all men who are celibate have to be eunuchs. Jesus himself never married. He came to serve us and to die, and marriage to a woman was not part of that equation. Jesus will have a bride, but she is the entire Church — as Paul states in Ephesians 5:23-32.

It appears from 1 Corinthians 7:5-6 and 9:5-6 that Paul had no wife, but he also recognizes he has that gift. In 1 Corinthians 7:25-40, he gives his opinion about marriage during the troubled times of the first century. He suggests that it was better not to marry during those dark days, because marriage would only bring trouble. At the same time, he recognizes that it is better to marry than to fornicate, and Paul treats the situation as a matter to be decided by each man according to his own judgment.

It's important to realize that the political world was unstable during those times, and persecutions against Christians were already going on. We all know it's easier to crush a man who has a wife and children to worry about. In other words, this is a passage that applies to times of instability and trouble. In the day-to-day world today, things are slightly different.

Celibacy has its benefits. Those who are unmarried can focus strictly on God's work without the distractions (good or bad) of married life. At the same time, it doesn't work if those who are *supposed* to be focused on God's work are actually secretly focused on sexual things.

There are times in all of our lives when we are required to be chaste, despite the bellows from our sexual urges. We all had to be teenagers, after all. But, we shouldn't force round pegs into square holes. It is better to be celibate if we are given that gift and can focus on God's calling for us. On the other hand, it is better to marry than to burn with lust.[1]

In the history of the church, we find that while priests, monks, bishops and cardinals, as well as the pope himself had devoted themselves to lives of celibacy. The reality is a large number of them broke those vows and kept mistresses. Not just one mistress, but many. It would have been better for them to have just married and lived within the holy bounds of marriage. Paul instructs both Timothy and Titus that bishops and other elders *should be* the husbands of one wife, so marriage is the general model for leaders laid down by Paul.[2] If Paul said they should be married, when was celibacy of the clergy mandated by the church?

Celibacy of the Priesthood:

Marriage is one of the seven sacraments of the Catholic Church, but so is Holy Orders — being set aside for the priesthood.

Several famous church men never married, including Saint Jerome and Saint Augustine. At the 325 Council of Nicaea, celibacy of the priesthood was suggested but voted down. In the 11th century, Pope Gregory VII tried to enforce celibacy for the priesthood, and it became an issue that led to further division between the Catholic Church in Constantinople and the Catholic

---
[1] 1 Corinthians 7:9
[2] 1 Timothy 3:2; Titus 1:6

Church in Rome. Eastern priests were marrying, while the pope in Rome required Western priests to remain celibate.

In 1074, Gregory VII made decrees against simony (the practice of selling church positions) and the marriage of priests. He stated:

> Nor shall clergymen who are married say mass or serve the altar in any way. We decree also that if they refuse to obey our orders, or rather those of the holy fathers, the people shall refuse to receive their ministrations, in order that those who disregard the love of God and the dignity of their office may be brought to their senses through feeling the shame of the world and the reproof of the people.[3]

Look at the pope's attitude toward marriage here. He suggests that priests who are married have disregarded "the love of God" and have neglected the "dignity of their office."

Does the Bible treat marriage this way? No. When Paul tells Timothy in 1 Timothy 3:2-6,12 that bishops and deacons should be husbands of one wife (not *no* wives, not *many* wives) he treats it as part of their being righteous men. Marriage is always treated as holy and good in the Bible. The writer of Hebrews declares that marriage is honorable. It's fornication that is shameful and wicked:

> *Marriage is honorable among all, and the bed undefiled; but fornicators and adulterers God will judge.*
>
> Hebrews 13:4

Pope Gregory VII was out of line. Surely, if priests and other clergy love God, they want to live in such a way as to avoid temptations. If this means remaining in a monastery and praying all day, then they should do that. If it means getting married and enjoying a wife and children, then they should do that. This appears to be a Romans 14 matter — one in which everybody must do according to his or her own conscience before the Lord.

---

3   Decree of Council at Rome 1074, [Mansi XX. P. 404], in Oliver J. Thatcher, and Edgar Holmes McNeal, eds., *A Source Book for Medieval History* (New York: Scribners, 1905), 134-135.

Marriage

Jesus declares that God made marriage in the beginning. Some people have developed the idea that sex is the result of sin, and that's not remotely true. God invented sex and procreation. He created us as sexual beings, and He told Adam and Eve to go forth and multiply, to produce children and fill the world. God said it was not good for man to be alone, and as Christians we know that marriage represents the relationship between Christ and the Church. Marriage was God's idea, and it's a good and holy thing.

> *And the LORD God said, "It is not good that man should be alone; I will make him a helper comparable to him."*
>
> Genesis 2:18

> *"Have you not read that He who made them at the beginning 'made them male and female?...For this reason a man shall leave his father and mother and be joined to his wife, and the two shall become one flesh'?...So then, they are no longer two but one flesh. Therefore what God has joined together, let not man separate."*
>
> Matthew 19:5-6

We have all erred in our lives. We have all made mistakes, and we learn from each one. God is a God of mercy, and He has every power to take our broken relationships and broken hearts and make amazing things happen in our lives when we trust in Him. I say this, because I know that there are very few of us who have gone through romantic relationships unscarred or shameless. However, with God there is always hope. If we know that God loves us, we can trust Him to move us forward from this point on.

Neglect of the Body

The Catholic Church recognizes that God invented marriage and that it is a holy institution blessed by God. However, there is a habit among all human beings — whether Christian or Buddhist or Islamic — to regard asceticism and the neglect of the body as the mark of the holiest people. People who can ignore their worldly desires are often seen as purer people, but the Bible actually doesn't support this. In fact, Paul warns us against this type of thinking, saying:

Therefore, if you died with Christ from the basic principles of the world, why, as though living in the world, do you subject yourselves to regulations - "Do not touch, do not taste, do not handle," which all concern things which perish with the using - according to the commandments and doctrines of men? These things indeed have an appearance of wisdom in self-imposed religion, false humility, and neglect of the body, but are of no value against the indulgence of the flesh.

Colossians 2:20-23

What the New King James here calls "self-imposed religion" the King James calls "will worship." It's the focus on rejecting our natural desires as an end in itself.

This is a much different thing than neglecting ourselves for a *purpose*. There are times we need to fast and pray — for instance, for a brother who is struggling with drugs or depression. Sometimes we might need to be cold or tired while helping our neighbors move into a new house or helping them get their firewood in. We might need to spend our money paying a neighbor's electric bill instead of buying those concert tickets we wanted. We might end up in a terrifying prison for smuggling Bibles into North Korea. However, when we neglect ourselves, it should always be for specific purposes. Suffering is not an end in itself. Being voluntarily cold and hungry for the sake of being cold and hungry is just empty misery.

Therefore, if we choose not to marry, it should be because that's something God has chosen for us. In the meanwhile, all of us, whether married or single, are called to serve God with all our hearts.

ALL THE SINGLE LADIES

While marriage is a holy blessing, there are times in all of our lives when we are not married, and we still need to serve God faithfully during those years. Most people will get married eventually, but while they are single, young people can take the precious time before marriage to develop their relationships with God. It is important to learn to depend on God and not another human as the source of emotional stability, strength and peace. Learning how to control themselves, to put their lives totally into God's hands, and walk with Him every day, will be a blessing to those young people (and their future spouses) when they do get married.

Chapter 17

Mary Adulation

The issue of marriage is an important one as we get into a particularly sensitive subject: Mary, the mother of our Lord.

Protestants and Catholics can make each other frustrated, hurt and angry no faster than in arguments about Mary the mother of Jesus Christ. Some Protestants have cast Mary aside in a way that is wrong. Some Catholics have held Mary up too high in a way that is wrong. There is emotion on both sides, and the wisest thing that each can do is take the Bible's words about Mary at face value.

Mary was the beloved mother of Jesus, and when Gabriel arrives to tell her she would bear a son, he greets her in Luke 1:28, saying, *"Rejoice, highly favored one, the Lord is with you; blessed are you among women!"*

The Bible treats Mary with great honor. Out of all the young women in Israel in those days, God the Father chose Mary to bear and raise Jesus. That's nothing small. In Luke 1:48, Mary declares in faith that all generations would call her blessed. It is right to call Mary "blessed" and to recognize her position as the one chosen by God for an absolutely one-of-a-kind privilege — that of carrying the Savior of the world. We should not cast Mary aside as though she were just any woman.

At the same time, it's also important to remember that Mary was a human woman. She provided Jesus with His human body, and God the Father provided Jesus with His divine nature. In some Catholic traditions, the faithful pray almost solely to Mary, as though they cannot pray directly to God, and this is extremely troubling. I'm treading here cautiously, but this is an issue that deeply concerns me.

As we approach this tender topic, it's important that we recognize that there was a problem in Rome; the old pagan

Figure 13: "Coronation of the Virgin by Diego Velázquez (c.1635-1636), Museo Del Prado.

religions from time immemorial had engaged in mother goddess worship, and there was severe danger of mixing honor of Mary with the worship of Mary.

Faithful Catholics will explain that they do not worship Mary. They regard her as a spiritual mother, and they seek her help. We can all appreciate this love for the mother of Jesus Christ. Yet, I have seen shrines to Mary in the corner of some Catholic households, and we see many movies in which people start praying the Hail Mary before they die rather than praying the Our Father. This raises questions in my mind. Do we feel that Mary is more tender and sympathetic toward us than the God who gave His Son for us? Did Mary die for us? Is it even right to pray to Mary at all?

It's important to realize that there truly was danger in ancient Rome of mixing Mary with the mother goddesses of old. The same powerful goddess of love and fertility was rehashed over and over as Inanna, Astarte, Ishtar, Isis, Ashtoreth, Aphrodite and Venus. We find statues of Aphrodite and her son Eros and Isis with son Horus — both accompanied by the crescent moon. In Roman Catholic art, we often find Mary holding Jesus on a crescent moon.

At the Council of Ephesus in A.D. 431, Mary was officially given the title "Mother of God." The intention was to recognize that Jesus was God, and Mary gave birth to Him. The emphasis was on Christ's deity — which came by His conception through the creative work of God the Father. As His human mother, the mother of the second member of the Trinity, Mary earned the title of Mother of God. Mary was certainly the mother of Jesus, but the Bible in no place describes her as "Mother of God." Despite its original intention, "Mother of God" offers a different picture of Mary than the teenage girl honored to carry the infant Messiah.

Admiration and honor of Mary developed century after century into what looked more like worship of Mary. Eventually, Mary came to assume many characteristics and positions that the Bible ascribes only to Jesus. Like Jesus, for instance, Mary is said to have lived a sinless life. Like Jesus, she ascended bodily into Heaven. Like Jesus, she acts as our mediator. None of these things are in the Bible, and that's where it gets scary. The Roman

Catholic Church has transformed the handmaiden of God in Luke 1:48 into the Queen of Heaven.

THE QUEEN OF HEAVEN

In Revelation 12, we find the picture of a woman crowned with 12 stars, with the moon under her feet and clothed with the sun. Some have seen this woman as Mary, and this has been the justification for considering her the "Queen of Heaven." However, this is an incorrect interpretation of these verses. While this woman does give birth to the man-child, who is clearly the Messiah, the woman portrayed is not Mary. She is *Israel*. From the time of Abraham, it was prophesied that the Messiah would come through Israel, and we can see by the description that this is who is intended. Revelation 12:1 is a reference to Joseph's dream in Genesis 37:9. Jacob immediately interprets the dream in the next verse, saying that the sun and moon are Jacob himself and his wife, and the 12 stars are his 12 sons.

Asherah (or Ashtoreth or Astarte) was the "queen of heaven" and we find throughout the Old Testament that Asherah worship was a plague in Israel. In the King James, her worship is translated "the groves" because the Israelites would set up poles or trees in her honor, but the actual word is Asherah. She is that female goddess that began as Ishtar and Inana in Sumer and Akkad — the land of ancient Babylon.

The very title "Queen of Heaven" is a scary one to give Mary, and we should all be warned. The Old Testament strictly forbade the worship of the Canaanite cultures in the Holy Land. Yet, the ancient mother goddess worship of Babylon and Persia and Greece and Rome made its way conveniently into the Christian religion of Rome through the role of Mary. Many Catholics are deeply insulted by the insinuation that their reverence for Mary has anything to do with ancient paganism. Yet, Gabriel never calls Mary, "Queen of Heaven." In Jeremiah, the "queen of heaven" was a pagan goddess the Israelites insisted on worshiping against the commands of the LORD.[1]

---

1 Jeremiah 7:18, 44:17-25

Mary Adulation

As we see Mary elevated to the *position* of a goddess (whether in word or in deed) we should be absolutely alarmed. Mary did not die for our sins. She is not a member of the Godhead. She is a human woman who needed a Savior just like the rest of us.

In 1854, Pope Pius IX declared that Mary was immaculately conceived, saying:

> The most Blessed Virgin Mary was, from the first moment of her conception, by a singular grace and privilege of almighty God and by virtue of the merits of Jesus Christ, Savior of the human race, preserved immune from all stain of original sin.[2]

The Catholic Church teaches that Mary had need of a Savior, but she was saved by the grace that enabled her to avoid ever sinning. The Catholic Church also teaches that Mary was assumed, body and soul, into heaven at the end of her life on earth. In 1950, Pope Pius XII made this belief official doctrine in the apostolic constitution *Munificentissimus Deus*.

To this day, Catholics pray the rosary, seeking Mary's mediation in their lives: "Holy Mary, Mother of God, pray for us sinners, now and at the hour of our death. Amen." They are not praying to Mary, as though she is a goddess. They are seeking her intervention on their behalf, as one who is beloved by the Lord and stands in the presence of God.

It's a touchy area. In some Roman Catholic households, Jesus is always and ever placed first. However, it's simply true that in many other Catholic households, family members pray first and foremost to Mary, as though Mary is more gentle, loving and understanding than God Himself.

The real question is, should we seek Mary's help at all? The Bible never suggests any such thing. We do not even know if Mary can hear us. The men of the New Testament knew Mary personally, and if anybody should have recognized her position as our advocate, it would have been them. They never mention her beyond her position as Jesus' birth mother. There is a unanimous consensus that we should only seek God

---

[2] CCC 491.

the Father through the Lord Jesus Christ by the guidance of the Holy Spirit. Mary is never made part of that equation.

There are all manner of arguments that can be made, but the bottom line is that the Bible never encourages us to seek the intercession of Mary, any more than we are to seek the intercession of Moses or King David or Abel or Noah. Instead, we are told we can go straight to the throne of God for help in time of need.[3] Therefore, if we seek God the Father directly, through Jesus Christ, we are only doing what the Bible actually *tells* us to do.

The biggest concern is the evolution of Mary to the position of a member of the Godhead. It's dangerous to give Mary a mediatory role in the place of Christ, because it contradicts the clear Word of God:

For there is one God, and one Mediator between God and men, the man Christ Jesus

1 Timothy 2:5

My little children, these things write I to you, so that you may not sin. And if anyone sins, we have an Advocate with the Father, Jesus Christ the righteous.

1 John 2:1

There are other teachings about Mary that directly contradict the plain meaning of the Bible:

1. Mary was a perpetual virgin.

There is no Biblical or even logical reason to think this. Matthew 1:25 explains that Joseph, *"knew her not till she had brought forth her firstborn son: and he called his name JESUS."* In other words, Mary and Joseph did not consummate their marriage until after Jesus was born. Mary and Joseph were married, and it would have been a cruel and unusual thing for them to spend their entire married life in a state of abstinence. There's no reason to teach that Mary remained a virgin. She didn't become any less holy or blessed by God for marrying Joseph, and the angel told Joseph not to be afraid to take her as his wife.[4]

---
3 Hebrews 4:16
4 Matthew 1:20

The Bible tells us Mary had other children after Jesus. John 2:12 tells us that Jesus went to Capernaum with his Mother, brothers and disciples. Matthew 13:55-56 names Christ's brothers as James, Joseph, Simon, and Judas and mentions his sisters as well. The Catholic Church dismisses these children from Mary by saying they are cousins and not half-brothers. Yet, the plainest meaning is that Mary and Joseph were married, and they had children after Jesus was born.

2. Mary was born without original sin.

We trust that Mary truly was "full of grace" as the Angel Gabriel said when he greeted her. We also recognize from Jude 1:24 and Galatians 5:16-25 that God is able to keep us from sinning when we walk in His Spirit. However, there is no need for Mary to have lived a completely sinless life, and in fact, the Bible only says that Jesus managed to accomplish this otherwise impossible task.

According to 2 Corinthians 5:21, 1 Peter 2:22, and 1 John 3:5 Jesus Christ was sinless, and that description is given to Christ alone. The writers of the New Testament could have told us that Mary was also sinless, and they failed to do so.

The plain meaning of the Scripture is that Mary is included with the rest of normal humanity. Romans 3:23 tells us that all have sinned, and Mary should naturally be included in that "all." In Luke 1:47, Mary declared, *"And my spirit has rejoiced in God my Savior"* — because Mary needed a savior just like the rest of us. Did she need a savior to help her *keep* from sinning? Yes, as we all do. Do we have any indication that she never sinned? No. Not in the Bible.

IDEALISM

We Christians often make the mistake of confusing faith with unrealistic *idealism*. Let me explain what I mean. We need to believe the things that God tells us are true. That's not idealism. That's simply taking God at His Word. On the other hand, we come up with ideas that have nothing to do with reality because we think they *should* be true — even if they're not.

For instance, we get this crazy idea that church pastors and elders, our spiritual leaders, are miraculously perfect. We expect them to be wise and righteous and patient and godly all the time. That's not realistic. We should have high expectations for our spiritual leaders, but we also need to remember that they are human beings who need our prayers. We need to remember that Satan has his sights on them. The best way to destroy a flock is to take out the shepherd, right? So, we need to serve those men and women by praying for them.

Ideally, the clergy should be men who are so devoted to God they no longer think about sex. This is how it *should be*, but it's not how it *is*. In the real world, men of God, who deeply love Jesus Christ and serve him as priests and pastors *still think about sex* — unless they have been given a very rare gift.

It is idealistic to suggest that the pope is always infallible when he speaks on matters of faith due to his high position. It's how it *should be*, but the reality is that popes have given many decrees that directly contradict the plain meaning of the Bible.

The Bible is never idealistic. The Bible is always realistic. Even Moses, who walked into the presence of God in the Tabernacle every day, so much so that he glowed.[5] Even Moses sinned by losing his temper at the waters of Meribah in Numbers 20:7-12.

Realistic doesn't mean "bad," by the way. It's whatever is true. Isaiah 11 describes a gloriously peaceful world in which the wolf lies down with the lamb — a future time when the Messiah reigns. The Old Testament is filled with promises of His righteous rule. The Bible promises a time when God will wipe away every tear and sin and death will be destroyed forever. However, the Bible tell us these things. We didn't have to dream them up ourselves.

Jesus was able to be sinless, because his Father was God. Mary's parents were just human beings like the rest of us. The human reasoning that says Mary must have also been sinless isn't supported by a straight-forward reading of Scripture.

Catholics should take care that in their love and admiration of Mary, they not place their devotion to Mary over and before their trust in the love, and care, and gentleness of God Himself.

---

[5] Exodus 34:34-35

At the same time, Protestants should take care not to treat Mary with contempt. She was given a unique and precious gift; she was entrusted with the job of giving birth to, and raising, the Savior of the world. That is not an honor to take lightly, and all Christians of all generations should recognize her position and call her "blessed" because she was blessed indeed.

Chapter 18

Saints and Angels

Figure 14: Statue of the decapitated Saint Denis, Notre Dame Cathedral, Paris.

We find in the Bible a multitude of references to Christians praying for one another. In the epistles, Paul repeatedly sought prayers on his own behalf,[1] and he prayed constantly for those in the churches.[2] Throughout the New Testament we are urged to pray with each other and for each other.[3]

Many people today seek the intercession of those saints who have died before us. Whether they are speaking to their dead relatives or to saints from long ago, many people want the assistance of those considered to be already in the presence of God. Multitudes of people go stand over the grave of a loved one, whether a father or a mother, a dead wife or brother. Little children are taught that the dearly departed are watching from

---
1 Romans 15:30; Colossians 4:3; 1 Thessalonians 5:25; 2 Thessalonians 3:1
2 Romans 1:9; 1 Corinthians 1:4; 2 Corinthians 13:7; Philippians 1:9-11; Colossians 1:9-12; 1 Thessalonians 5:23
3 Matthew 5:44; Ephesians 6:18; 1 Timothy 2:1; James 5:16

137

heaven. Before filming the famous flogging scene in the 1989 movie *Glory*, Denzel Washington sought help from the spirits of the slaves who had died in the centuries before him.

Is this right to do? A vast number of Christians try to speak to the spirits of those who have passed away, but is there any justification for this in the Bible?

This is an interesting issue, and one that causes much debate. We know it is right to ask for the help and prayers of those who are around us right *now*, but is it also good to ask for Saint Thomas or Saint Teresa to speak to God on our behalf? Should we even be seeking the guidance of our dead parents or other family members?

On one hand, we see the 24 elders in heaven before the throne of God in Revelation 5:8, and they are holding vials of beautiful smells, which are the prayers of the saints. On the other hand, we don't know whether those in heaven can hear our prayers the way that God can. The only being in the universe we know is omniscient is God alone; He is the only spiritual being we can be certain hears us. In 1 Timothy 2:5, Paul says, "For there is one God and one Mediator between God and men, the Man Christ Jesus."

We *do* know that the living saints around us can listen to us and pray on our behalf, and we can gather together and seek the Lord together. The Lord directly instructs us to pray with our brothers and sisters in Christ. As Jesus told us:

> *Again I say unto you, That if two of you shall agree on earth as touching any thing that they shall ask, it shall be done for them of my Father which is in heaven. For where two or three are gathered together in my name, there am I in the midst of them.*
>
> Matthew 18:19-20

We have the idea that saints in heaven before God's throne can petition the Lord on our behalf, and that's better because they are already glorified in His presence, but this raises a very important issue. We need to understand that God doesn't look at us any differently than He does the saints who are already in His presence. Do we appreciate that? We are already purified and justified in the sight of the Lord! We can come to God having confidence that we are already in good standing with Him, because we are covered by the blood of Jesus. His righteousness is already imputed to us. When we pray to God, He sees us as His children, holy and pure. We can pray to Him with that understanding, because we aren't depending on our own righteousness. The righteousness of Jesus covers us right now, just like those already rejoicing before the Lord!

When Jesus taught his disciples to pray, he taught them to pray directly to God the Father: "Our Father in heaven, Hallowed by Your name…"[4] He told us He would hear us when we gathered together to pray in His name. The direct teaching of Christ is always going to be the wisest route to take.

AGE-OLD VENERATION

Veneration of the saints is a practice that goes back many many centuries. Christians throughout the ages have believed the ancient saints had power due to special attributes. The idea of patron saints came about because certain saints had specific talents or areas of interest during their lifetimes. Saint Francis of Assisi was notably fond of animals and nature, and today he is considered the patron saint of ecology. Is something lost? Pray to Saint Anthony, the patron saint of finding lost things. Do you need help with your singing? Pray to Saint Cecilia, the patron saint of musicians, who was herself a singer.

With the binding of Christianity to pagan Rome, a wide variety of practices got mixed into the new state religion — practices which had little to do with anything taught in the New Testament. The pagan people of Rome were accustomed to religious ceremonies, and they were unfamiliar with personal one-on-one communication with a single Creator. The trappings of paganism — with its rituals and extensive requirements and distance from the gods — these all perpetuated in newly Christian Rome.

It was very easy for the previously pagan world to move onto veneration of saints in an unhealthy way. They didn't merely seek

---
[4] Matthew 6:9; Luke 11:2

the prayers of these exalted saints on their behalf, but during history we find people prayed *to* the saints themselves. This was an easy transition for those in post-pagan Rome, who had been required to heave aside their pantheons of gods.

The saints were not just remembered and honored, but statues of them were created. The basic idea was that man's virtues did not die with his spirit, but protective and healing powers continued to reside in his body whether whole or turned to ash. Anything which had come in contact with the saints was believed to have special powers and was worthy of veneration by extension. This was a concept called *beneficent contagion*. Those who touched these saintly remains were believed to have access to their power. Even gazing upon a relic of a saint was said to convey the grace of the departed saint. In many cases, ancient straight-up idol worship reappeared in the Christian-looking clothes of saint veneration.

Those of us who know the Holy Spirit in our own lives know how sad this behavior was (and still is in some circles). The precious Christians seeking to touch a piece of a saint had access to the *same* healing powers, the *same* protection, the *same* wisdom and guidance as the saints of old. The Holy Spirit that moved the ancient saints is available to us still today. We have no need to chase after aged crumbs on the carpet when fresh food is available to us on the table if we just sit up in our chairs and look to our Heavenly Father.

To this day, in the din of flickering candles in cathedrals across France, one can find people kneeling in front of the stone statues of Joan of Arc. They can be seen praying to this young warrior woman burned at the stake because she dared to say she heard from God herself. If people buy candles from the church, they can pray to that girl frozen in stone, believing her to be a faithful mediator to God on their behalf. They don't know whether precious Joan can hear them, but they know that God can hear them. Why don't they go straight to God, who loves them with a great love?

DECEPTIVE SPIRITS

It's natural to want to speak to those relatives who have passed away. We miss them and long to pour our hearts out to them. However, we need to take very seriously the reality that we have deceptive spiritual enemies. The Bible strongly warns us against trying to communicate with the dead. The only time the Bible records that anybody succeeded was when the witch at Endor allegedly brought up the spirit of the dead prophet Samuel in 1 Samuel 28:6-18; and this was regarded as a wicked thing to do. The only reason Saul felt required to petition Samuel was because God had turned His back on him.

The Bible is absolutely firm against any kind of necromancy. Deuteronomy 18:11 continues a list of people considered an abomination, including: "... *a medium, or a spiritist, or one who calls up the dead.*" The Israelites were commanded in Leviticus 20:27:

> *A man or a woman who is a medium, or who has familiar spirits, shall surely be put to death; they shall stone them with stones. Their blood shall be upon them.*

To this day we find people who believe they've been visited by the spirits of their dead relatives. These spirits *know* things and they can be convincing, but we should never let ourselves be tricked by them, because deceptive unclean spirits abound. In 1 John 4:1, we are told to test the spirits to see if they are from God. Any spirit of the Lord will confirm that Jesus Christ is the Lord, that he is God in the flesh. In their grief and longing for contact with their beloved ones who have died, many people have been tricked by evil spirits that are ready to take advantage of those who are most vulnerable.

VENERATION OF ANGELS

Another dangerous trend we still see today is the worship of angels. The Bible makes it clear that angels are servants.

Hebrews 1 reminds us that they are ministers sent by God on our behalf. They are never to be objects of our worship, and we should never idolize them — or even seek them out directly. They are messengers. In Revelation 19:10, John starts to fall down at the feet of the angel who is his guide, and the angel stops him and does not accept his worship. "Worship God," the angel tells John.

Angels are beautiful beings, and even people who do not believe in God are willing to believe in angels. However, 2 Corinthians 11:14 warns us that Satan can appear as an angel of light, and people can be deceived by the fallen versions of these glorious beings. Any angel who accepts worship is not of God.

This is why it is vital we all know the Word of God thoroughly. There are intelligent, convincing, evil spiritual beings out there, and the only way to keep from being tricked is to already know what the Bible says.

CHAPTER 19

THE LATIN VULGATE

In the first several centuries of Christianity, most of the Greek speaking world was able to read both the Septuagint, the Greek version of the Old Testament, and the Koine Greek of the New Testament. Constantine commissioned 50 Bibles to be copied in his day, which was a big deal since the copies had to be produced by hand. As Latin became more common, Latin translations of varying quality popped up. Christian ascetic Jerome (A.D. 340-420) approached Pope Damsus and insisted on the importance of a single, authoritative Latin version based on the original Greek and Hebrew. Damasus gave Jerome the go-ahead to make the translation, and Jerome began the work in A.D. 382. For the next 23 years, Jerome labored almost as a hermit in Bethlehem translating the Old and New Testaments into Latin.

Figure 15: "Saint Jerome in his Study" by Domenico Ghirlandaio (1480), Chiesa di Ognissanti, Florence.

When Saint Jerome's Vulgate was completed in A.D. 405, it was reproduced across the Latin-speaking Empire. Monks labored in monasteries, carefully reproducing manuscripts so that the Latin-speaking world had the Word of God available to it. Unfortunately, the printing press would not appear for another millennium, and each copy of the Bible was extremely precious. Not every village priest had one available.

THE APOCRYPHA:

When Saint Jerome first translated the Vulgate, he was against including certain books that had been written during the 200 years before Christ. These were left out of the Hebrew Old Testament, and it's not certain when they appeared in the Septuagint. They included 14 books most likely all originally written in Greek. The books of Ecclesiasticus, the Wisdom of Solomon, 1 & 2 Maccabees, Tobit, Judith, Bel and the Dragon, Baruch, and verses added to the end of Esther are today regarded as inspired Deuterocanonical books in the Roman Catholic Bible; while 1 & 2 Esdras, The Prayer of Manasses, The Song of the Three Holy Children, and The History of Susanna are not regarded as inspired. The New Testament writers never quote these extra books, though some early Church fathers quote them or refer to them. Under pressure, Jerome finally added these additional books to the Vulgate, placing them between the Old and New Testaments and giving them their name, "the apocrypha," which means, "things that are secret."

Fourteen Books of the Apocrypha

RCC Regards as Inspired	Date Written	Not Regarded as Inspired	Date Written
Ecclesiasticus (or Sirach)	Second century B.C.	1 Esdras	100 B.C.
Wisdom of Solomon	65 B.C.	2 Esdras	65 B.C. - A.D. 120
1 Maccabees	Second century B.C.	The Prayer of Manasses	First century B.C.
2 Maccabees	Second century B.C.	The Song of the Three Holy Children	100 B.C.
Tobit	Third century B.C.	The History of Susanna	First century B.C.

Bel and the Dragon	100 B.C.		
Judith	Second century B.C.		
Extension to Esther	100 B.C.		
Baruch	First century A.D.		

These books date to the intertestamental period, a time when the Jews believed that prophecy had ceased. The first book of Maccabees is considered a reasonable history of the events involved in the Maccabean revolt against the Seleucid ruler Antiochus IV, but the Jews did not regard it as divinely inspired material. Ecclesiasticus gives historians some useful tidbits about life in the second century before Christ. However, while Tobit and Judith are interesting stories, they are both roundly recognized as works of fiction.

During the Reformation, Protestants treated the apocryphal books as useful but not inspired. At the fourth session of the Council of Trent, the Roman Catholic Church declared nine of the apocryphal books equal to the others as holy Scripture, saying:

> But if any one receive not, as sacred and canonical, the said books entire with all their parts, as they have been used to be read in the Catholic Church, and as they are contained in the old Latin vulgate edition; and knowingly and deliberately contemn the traditions aforesaid; let him be anathema.

Today, the Roman Catholic Church calls these nine books the Deuterocanonical books — that is, forming a second canon.

THE VULGATE OF SIXTUS V

Pope Sixtus V (1585-1590) did a lot to bring order and lawfulness to Rome, executing brigands so that "heads on stakes were more common than melons." He taxed the populace to dangerous amounts, but he used the money toward public works and building projects.

One of the most significant things produced by Sixtus V was his *Vulgata Sixtina* — his authorized version of the Latin Vulgate. By the 16th century, there were a variety of Vulgate manuscripts floating around that differed from each other in small ways, and the Council of Trent in 1546 had called for an authoritative version to be produced. Earlier popes had not worked hard on this, and in 1589 Sixtus V jumped into the project. He had a committee under Cardinal Carafa produce a manuscript, but Sixtus rejected it and spent the next 18 months working to refine it. He was an insomniac and took on the herculean task with only one assistant.

On March 1, 1590, Sixtus used the bull *Aeternus Ille* to declare that his new version of the Vulgate was the authentic version. In reality, it was a disaster. Sixtus had added phrases at his own whim and omitted entire verses. It was filled with numerous and embarrassing errors.

Sixtus V died in August that year, and almost immediately the College of Cardinals stopped sales of the new Vulgate and tried to round up and destroy any copies out in the public hands. Rather than admit the pope had erred badly, the decision was made to blame it all on the printers.

The newly elected Pope Clement VIII took charge of the problem and ordered a list of scholars to revise the *Vulgata Sixtina* and fix the errors. They went to work, and in 1592 the *Vulgata Sixto-Clementina* went to press. Clement issued the bull *Cum Sacrorum* on November 9, 1592 to declare that no word of his Vulgate version could be changed or even have variant readings in the margins.

Clement's version of the Vulgate was used into the 20th century, but it too received criticism. Both versions opened up the Roman Catholic Church to jeering from the Protestants. In the first edition of the King James Bible in 1611, the translators mocked Sixtus V and Clement VIII because they had both authorized versions of the Bible as authentic and perfect, yet their two versions differed from each other in thousands of places:

The Latin Vulgate

> [D]id not the same Sixtus ordain by an inviolable decree...that the Latin edition of the Old and New Testament, which the Council of Trent would have to be authentic, is the same without controversy which he then set forth, being diligently corrected and printed in the printing-house of Vatican? Thus Sixtus in his preface before his Bible.
>
> And yet Clement the Eighth his immediate successor, publisheth another edition of the Bible, containing in it infinite differences from that of Sixtus, (and many of them weighty and material) and yet this must be authentic by all means...Again, what is sweet harmony and consent, if this be?[1]

What sweet harmony between these two! The sarcasm clearly rings through despite their 17th century English.

Clement's version had to be corrected in a variety of ways in further editions, but even then it had some extreme issues. In his preface to the 4th edition of the Stuttgart Vulgate, Roger Gryson claims that the Clementine Vulgate, "...frequently deviates from the manuscript tradition for literary or doctrinal reasons, and offers only a faint reflection of the original Vulgate." In other words, Clement (or his scholars) changed the plain meaning of the words to suit themselves and the doctrines they wished to advance.

In 1611, The King James Version of the Bible was authorized by the Church of England. From 1604 to 1611, fifty scholars translated the Bible from the Greek and Hebrew texts — specifically, the Greek text developed by Erasmus of Rotterdam sometime between 1512 and 1516 and the Hebrew Masoretic text. King James wanted this version to contain English that the common people could understand, using common idioms of the day. Those 50 scholars did quite a decent job, producing one of the greatest works of English literature today, still read and memorized by multitudes.

Of course, the King James Version cannot be considered perfect either. It is a human work, and it has its own minor

---
1 Preface to the 1611 King James Version: 14:20-21,23.

problems. For example, in Acts 12:4, the KJV uses the term "Easter" when the original Greek actually uses the word *pascha*, Passover, not Easter. Only the original autographs, those written by the prophets and apostles themselves, can be considered "God-breathed" according to Paul's description in 2 Timothy 3:16. All translations are simply humanity's best efforts to put those inspired words into the languages of the peoples of the world.

CHAPTER 20

THE EUCHARIST

Jesus Christ initiated the Eucharist during the Last Supper, on the night of His betrayal. In Matthew 26:26-28 Jesus pronounced over the bread, *"This is my body"* and over the wine, *"this is my blood."* Multitudes have been slaughtered at the stake over what exactly Jesus meant by these words.

THE ELEMENTS

Who in their right mind would ever disagree with Mother Teresa? That worthy woman once said:

> It is beautiful to see the humanity of Christ…in his permanent state of humility in the tabernacle, where he has reduced himself to such a small particle of bread that the priest can hold him in two fingers.

The whole world can stand in reverence of Mother Teresa. What she's saying is more than a metaphor, though. According to Roman Catholic teachings, Christ's literal body can be transformed into a wafer and of bread. These elements physically became the Lord's body and blood during the Last Supper; Christ offered them as a sacrifice to the Father and then gave them to the disciples to eat and drink.

When the priest consecrates the wafer, a miracle is said to take place, transforming the element into the physical body of Jesus (including His hair and bones). The church of the Middle Ages took Jesus' words literally, teaching the concept of "transubstantiation" — that the bread and wine mystically *become* the body and blood of Christ when blessed by the priest. It is then called the "Host" and it is worshipped as God. It is said to contain the body, the blood, the soul and divinity of Christ, and it becomes spiritual and physical nourishment. As each believer partakes of the Host, it becomes part of that person; it transforms and makes that person more righteous. Pope Innocent III included this doctrine of transubstantiation at the Fourth Lateran Council in 1215.

Before we go further, let's take a quick look at Innocent III.

THE MASSACRE AT BÉZIERS

Pope Innocent III was an interesting character who can be remembered for certain exploits, particularly the Albigensian Crusade against the Cathars. The Cathars were a group of dualist heretics who believed in a good god and an evil god, and at first Pope Innocent III sent ministers to try and convert them. However, after one of his legates was killed in 1208, Pope Innocent declared a holy war on the Cathars. He promised that any who joined the holy fight would be able to keep the properties they took from these heretics, and men joined the crusader army by the thousands.

On July 22, 1209, the pope's army marched into the city of Béziers, France where there was a large Cathar population. First the army slaughtered 20,000 people with the sword. They then burned the city and murdered all the residents — an estimated 60,000 people in all. Many of the people of the city were innocent of heresy, but it didn't matter. The papal legate, Arnold the Abbot of Cîteaux, was asked what to do, because the crusaders didn't know how to tell the good people from the bad. He reportedly said, *Caedite eos. Novit enim Dominus qui sunt eius.* "Hew them all down. The Lord knows who are his."[1] After the massacre, a proud Abbot Arnold wrote to the Pope:

> Our men spared no one, irrespective of rank, sex, or age, and put to the sword almost 20,000 people. After this

---
[1] The Cistercian monk Caesarius of Heisterbach (ca. 1180 – ca.1240) is the lone historian on this massacre. He describes it in his *Dialogus Miraculorum*, Vol 1.5.XXI: "The Albigensian Heresy."

great slaughter the whole city was despoiled and burnt, as Divine vengeance raged marvelously.

Innocent III wrote back, pleased by the whole affair, confident that the destruction of the great city of Béziers sent many people to heaven. He wrote that it allowed, "as many as possible of the Faithful to earn by their extermination a well-merited reward."[2]

This sparked a ruthless campaign which rooted out all heretics across the land. People were hunted down and prosecuted in ways so despicable that words are ineffective in conveying the sheer magnitude of the terror. Six years later, this same Pope Innocent III held the Fourth Lateran Council in which transubstantiation was written into law.

Figure 16: "The Last Supper" by Fritz von Uhde (1886), Staatsgalerie Stuttgart.

IN REMEMBRANCE

What did Jesus actually mean when He spoke those words at the Last Supper?

In Luke 22:19, Jesus said, *"This do in remembrance of Me."* Paul repeats this sentiment in 1 Corinthians 11:24-25, saying

---
2 Both letters are recorded in Innocent's Register, Book. XII, numbers 108 and 136.

in 11:26, *"For as often as ye eat this bread, and drink this cup, ye do shew the Lord's death till he come."* In other words, the Last Supper was the Passover, and Jesus instructed his disciples to remember his sacrifice every time they ate the Passover. In doing so, they were proclaiming Christ's death.

A century and a half before the official Reformation, certain Christians disagreed with the transubstantiation view. English priest and Bible scholar John Wycliffe (1330-1384) notably argued that the Eucharist was a form of holy *remembrance*, a proclamation of Christ's death on our behalf.

Wycliffe was a respected Catholic theologian in his day, and he insisted that the wine and bread were not literally flesh and blood but were symbols used to help us remember Christ's sacrifice. In his teachings, he repeatedly tried to explain the idea of figurative language versus literal language in the Bible, something the people of his day didn't seem to understand. He taught that the bread of the Eucharist signified Christ's body while it remained actual bread, and the wine signified Christ's blood while it remained wine.

Wycliffe read and studied the Bible daily, contrary to much of the Christian world in the late 1300s before the printing press. Reading his arguments in this respect, it's easy to hear his frustration. He declared:

> The nature of the bread is not destroyed by what is done by the priest, it is only elevated so as to become a substance more honored. The bread while becoming by virtue of Christ's words the body of Christ does not cease to be bread. When it has become sacramentally the body of Christ, it remains bread substantially…

> Therefore, let every man wisely, with much prayer and great study, and also with charity read the words of God in the Holy Scriptures … Christ saith, 'I am the true vine.' Wherefore do you not worship the vine for God, as you do the bread? Wherein was Christ a true vine? Or, wherein was the bread Christ's body? It was in figurative speech, which is hidden to the understanding of the

sinners. And thus, as Christ became not a material nor an earthly vine, nor a material vine the body of Christ, so neither is material bread changed from its substance to the flesh and blood of Christ.[3]

Wycliffe denounced the doctrine of transubstantiation, and by doing so, he earned the obvious ire of the church leadership. People were imprisoned and burned at the stake over this disagreement. It came down to a question of whether Christ was sacrificed just once, or whether He is sacrificed over and over again, at one Mass after another, when the priests bless the elements of the Eucharist.

We can remember the sacrifice of Christ every day for all our lives, honoring Him for His great love for us — for saving us through shedding His blood. That sacrifice is the most important action ever taken in the history of the world. However, Christ was only sacrificed once — once for all sins forever. Hebrews 10:12 tells us, *"But this man, after he had offered one sacrifice for sins for ever, sat down on the right hand of God."*

When we partake of the Eucharist, we are not sacrificing the Lord again. We are partaking in an object lesson by which we ponder the precious gift he has given us.

My Catholic friends explain that Christ is omnipresent and so he can be everywhere. That's true in the spiritual sense. However, Jesus truly had one body and that body is now (according to Hebrews 1:3) seated at the right hand of God and is not distributed in wafers worldwide. The Lord said he had to go so that he could send us the Holy Spirit, who sheds his love abroad in our hearts.[4]

This tradition has been taught as a most serious doctrine of the Roman Catholic Church, if not *the* most important. The question remains, was the Last Supper statement by Jesus meant to be *symbolic* or were the wine and bread *literally* transformed into blood and flesh of our Lord?

---

[3] John Wycliffe, "Archives: Wycliffe Causes Controversy Over Eucharist," Christian History, no. 3 (1983).
[4] John 15:26, 16:7; Romans 5:5.

Figurative Language in the Bible

We know that Jesus repeatedly uses figurative language in His teachings. He refers to Himself as a temple (John 2:19-21), the door to the sheep (John 10:7-8), the true vine (John 15:1), the bread of life (John 6:33-35), the good shepherd (John 10:11), the light of the world (John 8:12), and the way, the truth and the life (John 14:6). Matthew 13:34 tells us Jesus spoke in parables and only in parables. Each time Jesus uses one of these metaphors about himself, He uses a state-of-being verb. He says, "I *am* the light of the world" and He says, "I *am* the true vine."

When Jesus holds up the bread and says, "This is my body," and "this is my blood" at the Last Supper, He is using a metaphor again. We know this for several reasons. Not only does He use metaphors regularly in His teaching and in referring to himself, but notice He was sitting there in His own body while He said this to the disciples. He didn't pull off a piece of himself to have them eat His flesh. He held up the bread and wine of the Passover meal. He was explaining to them that the whole reason for the Passover in the first place was to represent Him and His death as the lamb — the lamb whose blood smeared the door post to keep out the Angel of Death.

At the Last Supper, Jesus Christ was preparing to go to the cross, to die for our sins. He became the ultimate Lamb of God, sent to take away the sins of the world as John the Baptist had declared in John 1:29. In 1 Corinthians 11:25, Jesus also explains that He is giving them a new covenant in His blood (the same new covenant God promised in Jeremiah 31:31-34.) Obviously, the cup was not the new covenant in itself, but rather the *symbol* of the covenant.

Jesus explains to His disciples that He is using figurative language with them, saying also at the Last Supper:

> *These things have I spoken unto you in proverbs: but the time cometh, when I shall no more speak unto you in proverbs, but I shall shew you plainly of the Father.*
>
> John 16:25

We can find other verses that let us know Jesus is speaking about figurative things, not literal physical things. In John 6, Jesus explains that He is the bread of life, and that those who want to be part of Him must eat His flesh and drink His blood. This disgusts a number of people who call it a "hard saying." However, Jesus explains in John 6:63 that, *"It is the spirit that quickeneth; the flesh profiteth nothing: the words that I speak unto you, they are spirit, and they are life."* He doesn't mean for the disciples to become cannibals. He's explaining to them spiritual ideas using proverbs — using metaphors.

In John 6:35, when Jesus says, *"I am the bread of life: he that cometh to me shall never hunger; and he that believeth on me shall never thirst,"* it's clear that He is using figurative language. It's clear, because every Christian who eats the Eucharist is still hungry and thirsty. Jesus is talking about spiritual things. He is talking about spiritual hunger and spiritual thirst. Jesus fulfills our spirits like no physical bread or wine ever can.

John Wycliffe, a faithful Catholic priest, understood these things. He understood that when Jesus called himself a "vine," He was saying it in a figurative sense. Jesus didn't mean He was an actual vine. He was trying to help the disciples understand that He was the source of their life and the source of any good works — "good fruit" — they produced. Jesus was never a literal door. He was never a literal shepherd. When we are born again, we don't go back inside our mothers to be produced a second time. The woman at the well wasn't given physical "living water." She was given knowledge of Jesus.

These are all metaphors and not literal pronouncements that Jesus uses to describe himself. As we read the full conversation of the night of the Last Supper, we find Jesus uses figurative speech throughout it.

We have to realize that the doctrine of transubstantiation developed in a world plagued by literary ignorance. In the illiterate Middle Ages, when there were few people who studied literature, it was easy for the priests to take Jesus' statements about the bread and wine as literal statements. They misunderstood Christ's intent, and that misunderstanding has been perpetuated until the present day.

Tradition

I have talked to Catholics about the Mass, because I have wanted to truly understand their answers and justifications, but they readily admit they too do not understand it all; it is, after all, an "awesome mystery."

The Bible tells us Christ was sacrificed once for all time, but the tradition of the Mass claims to sacrifice Him again and again. The Fourth Lateran Council of Pope Innocent III chiseled into stone another manmade tradition that causes confusion. Many Catholics feel they must receive the "Host" every week in order to have the Lord with them. However, Jesus told his disciples in Matthew 28:20, *"… I am with you always, even to the end of the age."*

The end of the age hasn't come yet, but we have great comfort that He is still with us by His Spirit.

Chapter 21

The "Angelic" Religions

It may not be politically correct, but Jesus doesn't leave room for competing religions. When He declares in John 14:6, *"I am the way, the truth, and the life. No one comes to the Father except through Me,"* He doesn't open other doors. Jesus is the Key. He is the way to salvation. There is no other.

Any time a person or church claims they alone possess the hidden will of God separate from the teachings of Jesus and the apostles, we need to watch out. These individuals are wielding the dagger of self-justification. We see it all over the world, and it's deadly.

All religions claim to have truth, and all religions offer some form of salvation. Yet, all non-Christian religions have something in common. They claim that we can make our *own* salvation. We can earn our way. Only the Bible teaches that we are helpless to be "good enough," that we must depend on Christ's righteousness and His sacrifice for us.

As a policeman, I testified in court as a witness in various trials. I saw attorneys twist the truth like a pretzel. It was often the power of manipulation which won the day in court, and a guilty person was set free to wander at will and commit more crimes. The attorneys were not about the job of determining the truth; they created a version of "truth" to produce a desired outcome. The evidence should speak the truth, but it is he who interprets the evidence that moves the minds of the judges.

Tradition

This is exactly the problem. The Bible says what it says and means what it says. Those who don't like what it says, however, like to twist its words to further their agenda rather than the agenda of God. We will now move on to various religious constructs that insist there are other ways to God than through Christ alone.

The Bible has an amazing quality of anticipating all manner of incorrect views that come later. We can look pretty much any heretical religious view, and we can find verses that deal with it — in advance. This is astounding. We find that Paul says something very interesting when speaking to the Galatians. He tells them:

> *But even if we, or an angel from heaven, preach any other gospel to you than what we have preached to you, let him be accursed.*
>
> Galatians 1:8

As a matter of fact, there are religions today that were said to have been founded by... lo and behold... angels!

Islam

Mohammed was an Arab merchant. He was a man of religious interests who came in contact with various sects along with Christianity and Judaism. In A.D. 610, while meditating in a cave in Arabia, Mohammed claimed he was approached *by an angel*. He was about 35 years of age, when a spiritual being appeared to him and told him to "recite."[1] Repeatedly, Mohammed said, "I cannot read," and repeatedly, the being physically pressed/pushed him. Finally, the being told him to "recite," commanding him, "in the name of your Lord, who created man from a clot of blood."[2] This visitation disturbed Mohammed, who told his wife Khadija that he was afraid for himself. Later, he claimed that the angel Gabriel made appearances to him and piece-meal revealed to him the Quran;

---
[1] *Quran* 81:19-29; *Sahih Muslim*, Book 1, Hadith 301
[2] *Ibid.*

the Muslim holy book. The spiritual being made additional visitations to Mohammed over a 23-year period.

Mohammed had the perspective that he was not creating a new religion, but that he was the last prophet from a line of prophets that began with Father Abraham. He regarded Moses and Joseph, son of Jacob, as his brothers.

In the Face of the Jews

I have been in Arabia in the dead of summer, with its relentless sun and endless sand. It was in this cruelest of environments that Mohammed formed his new faith.

Mohammed claimed to be the last and final prophet anointed by God. He opposed the idol worship he saw at the Kaaba in Mecca, where the people honored a multitude of pagan gods. He had accepted certain aspects of Judaism, as well as parts of Christianity. Then, he learned that Jewish tribes had helped an enemy, the Quraish tribe of Mecca. As a result, eight hundred men of the Median Jews were beheaded. The remaining women and children were sold into slavery. Mohammed himself took a Jewish woman whose husband and all male relatives had been killed.

He returned to Mecca, the pilgrimage center of paganism, and told his followers to no longer face Jerusalem when praying, but to bow toward *Mecca* the home of the Kaaba. Mohammed sent out a message that the Muslims had replaced the Jews as God's chosen people.

The word "chosen" does not carry the same meaning in Islam as we find in the Bible, however. The Jews regard their position as "chosen" as a distinct responsibility to follow God and His commandments. They recognize they are responsible to actively bless the world in which they live. In Islam, the idea of being "chosen" means superiority.

From its inception, Islam has had a systemic vitriol toward the Jews — a continuation of Mohammed's personal hostility that began in the seventh century. It changed most of the world then, and it holds much of our world hostage today. In the centuries that followed Mohammed's death, much of the then-Christian and Jewish world was conquered by Islam. The Persian and Byzantine Empires had been weakened by years of fighting with each other, and the Muslims had little difficulty conquering the lands of these weary empires. The strategy used by the Muslims is *jihad* — "struggle." While jihad can be a struggle against sin or struggle against personal weakness, Jihad in the Quran often has a military sense. For instance, Sura 8:39 states, "Fight them, till there is no persecution and the religion is Allah's entirely..."

In the seventh and eighth centuries, Muslims subjugated lands that extended from Spain to India. Islam ruled the seas with marauding fleets and controlled caravan trade with China. New cities grew out of the heaps of sands. Conquered peoples were forced into submission to Allah. Muslims swept across vast tracts of land like a howling, desert sandstorm, conquering Egypt and spreading across the northern coast of Africa.

The Muslims even began to invade Europe. Arabs swarmed into Spain in the early eighth century, crossed the Pyrenees and held the coast of France. They were stopped at Tours, France by the Franks in 732. The armies of Europe would continue to fight the invaders off and on for the next several centuries, often losing more ground than they gained. Today, Islam is the fastest growing faith in sheer numbers in the world.

THE ISLAMIC MESSIAH

Interestingly, the Quran holds claim to the Jewish fathers and prophets of old. While the Quran honors Ishmael as Abraham's firstborn, Isaac is also revered. The Quran does not name which son was almost sacrificed in Abraham's faith test, and there has been a long debate among Muslim scholars over the issue. However, Abraham and Ishmael are the father-son pair said to have built the Kaaba.

The Quran does not deny that Jesus existed. In fact, the Quran teaches that Isa (Jesus) was the Messiah, a prophet who performed miracles[3] and was assumed into Heaven.[4] The Isa of the Quran

---
3   *Quran* 3:49-51
4   *Quran* 3:55,169

was born of a virgin and is often referred to as the "son of Mary."[5] However, the Quran insists that Jesus was just a messenger, that God was not his Father, and that there is not "three" — not a Trinity.[6]

Islam teaches that while Jesus was the Messiah and will return one day to judge the world, Jesus did not die on a cross for our sins.

Paul warned us against believing anybody, even an angel from heaven, who teaches any other gospel than the one taught by the New Testament writers. The Muslim Jesus, as portrayed by the Quran, absolutely presents a different gospel. While the Jesus of the Bible declares that He is God's Son and that salvation comes through Him,[7] the Muslim Isa's "good news" is to confirm the Quran and to promote worship of Allah alone.

The men who wrote the New Testament knew Jesus personally. They walked with Him for years, and after His death and resurrection were filled with His Spirit, as evidenced by their ability to heal and prophesy and speak in different tongues. They went to their deaths for the truths they proclaimed. They taught the Gospel, the Good News of salvation by the death and resurrection of Jesus Christ, according to a multitude of prophecies in the Hebrew Scriptures.

Islam has a completely different history, in which a solitary man had repeat visits from a spiritual visitor. Based on those many visions, he declared that the followers of Jesus were all wrong.

Here is the odd thing. The Quran recognizes the virgin birth of Jesus and Jesus' ability to perform miracles. It recognizes the sinlessness of Jesus and His blessedness by God. It recognizes that Jesus will return one day. Yet, while Mohammed was not born of a virgin, performed no miracles, was not sinless, and is not the one who will return, Islam makes Mohammed the most important prophet. None of this bodes well for the religion of Mohammed.

---

5   *Quran* 3:45-49; 19:20-21;
6   *Quran* 4:171; 17:111; 19:88-92; 37:152;
7   John 3:16, 14:6

Mormonism

Another religion birthed from an angelic vision was Mormonism. As a teenager, Joseph Smith had a vision while praying in the woods. In the *Pearl of Great Price*, Smith relates:

> I saw two Personages, whose brightness and glory defy all descriptions, standing above me in the air. One of them spake unto me, calling me by name, and said, pointing to the other — 'This is My Beloved Son. Hear Him!'[8]

In 1823, Smith claimed the angel Moroni appeared to him and told him the location of a buried box containing golden plates. These tablets were eventually translated into the *Book of Mormon* from "reformed Egyptian" using two "seer stones" — allegedly the Urim and the Thummim — to receive the translation word-for-word from God.

Joseph Smith stated, "I told the brethren that the Book of Mormon was the most correct of any book on the earth..."[9]

Smith claimed many more angelic visitations occurred; between 1831 and 1844 he received 135 direct revelations he believed came from God the Father, Jesus the Son, and many spirits of the dead.[10] Record of these revelations are printed in the book *Doctrine and Covenants*. Joseph Smith added other books to the canon of the Mormon Church, including the *Pearl of Great Price*, which contains the *Book of Moses* and the *Book of Abraham*.

Mormons believe they have the one and only true religion. In 1854, Orson Pratt argued that, "All other religions are entirely destitute of all authority from God," and Joseph Smith said Christian pastors are "of their father, the devil."[11] Smith claimed the Bible had been corrupted over the ages, and by his inspiration he claimed the ability to revise it.[12]

The Mormon Church's focus on family and community and moral living offer good things for our society. Christians might

---
8   *Pearl of Great Price*, 2:17.
9   Joseph Smith, *History of the Church*, Vol. 4 (1839-1856), 461.
10 John Ankerberg and John Weldon, *The Facts on the Mormon Church* (Harvest House, 1997), 7.
11 *Ibid*, 8, 13.
12 Claudia L. Bushman, *Joseph Smith: Rough Stone Rolling* (New York: Alfred A. Knopf, 2005) 133.

chuckle at the Mormon prohibitions against coffee and tea, but these things are not important. Paul in Romans 14 tells Christians not to judge each other over small, questionable things.

The real question is whether Mormonism is based in truth. Does it teach another gospel than the good news of the New Testament? If the messages that the spiritual visitors gave Joseph Smith contradict the Gospel of Jesus Christ, we need to reject them. If the teachings of Joseph Smith contradict the Bible as a whole, we need to reject them.

The most difficult issue with Mormonism is that it uses vocabulary that can sound very Bible-based, but Joseph Smith appears to have been either spiritually misled or an outright fraud.

First, there are serious Bible prohibitions against having familiar spirits and against speaking with the dead.

> *And when they say to you, "Seek those who are mediums and wizards, who whisper and mutter," should not a people seek their God? Should they seek the dead on behalf of the living? To the law and to the testimony! If they do not speak according to this word, it is because there is no light in them.*
>
> Isaiah 8:19-20

Any spirit that is from God should confirm the words of the Bible, but Joseph Smith had contact with individuals long dead, and the Mormon Church teaches its adherents to "seek after" their dead. They are baptized for the dead and are concerned with bringing redemption to their dead relatives. Wilford Woodruff is quoted as saying:

> The dead will be after you, they will seek after you as they have after us in St. George. They called upon us, knowing that we held the keys and power to redeem them. I will here say, before closing, that two weeks before I left St. George, the spirits of the dead gathered around me, wanting to know why we did not redeem them.[13]

---

[13] *Journal of Discourses* 19:229-230.

This is a fantastic admission for a Mormon leader to make, because the Bible specifically and adamantly tells us not to speak to the dead.[14]

It should concern any Christian that Joseph Smith declared the Bible to have been corrupted, and that he placed his own translations and inspirations on par (or above) the Bible. This is what cult leaders do; they say, "I have the only revealed truth." (The Dead Sea Scrolls actually have done a great deal to demonstrate how faithfully the Scriptures have been copied over the millennia.)

There are other indications that Smith's writings are fraudulent. The *Book of Mormon* quotes the Old Testament extensively, but Smith's supposedly word-for-word translation from God amazingly matches the King James Version verbatim. The original *Book of Mormon* was filled with grammatical errors, which was well-recognized by Mormon historians like B.H. Roberts.[15] The typesetter said Smith wouldn't let him fix the errors,[16] and Roberts acknowledged:

> But after due allowance is made for all these conditions, the errors are so numerous, and of such a constitutional nature, that they cannot be explained away by these unfavorable conditions under which the work was published.[17]

Besides these things, the alleged history in the *Book of Mormon* has left no evidence. We can find archeological evidence and the locations of places described in the Old Testament, but the locations described in the *Book of Mormon* cannot be found in the real world. Also, despite the claims of *the Book of Mormon*, DNA evidence from Native Americans show they are not genetic Hebrews, but originated in the Altai Mountains of southern Siberia.[18]

---

[14] Deuteronomy 18:10-13.
[15] B.H. Roberts, *Defense of the Faith*, Vol. 1 (1907), 280-281, 300-301.
[16] George W.M. Reynolds, *The Myth of the Manuscript Found* (Salt Lake City: Juvenile Instructor Office, 1883), 59.
[17] Brigham H. Roberts, *Defense of the Faith*, Vol. 1. (1907), 295.
[18] S.L. Zegura, et al., "High-Resolution SNPs and Microsatellite Haplotypes Point to a Single, Recent Entry of Native American Y Chromosomes into the Americas," *Molecular Biology and Evolution* 21, no 1(2004), 164–175, doi:10.1093/molbev/msh009.

In 1842, Smith published the *Book of Abraham*, which he supposedly translated from Egyptian papyri purchased from a traveling exhibit in Kirtland, Ohio in 1835. Hieroglyphics had not been deciphered in those days, and Smith presumed to produce a translation, which became the *Book of Abraham*. Tragically, the papyri were thought to have burned in the Great Chicago Fire, but they were found again in 1966, tucked away in the New York Metropolitan Museum of Art. The Latter Day Saints community was overjoyed as the papyri were validated as the ones from Joseph Smith's collection (complete with drawings of a Mormon temple and Ohio maps on the back). When the papyri were examined and the hieroglyphics translated by experts, however, the contents turned out to be from the *Book of Breathing*, which was derived from the *Book of the Dead*.[19] This discovery makes excellent sense. The *Book of the Dead* and its derivative funerary texts are Egyptian documents known to the world, and we would expect versions of them traveling in an exhibit. Smith's "translated" history of Abraham, including an additional creation story, is original to Smith. The fact that he gleaned his *Book of Abraham* from the *Book of Breathing* indicates that Smith's translations came either from a deceptive spirit or were just plain made up.

Mormonism teaches a mixture of beliefs, focusing on a religious system of good works and personal righteousness for salvation. Mormons will declare that Jesus died for our sins, and they claim to revere the Bible as the Word of God. However, Jesus, God the Father, and the Holy Spirit are different people in Mormonism than we find in the Bible. The Mormon members of the Trinity are completely separate individuals who are unified only in the sense of having a single purpose. They are called a "Godhead," but they are not one God. The Jesus of Mormonism was the result of a sexual act between God the Father and Mary.

The Old Testament gave us the old covenant, one that required following the Law and depending on the sacrifice of lambs and bulls for forgiveness of sins. The New Testament

---

[19] J. Warner Wallace, "How the Book of Abraham Exposes the False Nature of Mormonism," June 20, 2014. http://coldcasechristianity.com/2014/how-the-book-of-abraham-exposes-the-false-nature-of-mormonism/ and Fawn M. Brodie, No Man Knows My History: The Life of Joseph Smith, 2nd ed. (New York: Alfred A. Knopf, 1971) 170–75) and Bushman, *Rough Stone Rolling*, 286, 289–290.

presents a new covenant, in which Jesus Christ is the eternal sacrificial lamb who died for the sins of the world in fulfillment of the Old Testament Scriptures. Hebrews chapters 7-10 go into this in depth. The New Testament treats the Old Testament as a shadow, a reflection of what Jesus would do to save us. He gives us new life, and the good works we do, we do because we are already in Him and are walking by His Spirit.[20] That's what the Bible teaches.

The *Book of Mormon* claims to be a final testament, but it doesn't actually offer a new covenant or even contain the majority of the doctrines of Mormonism. The Book of Mormon seems to confuse New Testament practices and Old Testament times. That's just it, though. The *Book of Mormon* appears to be filled with confusion.

For instance, the Book of Mosiah is supposed to date to the second century B.C., before the birth of Christ. It makes sense it would use the terminology of the old covenant. However, Mosiah also declares that the Holy Spirit was poured out before Christ even came,[21] and the Church of Christ was founded long before Christ.[22]

In practical application, the *Book of Mormon* and other teachings/ books by Joseph Smith are often taught primarily to the neglect of the Bible. While, the *Book of Mormon* is not the source for Mormon doctrines, it opens the door to all of Mormon teachings, which do contradict the Word of God. The Mormon Church has modern day prophets and apostles who claim to speak directly to Jesus Christ in the Mormon temples, and their words can override the Scriptures. Mormons often depend far more on their prophet than on the Holy Spirit, on the teachings of Joseph Smith than on the Bible, and on their own good works instead of the blood of Jesus Christ. These things are dangerous.

As of 2016, the world held roughly 15.9 million Mormons.[23] Unfortunately, these worship God according to Joseph Smith's interpretations of "true" religion, following the traditions he set

---
20 Galatians 5:16-26; Ephesians 2:8-16
21 Mosiah 25:24
22 Mosiah 18:17, 23:16
23 LDS, *2016 Statistical Report for 2017 April Conference.*

up rather than following the Bible. We would encourage all God-fearing Mormons to look into these things in more depth.

Chapter 22

Archeology and Calvary

I now want to address, in my opinion, a principal false tradition of the Protestant faith archeologically speaking.

As we have traveled a long road to find the buried bones of Church traditions, we have seen that Catholic traditions emerged in the soil of the Middle Ages. Do we have examples of Protestants making for themselves traditions? Definitely.

I recently wrote a book about the site of Jesus' crucifixion and burial. When Emperor Constantine's mother Helena went hunting for the True Cross of Christ,

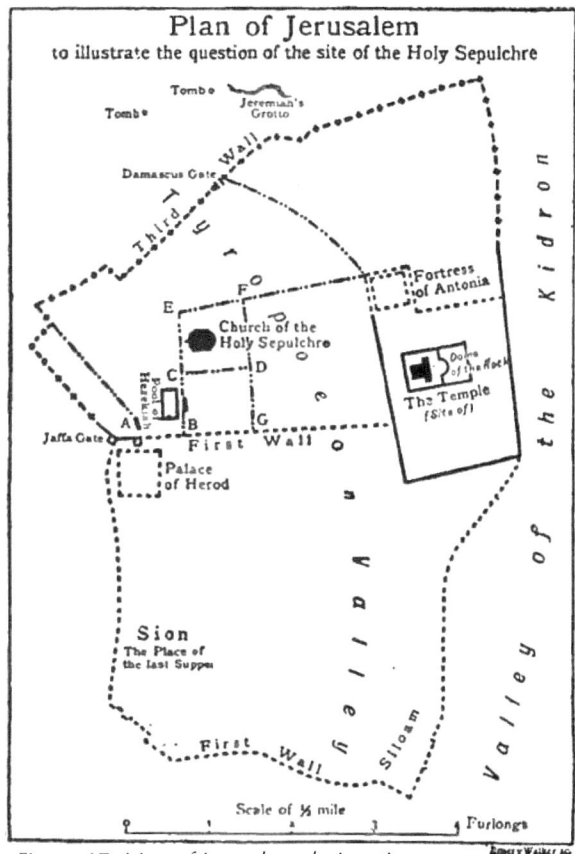

Figure 17: Map of Jerusalem designating site of Gordon's Calvary and Church of the Holy Sepulchre. Source: 1911 Encyclopædia Britannica.

169

Tradition

she defined where Christ's tomb was located for all of Christendom. That location is where we find the Church of the Holy Sepulchre today. I would like to show how Protestant tradition crept into this subject without much critical examination.

The Church of the Holy Sepulchre was the unchallenged location for Calvary since the fourth century. In 1883, a famed British officer named Major-General Charles Gordon boldly challenged the pedigree of the Holy Sepulchre as the place of Golgotha. His proposed site for the crucifixion of Christ was north of the Damascus Gate. While living for a time in Jerusalem, General Gordon observed what he believed was a skull-like formation in a rock cliff at Jeremiah's Grotto, near his temporary residence. To him, Scripture suggested this as the "place of the skull" and, conversely, Christ's execution location.

In Matthew 27:33, Golgotha is called the "Place of the Skull." In the cliff face, Gordon observed a geological display of two small indentations, like sunken eye sockets, and other rough

Figure 18: Skull Hill from the south, c. 1900.

"facial" contours that fit the appearance of a skull. Two things convinced Gordon this was the real Golgotha — the skull—like facial feature he saw in the cliff and an ancient tomb nearby. In a letter to his sister written on January 17, 1883, (his second day in Jerusalem) Gordon wrote:

I feel, for myself, convinced that the hill near the Damascus Gate is Golgotha. ... From it, you can see the Temple, the Mount of Olives and the bulk of Jerusalem. His stretched out arms would, as it were, embrace it: "all day long have I stretched out my arms" [cf. Isaiah 65:2]. Close to it is the slaughter-house of Jerusalem; quiet pools of blood are lying there. It is covered with tombs of Muslims. There are many rock-hewn caves; and gardens surround it. Now, the place of execution in our Lord's time must have been, and continued to be, an unclean place ... so, to me, this hill is left bare ever since it was first used as a place of execution. ... It is very nice to see it so plain and simple, instead of having a huge church built on it."

Due to Gordon's heroic status as a war veteran, the designation of the site steadily gained acceptance. Since Gordon was an avowed Protestant like the majority of his English countrymen, the notion of a site other than the Catholic Church of the Holy Sepulchre was appealing. Through Gordon, an entirely new tradition on the location of Christ's execution, burial, and resurrection was conveniently born to the delight of British Protestants.

However, both Gordon's Calvary and the Church of the Holy Sepulchre are fraught with geographical flaws. Simply put, they do not align with Scriptural descriptions.

All across Israel there are many "holy sites" which are based on, at best, questionable historic lineages. Tour guides with an ounce of integrity would freely confess that many of the locations they show tourists have little to do with historical reality. A cleric raised his bony finger in some dusty backyard part of the Holy Land a millennia ago, and today there's a guided tour. A location might have no legitimate historical value, but religious throngs from tour buses crowd the polished marble floor of the locations' gift shop.

Don't misunderstand me. Israel is truly an archeologist's dream. A large number of the places described in the Bible have been excavated and verified. Some popular tourist destinations make for accurate historical lessons, but the fact remains that many do not. In 1883, Charles Gordon made a stunning pronouncement that he had discovered the true location of Calvary, and in time it became a sensation.

I first learned about General Gordon as a teenager in an old darkened theatre while watching the movie, *Khartoum*. Set in 1886 in Sudan, Charlton Heston starred as Major-General Charles Gordon. I recall the film's spectacular desert scenery, framing rows of regimental British soldiers riding atop bellowing camels, poised for battle. The wide screen was soon filled with a cloud of dust as opposing warriors charged into the fray with flags unfurled and the glint of sabers clashing under a cloudless desert sky. At the end of the movie, Gordon made his last stand. The Muslim warriors breached the walls of the besieged British fortress at Khartoum and swarmed in for the kill. Charlton Heston made a heroic Gordon, standing ramrod stiff at the top of a flight of steps, completely fearless in the face of certain death.

A horde of frenzied, screaming warriors raced up the steps toward Gordon and then suddenly and inexplicably stopped. The Mahdists had been rioting in wild and unrestrained fashion, shooting and shouting. When confronting Gordon, they froze like statues in a haze of lingering rifle smoke. Gordon did not twitch. He simply stared down the paralyzed mob, his sword at his side. In that instant, a lone spear hissed through the air and embedded deep into Gordon's chest. The Muslims erupted into a frenzied rampage again. The camera then panned to a building set ablaze, sparing us the gruesome scene.

Who was Major-General Charles Gordon really? He joined the army when he was only sixteen years old and quickly found himself commissioned to the Royal Engineers in 1852 at the age of 19. His bravery in the Crimean War earned him a reputation as a courageous and devoted soldier. During the bloody Taiping Rebellion in China, he further distinguished himself, playing a major role in halting the violent insurgency.

Gordon also stood out for his oversized and egocentric lust for authority. His dominating personality caused Lord Cromer to describe him as "mad or half-mad." An incessant smoker, heavy drinker, and (paradoxically) unapologetically fervent man of prayer, Gordon became to those around him infuriatingly eccentric, though in battle, he was a magnificently courageous soldier.

It should shock no one that Hollywood's portrayal of Khartoum was far different than actual events. Gordon may have been sleeping in the early hours of January 26, 1885 when the din of war drums cut through the darkness. It's said that a traitor opened the gates, letting in the rebels who raced through the streets amid rapid rifle reports. Dervishes stormed the walls screaming "DEATH TO ALL!" Gordon hastily donned his regimental uniform, grabbed his pistol and, with a sword at his side, went down to confront the invaders. He emptied a revolver into the sea of enemies as he was hit by three different spears and a rifle shot. In the fury of the moment, no one actually saw Gordon die. His head was severed and carried in a leather bag to the Mahdi's camp. On February 5th, news reached London that Gordon was dead. England's anguish was compounded by the grisly report that his head had been paraded through the streets on a pike.

Gordon's remains were never found, but his fame lived on. An impassioned period of national mourning followed, as shop windows across London displayed pictures of the dead hero draped in black bunting. A public outpouring of grief spilled far beyond Britain — into Paris, Berlin, and as far as New York. Distraught as well as outraged, Queen Victoria wrote a scathing note to Prime Minister Gladstone, practically accusing him of indirectly murdering the general. Songs and poems sailed off the printing presses as tributes to Gordon appeared throughout England. Books, pamphlets, and articles contributed to Gordon's mounting status in legend.

Gordon's Calvary became a spiritual Mecca for zealous patrons who idolized the general. His theory hadn't gained much traction until his spectacular death, but the rocky skull face now won hearts as the execution site for Christ. The stone cliff shot to heights of prominence as the true place of the crucifixion. The evangelical Gordon was the "penultimate symbol of Victorian England's perception of the Holy Land."[1] In the emotional wake

---

[1] Seth J. Frantzman and Ruth Kark, "General Gordon, The Palestine Exploration Fund and the Origins of 'Gordon's Calvary' in the Holy Land," *Palestine Exploration Quarterly* 140, no. 2 (2008): 119-136.

of Gordon's heart-wrenching death, a prideful nation, wrestling with issues of faith, science, and culture, seized upon his brash proclamation of a new monument to Christ the King.

Unfortunately, the "Golgotha" that Gordon endorsed was riddled with scriptural and geographical flaws. I cannot help but wonder, "What if…?" What if Gordon hadn't died at Khartoum? He certainly wouldn't have attained his adored status across England. There would likely be no tourist site known as "Gordon's Calvary."

Gordon's Calvary, also known as "Jeremiah's Grotto," is one of the more beautiful and serene settings in Jerusalem. I have been there and enjoyed it as a lush, cool oasis amid Jerusalem's clamor, chaos, and traffic. Visitors describe their "genuine experiences," in some cases, prompting them to linger for hours, meditating and praying in the manicured garden's shady calm. Some raise hands toward heaven, bathing the stone fortifications in songs of praise. I have felt a serene tranquility there myself.

Whether the real location of Christ's death or not, our God delights in sincere praise and prayers whenever — and wherever — they're offered. A heart made holy by the eternal event on the cross matters more than the precise ancient location of that cross.

The Garden Tomb

With Gordon's Calvary came renewed interest in the nearby Garden Tomb. Canon Tristan of Durham considered the place "simply priceless." In 1892, the highest dignitaries in the English Church threw their full support toward the land's purchase, and in 1893-94, a huge influx of subscribers, trustees, donors, scholars, artists, clergy, and patrons secured the purchase of the land. This lifeless, dry, scab of dirt was irrigated and transformed into a landscape of lush serenity that still holds exquisite beauty today. In an attempt to appease most, the trust deed included these words, "That the Garden and the Tomb be kept sacred as a quiet spot, and preserved on the one hand from desecration, and on the other hand from superstitious uses."

Those who doubt the legitimacy of the Garden Tomb have just cause. Gordon would be crushed to learn that this location, where he believed the Lord once lay, was actually chiseled out in the wrong era.

I recently met with famed scholar and archaeologist, Gabriel Barkey, who has done extensive analysis at Gordon's Garden Tomb. He told me the tomb there could not be the tomb of Christ, because it was carved out of rock before the seventh century B.C. Christ was laid in a brand new tomb, which Matthew 27:60 says Joseph of Arimathea had recently hewn from a rock. Though Gordon chose it because of its close proximity to "Skull Mountain," the Garden Tomb was at least 700 years old by the time Jesus died. Luke 23:53 and John 19:41 confirm that the tomb of Jesus was new when Christ was laid there, and nobody had ever been buried there.

I also found compelling graphic evidence which suggests the cliff of Gordon's Calvary did not always resemble a skull. A drawing of this same area from by a man named "Sandy" in A.D. 1610 depicts Gordon's cliff with nothing resembling a skull-like aspect. Other photos as recent as the 1930s indicate what seems to be radical erosion of the shale-like limestone cliff. Using even the most facile powers of observation, there can be little doubt the area's capricious winds and rains continuously and relentlessly modify the cliff's appearance.

In an article for *WorldNetDaily*, Jeff Baggett noted:

> The Jerusalem site many Christians believe is "the Place of the Skull" has been forever altered. Located behind Jerusalem's bus station and adjacent to the Garden Tomb, the rocky escarpment with its two cavernous 'eyes' has been linked to the events of Jesus' passion since the mid-19th century. Recent storms and erosion however caused the collapse of the skull's 'nose.[2]

Taking into account the cliff's steady, rapid, and irrefutable decay, it defies logic that it resembled a skull nearly 2,000 years prior to Gordon's visit to Jerusalem. The true source of Gordon's error, it turns out, is that he misunderstood the Bible's description of the Calvary location. Dr. Ernest Martin explains:

---
[2] Jay Baggett, "Possible 'Place of the Skull' Loses its Nose," *WorldNetDaily*, March 4, 2015, http://www.wnd.com/2015/03/sudden-change-at-jesus-place-of-the-skull/.

The New Testament writers were not actually suggesting that the place of Jesus' crucifixion, the "Place of the Skull," looked like an actual skull. They were, rather, referring to the term's original Aramaic meaning translated as the "place of the head" or "the poll."[3]

> And they brought Him to the place Golgotha, which is translated, Place of a Skull. Then they gave Him wine mingled with myrrh to drink, but He did not take it. And when they crucified Him, they divided His garments, casting lots for them to determine what every man should take. Now it was the third hour, and they crucified Him.
>
> Mark 15:22-25

There have been significant debates over what Mark meant when he described Golgotha as the "Place of a Skull." It may be the location where David buried the skull of Goliath, or it may be ground that was littered with skulls from crucifixion victims.

New Testament Greek scholar Dr. William Welty, Executive Director of the ISV Foundation, helped me better to understand the historic and cultural antecedents of these scriptural references. I asked him to explain his understanding of the "Place of a Skull" and received a thorough civic and linguistic exegesis:

> We may eliminate on linguistic grounds the common notion held by those who have read the crucifixion narratives only in the English language translation that the term 'Place of the Skull' used by the Gospel writers to describe the crucifixion site refers to the apparent shape of the mountain. This is because the term does not refer to the geological appearance of the hill, but rather to the purpose for which the place was utilized. It was not a first century Israeli or Roman practice to name geological features after their visual appearance. Instead, if they were not named after a person of public importance or of historical significance, sites were named as an indicator of their public function. Accordingly, it is highly unlikely

---

[3] Ernest L. Martin, *Secrets of Golgotha: The Lost History of Christ's Crucifixion* (Portland, Oregon: ASK Publications, 1996) 100.

that the area known today as Gordon's Calvary was the site of the Messiah's death.

It's suggested that the term should be "Skull Place," which is the literal translation of the Greek phrase *Kraniou Topos (*Κρανίου Τόπος*)*. This refers to the known use of an elevated portion of a hill directly east of the City of David. This area was probably used for undertaking head counts for census enumerations and other similar public functions. Think of the area as a form of public staging area where crowds of people were processed for a variety of civil and criminal administrative purposes. This would also be an appropriate place for a public execution.

As with Gordon's Calvary, or any other suspected Biblical site, heightened emotional attachments to a place does not certify it as the real location no matter how passionate one's declaration may be. Thus, we find a tradition started fewer than 150 years ago by a well-admired general slain in battle. It was promoted by Protestants who wanted a site to compete with the Catholic Church of the Holy Sepulchre. Today, there is a gift shop at the Garden Tomb. Multitudes visit it every year as though it truly is the tomb from which Jesus emerged on Resurrection Sunday. I have been there many times and, yes, it is a very calm and tranquil place where I often pray. But it is not where Christ was buried. Gordon's Calvary as the crucifixion site of Jesus is a man-made tradition — and it took just a few years to solidify in the public mind.

Traditions are all born the same way, whether Catholic or Protestant or Evangelical. Once a tradition takes root, it is protected and honored, especially as the dollars keep flowing in.

CHAPTER 23

GALILEO

One of the most troublesome traditions of the Middle Ages was the lack of freedom to interpret the Bible on one's own. The church leadership alone claimed the authority to decipher the Scriptures. Most school children think that Galileo was persecuted because his scientific discoveries conflicted with the religious views of the day. That's not actually the case. Galileo dared to offer insights about the Bible, and when he was censured for it, he warmly criticized the pope who had been his friend. That's what got Galileo into trouble.

In 1609, Galileo heard rumors of a spyglass contraption. A German optician Hans Lippershey had found a way put a lens in a tube in such a way that it would magnify distant objects two or three times. Galileo took the same basic idea and created a device involving a lead tube and ground concave lenses. This invention made celestial objects appear 3-9 times larger than they were seen with the naked eye. That was his first effort. Eventually, Galileo developed a spyglass that made objects appear 30 times nearer.

On a cold January night, Galileo wrapped a heavy coat around him and climbed to the highest room of his house and onto the roof. There he set up his spyglass innovation. A vaporous mist puffed into the cool air as he placed his eye to the device.

He gazed on a universe more closely and clearly than anyone had ever recorded. He remained on the roof until dawn erased the stars from sight. Galileo performed this activity every night, charting a full month of star and planet movements. Using his handmade telescope, Galileo made important discoveries, many of which he published in his 1610 book *Starry Messenger*. He found that:

- Sun spots are part of the surface of the sun (which means Aristotle was wrong about the perfection of celestial bodies).
- The moon has mountains and valleys just like Earth.
- Venus has phases like the moon, suggesting that it orbits the sun.
- Saturn has "ears" — which we now know are its rings.
- Stars are more distant than planets.
- There are stars that can't be seen without a telescope.
- The Milky Way is made of stars.
- Jupiter has moons (which means Aritstotle was wrong about Earth as the sole center of the universe).

In his journal, Galileo wrote, "I render infinite thanks to God for being so kind as to make me alone the first observer of marvels kept hidden in obscurity for all previous centuries."

Galileo's *Starry Messenger* was a popular book and was initially received well in Rome. He named Jupiter's moons the "Medicean planets" after the Medici dukes of Tuscany, which pleased the powerful family. Galileo even earned a position as the duke's mathematician and philosopher. The Roman Catholic Church hadn't made a firm doctrine on the habits of celestial bodies just yet, and the Jesuits and the pope treated the scientist warmly.

Then, Galileo made a mistake. During breakfast one morning, the elderly Princess Christina, Grand Duchess of Tuscany, commented that the Bible said the Earth stood still and the sun moved around it. Rather than letting it go, Galileo wrote the Grand Duchess Christina a letter, explaining his position that the Bible would match up with science if it were interpreted correctly. He suggested that God wasn't concerned with teaching astronomy through His Word, and it was not a salvation issue. He famously concluded in his letter to her,

"I would say here something that was heard from an ecclesiastic of the most eminent degree: 'That the intention of the Holy Ghost is to teach us how one goes to heaven, not how heaven goes.'"

This is where Galileo got into trouble, because the church frowned on his making his own interpretation of the Bible. As his letter to Princess Christina circulated, Galileo's enemies jumped on it and sought an Inquisition to look into the matter. Pope Paul V ordered theologians to determine what the Bible said about the universe and the movement of the celestial bodies. In February of 1616, it was officially determined that teaching that the Earth moved about the sun was heretical and absurd. Galileo was forbidden to teach these Copernican ideas, and all materials teaching a heliocentric view were banned. The Inquisition made an injunction against Galileo, ordering him:

> ...to abstain completely from teaching or defending this doctrine and opinion or from discussing it... to abandon completely... the opinion that the sun stands still at the center of the world and the earth moves, and henceforth not to hold, teach, or defend it in any way whatever, either orally or in writing.[1]

That was it. Galileo was highly respected, but he was sent home. However, as the old saying goes, "Familiarity breeds contempt." Galileo's personal closeness to the highest classes of Italian society gave him a boldness few others would have conveyed. Galileo behaved himself for many years, even when he was wrongly told not to argue that the Earth rotated around the sun. Galileo had a long history of arrogance, and he developed an attitude. As the years went by, he lost his prudence on the matter, and in 1632 Galileo published his famous *Dialog Concerning the Two Chief World Systems*. In this sardonic satire, he promoted the heliocentric view of the universe while making direct fun of the pope and anybody who affirmed the geocentric view.

---

[1] John L. Heilbron, *Galileo* (Oxford: Oxford University Press, 2010), 218.

TRADITION

Figure 19: Galileo facing the Roman Inquisition, painting by Cristiano Banti (1857), private collection.

Pope Urban VIII was a personal friend of Galileo at this time, but he was not entertained by the book. Galileo was brought before the Inquisition again, and he back-pedaled madly. In the end, Galileo was *not* tortured and killed. Instead, he was placed under house arrest and his book was banned. Galileo was forced to renounce his views, and Urban VIII ordered copies made of the renunciation papers and sent them far and wide to be read in all the churches. This humiliated Galileo. He was not tortured physically, but this must have torn him up inside. He remained on house arrest until his death in 1642 at the age of 77.

The battle between Galileo and the Roman Catholic Church was not about whether Galileo believed the Bible. He simply argued a different interpretation of the Bible than the official theologians. Despite his own personal failings, Galileo admired the God of the Bible with all of his heart. "When I consider what marvelous things men have understood," Galileo wrote, "what he has inquired into and contrived, I know only too clearly that the human mind is a work of God, and one of the most excellent."[2] The issue here isn't whether the Bible or the church is anti-science.

The issue here is to point out the danger of holding on to human traditions — to the neglect of the truth! According to tradition, nobody but those approved by the pope were permitted to explain the meaning of the Scriptures. Yet, because of bad biblical interpretation, multitudes were given a completely wrong view of the solar system for two centuries — until books teaching the heliocentric view were finally taken off the Vatican's banned books list in 1835.

---

[2] Paul C. Poupard, *Galileo Galilei* (Pittsburgh: Duquesne University Press, 1983), 101.

CHAPTER 24

JIM IRWIN

Galileo was the first to really explore the surface of the moon. His eyes wandered across the moon through his telescope, observing its craters and mountains. When he saw the vast plains, he first took them for great seas. To this day they are called the "Seas of the Moon."

I too have a connection to Galileo. I am not a scientist, but I knew a man that explored the moon; possibly in the very same spot Galileo scanned on a frosty winter's night back in 1610.

This is the story of my friend Jim Irwin, who linked mind and hearts with Galileo in a very unique way. Let me explain.

In the summer of 1971, Jim Irwin trudged through the mantle of dust that blanketed the moon. He stopped and raised his visor and, with oxygen hissing in his helmet, he saw it — the blue, green, brown and white ball we call our home. It was like a Christmas tree ornament suspended in the black canopy of space. Jim told me that everything about space wants to kill, wants to rob you of life. It's an unsympathetic and hostile place, where life without a space suit has no chance to live.

Yet this ball called "Earth" was warm, green and sparkling with life. So, it was there, while standing on the threshold of infinity, he knew that the Earth was not the result of

Figure 20: Apollo 15 Lunar Module Pilot James Irwin, NASA (1971).

185

some random chaotic explosion. He realized it was the result of a Master Craftsman that breathed life into existence; and made us a refuge of safety and a home in the deadly harshness of space.

Just as Galileo saw the details of the moon from a distance, Jim was one of a few who was able to look at the Earth from a distance and see its grandeur. He saw its vitality from his new perch on a chunk of lifeless dust and rock floating in the vast, black emptiness.

Jim told me he was not so much awed by all the technology; he had worked with much technical equipment. No, it was the wonders of the universe that enveloped his mind and heart. He told me once that, "Man walking on the moon was not anywhere as important as Jesus walking on the earth."

Jim was also the first man to speak a verse from Psalms on the moon. While gazing at the high mountains of Earth's satellite, he said, *"I will lift up my eyes unto the hills from whence comes my help."*

Jim was a good friend who has since passed away, but he always lifted his eyes to God for His strength, wisdom, knowledge, and eternal hope. He found these things only in Jesus Christ. King David never knew that Jim Irwin would walk on the moon, but he and Jim both understood the words David declared in Psalm 19:1-3:

The heavens declare the glory of God;

And the firmament shows His handiwork.

Day unto day utters speech,

And night unto night reveals knowledge.

There is no speech nor language

Where their voice is not heard.

Part III
A Walk Through Church History

Chapter 25

The Early Church

In Acts 7, Luke records the final message and the death of the first Christian martyr, Stephen. This was an important memory for Paul, who explains in Acts 22:20 that he, as a young man, stood by and held the coats of those who stoned Stephen. The Jewish authorities came against the early Christians, and in Acts 9 Paul was on his way to Damascus to hunt down the Christians there when God interrupted his plans and changed his life.

The early Christians knew persecution from the very beginning. Acts 12:2 tells us that Herod (Agrippa) had James, the brother of John, killed with a sword. Peter was imprisoned that same chapter, but the Lord sent an angel to rescue him. There was no glory for those early church leaders as they faced opposition on every side. In 2 Corinthians 11:23-27, Paul describes the many sources of suffering he had faced in his work as a missionary. Eight different times he was either whipped or beaten with rods. He spent time in prison, in shipwrecks, in cold and fasting.

Every one of the apostles was martyred with the exception of John. Peter was executed upside down on a cross in about A.D. 66. Paul died that same year, being beheaded by Nero. Peter's brother Andrew went to preach to the Scythians, and he was crucified in Achaia in A.D. 61. Eusebius spends extensive time describing how James the Just was thrown from the pinnacle of the Temple in Jerusalem and then clubbed to death.[1] According to tradition, Simon the Zealot and Jude "Thaddaeus" preached in Libya and Persia. Justus Lipsius made famous the tradition that Simon was sawed in half. Philip preached in Greece and

---
1 *Ibid*, II.23.1-25

Egypt and traditionally was executed in Hieropolis upside down on a cross like Peter. Bartholomew "Nathanael" preached as far as India and was reportedly skinned alive in Armenia in A.D. 72. Matthew was killed in Ethiopia, and Thomas was stabbed to death in India.

The Roman historian Tacitus (A.D. 54-120) gives us a gruesome picture of Nero's persecution of the Christians. Claudius and Nero were only the first emperors to slay the Christians. There followed persecutions under at least eight of the Roman emperors over the next 250 years. Not all the emperors targeted Christians, but there was sufficient trouble to send the Christians underground, and Christian symbols of the fish and dove, ships and anchors, and the Good Shepherd can still be seen etched in the walls of the catacombs under Rome.

Then something astonishing happened in the year A.D. 312. A Roman emperor actually claimed to be converted to Christianity, and in a most dramatic way. Emperor Constantine allegedly saw a "vision" of a cross floating in front of the sun. In the evening before the great battle of Milvian Bridge, just as the sun was about to slide into the distant purple hills, an apparition appeared to an astonished Constantine. There it was; the shape of a cross stretched across the burning orb, and beneath the sun an inscription declared *In Hoc Signo Vinces* — "In this sign may you prevail."[2]

Constantine did prevail; he went on to defeat Maxentius the next day and solidified his reign as Emperor of Rome. In a manner that reflects a sense of superstition rather than a true love for Christ, Constantine adopted the religion of the cross. He used the device of Jesus Christ's torture and death and made it into the new logo for his faith. Who could doubt the veracity of the vison claimed by the emperor?

Once Constantine converted, the Christians were able to come out of the catacombs and the dark dens where they had been hiding. After centuries of savage persecution, they were welcomed into the light of day. Constantine decreed there would be no more attacks upon them. He built a large number of churches, including the original St. Peter's Basilica in Rome and

---

[2] Michael Kerrigan. *Dark History of the Catholic Church* (London: Amber Books Limited, 2014), 346.

the Church of the Holy Sepulchre in Jerusalem. He appointed Christian bishops to high posts, and when his Christian advisors told him he needed to put a stop to magic and private divination, he listened and did so.

Figure 21: "Bishops of Rome advaunced by Emperours, Constantinus, Theodosius" by John Foxe (1563).

However, Rome still faced the problem of syncretism. Constantine apparently never renounced his dedication to sun worship. On March 7, 321, Constantine established Sunday as the day of rest, with special recognition of the sun:

> On the venerable Day of the Sun let the magistrates and people residing in cities rest, and let all workshops be closed.[3]

We can suggest Constantine was a shrewd politician who understood that he had an entire empire of pagans to bring into the Christian fold. He therefore used terms they understood to bridge the gap — associating the God of Jesus Christ with the sun god worship that pervaded the empire. We can also suggest that Constantine never completely gave up his own sun worship. In Egypt, the sun god was Ra. In ancient Indo-Iranian mythology he was Mithra, the god of light. In Rome he was Helios, or Sol,

---
[3] *Codex Justinianus*, 1.iii, Tit. 12.3; as translated in Philip Schaff, *History of the Christian Church*, Vol. 3 (Edinburgh: T&T Clark,1884), 380.

or Apollo. This newly formulated Christian religion by Constantine was like a braided cord that wound the threads of old pagan influences around the original Christian teachings of Jesus and His apostles.

After Constantine's dramatic conversion, the Roman people were told to pray facing the east, where the sun rises. We know that faithful Muslims today stop what they are doing and pray east toward Mecca five times a day, but Constantine's Christians were doing the same hundreds of years before Islam.

Constantine remained a high priest to the sun until almost the day he died, but he also called himself bishop of bishops, which may be why we still find sun god symbolism at the Vatican to this day. There is a giant sun emblem behind the papal throne and a sun emblem on the Pope's monstrance that holds the Eucharist. After his death, the Eastern Church eventually declared Constantine a holy saint, while the Roman Senate moved to declare him a pagan god.[4]

Constantine was hardly a model Christian leader. His paranoia led him to have his firstborn son Crispus executed, and later his wife Fausta as well. He served as the high priest of Rome's sun worshipers. According to the *Oxford Dictionary of the Christian Church*:

> …When Constantine dedicated the new city of Constance on May 11, A.D. 330, he adorned it with treasures taken from the heathen temples throughout the east.

Constantine moved the capital of his new empire to Byzantium in modern-day Turkey and renamed it Constantinople. The Eastern and Western halves of the Roman Empire were on the verge of a schism, and one of Constantine's successors, Theodosius, was the last emperor to reign over both halves.

Before the Roman Empire made its final great divide, on February 27, A.D. 380, Theodosius (along with Gratian and Valentinian II) issued decrees that not only legalized Christianity, but made it the Roman Empire's official state church. The Nicene Creed had been developed at the Council at Nicaea in 325 as

---

[4] Justo L. González, *The History of Christianity Volume I* (Harper Collins, 2010) 141.

a statement of faith. With the Edict of Thessalonica, Theodosius went to town against the Roman paganism that had ruled the empire for so long. He closed Roman temples, banned blood sacrifices, and punished witchcraft. Pagan images and holy sites were vandalized, and the people of the empire were required to work on former pagan holidays.

Drawing the entire Roman world into the arms of Jesus Christ, however, was not as simple as signing a few papyri documents and closing the temples of Jupiter. Roman soldiers and citizens who had been raised on the gods and idol worship were suddenly required to convert to a religion they didn't understand. Roman soldiers who had been saturated in immorality and idol worship were suddenly forced to worship a new Supreme God — and they had to do so alongside lowly Christians.

On the other hand, humble Christian bishops, full of the indwelling light of Jesus, had worshiped the Lord in the shadows. They were now free to come out into the public eye and take public offices. They were able to advise the leaders of the known world and give the words of Christ a public voice.

Despite the words of the faithful speaking in the ears of the emperors, the trappings of paganism remained throughout the fragmenting empire. Former cardinal John Henry Newman noted:

> We are told in various ways by Eusebius, that Constantine, in order to recommend the new religion to the heathen, transferred into it the outward ornaments to which they had been accustomed in their own... The use of temples, and these dedicated to particular saints... incense, lamps, and candles; votive offerings on recovery from illness; holy water... turning to the East, images at a later date... are all of pagan origin, and sanctified by their adoption into the Church..[5]

At the very beginning, the Christians met together in each other's homes. During times of severe persecution, they moved from these houses down into the catacombs under Rome's

---

5   John H. Newman, *An Essay on the Development of Christian Doctrine* (London: James Toovey, 1845) 359.

streets. From there, they were suddenly free and urged to open worship in ornate church buildings. Officiating ministers went from wearing simple, everyday clothes to luxurious garments. Under the New Testament, church leaders were deacons or elders or bishops. Under Constantine, the official title of "priest" also began to be used, just as it was in their pagan counterparts.

This strange yet strategic alliance was a welcome respite of peace, and certainly it felt like a great and mighty victory for those early Christians. The leader of the Roman Empire was a promoter of Jesus Christ! Yet, the combining of Christianity with pagan Rome created a syncretism with vestiges that remain until this day.

Jesuit priest Josef A. Jungmann describes these circumstances of sun and pagan worship as a confluence of two religious worlds:

> [V]arious customs of ancient Roman culture flowed into the Christian liturgy...even the ceremonies involved in the ancient worship of the emperor as a deity found their way into the church's worship, only in their secularized form.[6]

Secular historian Will Durant describes the alliance of church and empire in chilling words. He noted that paganism in Rome continued:

> ...in the form of ancient rites and customs condoned or accepted and transformed by an often indulgent Church...An intimate and trustful worship of saints replaced the cult of the pagan gods, and satisfied the polytheism of simple or poetic minds. Statues of Isis and Horus were renamed Mary and Jesus.[7]

During the years of persecution, the symbol of Christianity was the fish, representing the disciples' role as fishers of men. The Greek word for "fish" — ICQUΣ — was made an acronym that became a statement of faith: Ἰησοῦς Χριστός Θεοῦ Υἱός

---

[6] Josef Jungmann, *The Early Liturgy* (University of Notre Dame Press, 1959), 130, 133.
[7] Will Durant, *The Story of Civilization Vol. IV* (New York: Simon and Schuster, 1950), 73

The Early Church

Σωτήρ — "Jesus Christ God Son Savior." Before the fourth century, burial sites of Christians were adorned with images of doves, anchors, peacocks, fish and palm branches. The *sun* was not a feature of any importance to early Christians and neither was the *cross*.

Figure 22: Early Christian symbolism in Rome.

Under Rome, the cross became the symbol of importance. Constantine's soldiers were largely illiterate peasants steeped in paganism, and few would have understood the cross as a symbol representing salvation. They would more likely have regarded it as nothing more than an ancestral wooded totem, yet the symbol of the cross has persisted to the present day as one of the most recognized and praised icons on earth.

CHRISTMAS

Nobody is certain exactly what day of the year Jesus was born. The Bible gives no dates. In A.D. 274, the Roman emperor Aurelian had established a feast day celebrating the birth of Sol Invictus on the 25th of December. Since Constantine worked to roll over the worship of the sun with the worship of God's Son, it's no surprise that a Roman almanac of A.D. 354 lists the birth of Jesus Christ "in Bethlehem of Judea" on December 25th.[8] The Eastern Church celebrated Christ's birth on January 6, and the Western Church decided to call January 6 "Epiphany"

---
8 This surviving illustrated codex is known as Chronography of 354 or the Philocalian Calendar.

— the day the Magi arrived — and the days between became "the 12 Days of Christmas." Of course, Jesus was probably born in the Fall, but the early Catholic Church didn't know that.

If Christmas is simply a holiday commandeered from the pagans, does this mean we shouldn't celebrate it? Let's think about that. In our day, we do not celebrate the birth of Sol Invictus, but the Savior of the world. Christmas is a time in our culture when we are freer to talk about Christ in public settings, to sing about Christ and rejoice that he came into the world to save us from our sins. We hear, "Hark, the herald angels sing, Glory to the newborn King!" playing over the sound system while walking through our workplaces. We can go caroling at our neighbors' doors, singing, "Fall on your knees; O hear the angels' voices; O night divine; O night when Christ was born." These are all excellent things.

We simply need to be aware that trappings of paganism were carried along into the new Roman version of Christianity. We need to recognize that certain traditions began in Rome that had nothing to do with Christ in the Bible.

OUTWARD V. INWARD

Consider the act of lighting a votive candle, one of the trappings left over from ancient paganism. There is nothing wrong with lighting a candle when praying, but there's nothing special or magical or required about lighting candles either. When we pray, God looks at our hearts and sees we are seeking Him, depending on Him and trusting in Him. We can light the candle if we like or not light the candle if we like. The outward show is never the important matter; it's always what is going on in our inner beings.

The trouble with "outward show versus the inner being" goes into the issue of differing Christian denominations as well. In the third century, Saint Cyprian said *Nulla salus extra ecclesiam* — "Outside the Church there is no salvation." If that is true, then which "church" are we talking about? Is the Church a physical church body on earth, whether the Roman Catholic Church or a particular Baptist or Presbyterian Church?

Or, is the Church simply the eternal body of believers saved by the blood of Jesus Christ? In which case the "Church" *means* "those who are saved." They may or may not be visibly part of a particular church body, but those who belong to God are known to God. As Saint Augustine said, "How many sheep there are without, how many wolves within!"[9]

In Revelation 7:9-10, we find a vast body of human beings from *"all nations, and kindreds, and people, and tongues"* worshipping the Lamb. God is the judge of who belongs to Him, and it is dangerous for any earthly institution to declare that "salvation comes from belonging to our church body." If Saint Cyprian meant that there is no salvation outside of this body of believers saved by Christ, then his statement is true by default.

In John 14:6, Jesus said, *"I am the way, the truth, and the life. No one comes to the Father except through Me."* That's it. If we place anything before Christ — even a church or a manmade law — then we're engaging in idol worship. The thief on the cross had no Eucharist, no good deeds, no candles, no confessionals. He had none of those things, yet Jesus told him they would be together in Paradise.[10] Jesus Christ died on the cross to pay for our sins and He defeated death by rising again. When we depend on his finished work, that's what saves us.

> *Then the angel said to them, "Do not be afraid, for behold, I bring you good tidings of great joy which will be to all people. For there is born to you this day in the city of David a Savior, who is Christ the Lord. And this will be the sign to you: You will find a Babe wrapped in swaddling cloths, lying in a manger." And suddenly there was with the angel a multitude of the heavenly host praising God and saying: "Glory to God in the highest, And on earth peace, goodwill toward men!"*
> Luke 2:10-14

---

9   St. Augustine. *Homilies on John*, 45.12.
10 Luke 23:39-43

ANTI-SEMITISM:

One of the results of the weaving of Christianity with Rome, was a marked disgust with the Jews who had rejected Jesus. In the Gospels, Jesus constantly presents himself as the Lord of the Jews first. Even when He heals gentiles in the Gospels, Jesus makes it clear that He has come to the lost sheep of the House of Israel.[11] His polemics against the scribes and Pharisees, like that in Matthew 23, focus on their hypocrisy, not their identity as Jews. Jesus the Jew, the Son of David, always presents himself coming in fulfillment of the Hebrew Scriptures. Paul explains in Romans 11, that gentiles who become Christians are grafted into the root of the tree of Israel. Christianity is the fulfillment of Judaism.

In the years that followed the deaths of Christ and the apostles, anti-Semitism crept into the gentile communities of Christian converts. In his *Dialogue with Trypho*, Justin Martyr (A.D. 100-165) and a Jew named Trypho, discussed Christianity versus Judaism. Justin Martyr makes an attempt to convert Trypho, but he also heavily criticizes the Jews as hard-hearted and rebellious, blaming them for killing Jesus and for persecuting Christians.

The newly Christian Roman emperor was harshly antagonistic to the Jews, which is clear from proceedings at the Council of Nicaea in A.D. 325. A dark, anti-Semitic tenor seemed to cling to Constantine's family, and the emperor expressed harsh animosity toward the Jews. He forbade the observance of Easter at the time of Passover, declaring:

> It is unbecoming that on the holiest of festivals that we should follow the customs of the Jews; henceforth let us have nothing in common with these odious people.

This prejudice of Constantine would become another moldering bone of church tradition that would be used to justify a range of convoluted Jewish bigotries. In the beginning, the Inquisition focused on Christian heretics, but it didn't take long

---

[11] Matthew 15:24

for Jews to be included in the attacks. In 1242, the Inquisition condemned the Talmud, and thousands of copies of Jewish books were gathered up and burned. In 1288, the French Inquisition began burning multitudes of Jews at the stake.

To this day, many churches still teach that the Church has replaced Israel, contrary to what Paul explains in Romans 11. Only during the past century have the hearts of Christians greatly warmed toward the Jews. Pro-Jewish and pro-Israel sentiments among American Christians today are healing relationships brutally damaged by nearly two millennia of enmity.

STATE RELIGION

While Constantine had legalized and elevated Christianity, he hadn't made it the required religion of the realm. It was Emperor Theodosius the Great who, along with Gratian and Valentinian II, officially made Roman Catholicism the state religion in the Edict of Thessalonica in 380. In part, this edict declared:

> We order those who follow this doctrine to receive the title of Catholic Christians, but others we judge to be mad and raving and worthy of incurring the disgrace of heretical teaching, nor are their assemblies to receive the name of churches. They are to be punished not only by Divine retribution but also by our own measures…

As Christians, we might think this a great thing. Christianity was officially made the religion of the empire, and Theodosius quickly went about the process of cleaning up the paganism rampant within his realm. However, true Christianity is not conformation to particular rules or rituals. It's not attending meetings on Sunday. Christianity is a matter of the heart. It's a devotion to Jesus Christ, the Son of God, and that devotion cannot be forced or manufactured. The pagans of the Roman Empire were required to accept Christianity, whether they understood it or not.

CHAPTER 26

MARTYRS AND RELICS

Rome caught fire in A.D. 64, when the Roman historian Tacitus was about eight-years-old. The event was popularly blamed on Nero; and Tacitus reports that Nero in turn condemned the Christians for the disaster and set about torturing them to death:

> In dying, they were made the objects of sport, for they were wrapped in the hides of wild beasts and were torn to pieces by dogs, or were nailed to crosses, or were set on fire and as the day declined, were burned to serve as nocturnal [lights]."[1]

The persecutions against Christians continued off and on for the next two centuries. In A.D. 156, during the reign of Roman Emperor Antoninus Pius, the beloved Bishop of Smyrna Polycarp was burned at the stake. It was a messy execution. The fire did not have enough straw or wood, or the intended fuel source was wet. In any event, Polycarp was not killed by the flame and had to be stabbed several times. Later, Polycarp's body was burned and his bones were gathered up and taken away by his followers.

It seems that this began the curious habit of collecting relics from the artifacts of saints.

RELICS

When Polycarp was executed, his followers carried away his bones. They were a part of Polycarp, who had long been loved

---
[1] Tacitus (116). *Annals*, XV:44.

and honored as the spiritual leader of Smyrna. It was said he'd been taught by John the apostle, and the people considered Polycarp's bones more valuable than gold or precious stones.[2] By the fourth century, collecting saints' bones or the residue of their ashes became common practice.

Early on, this was criticized as a pagan habit. One of the first critics of keeping relics was the fourth century priest Vigilantius. According to Jerome, Vigilantius stated:

> Under the cloak of religion we see what is all but a heathen ceremony introduced into the churches: while the sun is still shining, heaps of tapers are lighted, and everywhere a paltry bit of powder, wrapped up in a costly cloth, is kissed and worshipped. Great honour do men of this sort pay to the blessed martyrs, who, they think, are to be made glorious by trumpery tapers, when the Lamb who is in the midst of the throne, with all the brightness of His majesty, gives them light?[3]

People were giving adoration to the ashes of the martyrs when God was there to be adored with or without the presence of relics. That seems like a reasonable complaint, yet Jerome responds by calling Vigilantius a "madman" and spends a great deal of paper space defending the practices of honoring martyrs' relics and holding vigils over their graves. Rather than recognizing a legitimate concern, Jerome is overtly abusive toward Vigilantius in this treatise and accuses him of being filled with devils.

EMPTY TOMBS

In the winding underground catacombs of Rome, not far from the Vatican, we find places that once held martyrs' bones. The catacombs have a macabre heritage. The thousands that were once interred in the underground stone cemetery are now all gone. Not a scrap of bone or even a brown tooth can be found lying in any of the carved-out niches. All human remains not

---

[2] See the *Catholic Encyclopedia* entry on "Relics."
[3] Jerome (A.D. 406). *Contra Vigilantium*. PL 23, 342. cf Ep. 109; Ad Riparium. Pl. 22. 907

consumed by the elements were long ago stolen away as holy relics to be venerated ... or sold. They scraped up the dust from those tombs as a holy residue.

The Greco-Roman religions viewed the dead as pollutants. No adult corpse could be buried inside the city walls or other occupied areas. The dead were placed outside the city, and many Christian deceased came to rest there. The early Christians had a different view of the dead; even the clothing scraps of the martyrs were believed to hold an ethereal power. Pieces of these saints might offer mystical healing, wealth, or spiritual blessings to the holders.

This morbid interest might seem superstitious, but there is actually biblical support for it. Acts 5:15 tells us that during his life, people hoped to have even Peter's shadow fall on the sick, because all those he prayed for were healed. Acts also speaks of miraculous power associated with pieces of cloth from Paul:

Now God worked unusual miracles by the hands of Paul, so that even handkerchiefs or aprons were brought from his body to the sick, and the diseases left them and the evil spirits went out of them.

Acts 19:11-12

We also see the case of Elisha, whose bones themselves gave life to a dead man:

Then Elisha died, and they buried him. And the raiding bands from Moab invaded the land in the spring of the year. So it was, as they were burying a man, that suddenly they spied a band of raiders; and they put the man in the tomb of Elisha; and when the man was let down and touched the bones of Elisha, he revived and stood on his feet.

2 Kings 13:20-21

These stories in the Bible gave hopeful folks interest in objects owned by the holy ones of old. Whether that interest was *healthy* is another matter. We find people can make an idol out of anything. After all, God instructed Moses to create the brazen serpent to bring healing to the Israelites in

Numbers 21 — but later in 2 Kings 18:4, King Hezekiah destroyed that brass snake because the people had started to burn incense to it. The danger was that people would begin to place their hope in a *thing* rather than in the love and mercy of God.

People desired bits and pieces of the apostles and saints who came before them but, even more, they longed to be close to anything associated with the Virgin Mary or to Jesus Christ himself. In its entry on "Relics," *The Catholic Encyclopedia* states:

> *If the shadow of the saints before they departed from this life, banished diseases and restored strength, who will have the hardihood to deny that God wonderfully works the same by the sacred ashes, the bones, and other relics of the saints.*

MIRACLES

In A.D. 386, two bodies were discovered buried in the basilica of Milan built by Saint Ambrose. Saint Ambrose wanted to have relics with which to consecrate the new basilica. He declared that he'd had a dream about where to find the necessary artifacts. He unearthed two bodies, which were declared to be the remains of martyrs Gervasius and Protasius. Saint Augustine mentions the events that surrounded the bodies of these two men:

> The miracle which was wrought at Milan when I was there, and by which a blind man was restored to sight, could come to the knowledge of many... the occurrence was witnessed by an immense concourse of people that had gathered to the bodies of the martyrs Protasius and Gervasius, which had long lain concealed and unknown, but were now made known to the bishop Ambrose in a dream, and discovered by him. By virtue of these remains the darkness of that blind man was scattered, and he saw the light of day.[4]

---
[4] St. Augustine, *City of God*, XXII.8.

St. Ambrose was being considered for expulsion from his bishopric by the Arian Empress Justina. After he dug up those two bodies, however, talk of expelling him ended and the bodies were venerated.

Relics became mandatory in the consecration of new churches. The second Council of Nicaea (A.D. 787) decreed that any new church must obtain a relic as soon as possible. Relics became a source of community pride and national prestige. Kings and queens across Europe paid huge sums for these prizes. If one country obtained an alleged piece of the cross of Christ, then another might boast that they had a glass vial that actually contained some drops of blood from Jesus *himself*.

We still adore relics to this day, don't we? Fans stand in line to earn the autograph of some celebrity or another, or wrestle in the stands over the prize of a homerun ball. We might not pay for splinters from the cross or finger bones of saints, but people have been willing to pay £9500 for John Lennon's toilet or $27,350 for a $10.50 check signed by Neil Armstrong on the day of his Apollo flight to the moon. (He didn't want to die in space owing his friend money!) The famous picture of Albert Einstein with his tongue out, autographed, sold for an incredible $74,340. Dorothy's original ruby red slippers from *The Wizard of Oz* were sold at auction for $660,000, and $956,000 was given for a tattered battle flag belonging to Confederate General, JEB Stuart.

Simple, material objects can become highly valuable to collectors, just because the people who originally owned them were considered significant. The saints of old were known to be filled with the Holy Spirit, and many people have longed to touch that holiness. The prized possessions of this world are placed prominently in display cases for all to see and admire. In the same manner, the Roman Catholic Church places their relics in display containers called reliquaries, and they are honored because of the saints who are said to have possessed them.

It's human nature to want to hold a fragment of history. It's human nature to want to link ourselves to the importance of people we admire. Relics are not exclusive to Catholics: when Buddha died in 483 B.C., his cremated ashes were supposedly saved by Indian monks. A bone believed to have belonged to Gautama Buddha is displayed at the Famen Temple in Fufeng County, China, and Buddhist pilgrims visit the temple just to see the bone fragment.

All over the world, in almost every culture, objects have been held in reverence due to their believed connection to some remarkable individual. The Topkapi Palace Museum in Istanbul, Turkey is said to hold the beard of Mohammed. One of the most visited relics in the world is the black rock of the Kaaba in Mecca. Millions of faithful Muslims journey each year to this shrine, fulfilling one of the obligations of their faith.

The Pilgrims

In the Roman Catholic Church, relics from a variety of saints are inexorably connected with miraculous healings. Some healings may have been a result of the placebo effect. Some might have been related to simple improvements of health as pilgrims traveled from the cold and damp environs of Europe to warmer and more arid sites in Spain or Israel. Some might have been complete lies and some might have been legitimate.

We do read of corroborated testimony from many witnesses regarding miraculous healings in correlation with relics. It takes only a few reports of divine healing to create *hope*. That hope drove the desperate to walk, limp, or crawl across long distances, seeking curative powers. Pilgrims often traveled in the harshest and most dangerous of conditions — across hostile lands, facing possible cold and heat, bandits and wild animals. Despite many dangers, the sick and dying sought the release from pain they believed only a relic would offer. If they lived through the journey, they trusted the wholehearted assurance by clerics of the shrine that they would find atonement, healing, or a spiritual touch from God.

Most of these tender souls would never touch the actual relic itself, nor even see the artifact of the dead saint. But just being close to a relic was to be in the very presence of a sacred person and the miraculous healing powers that they were alleged to possess.

Figure 23: Reliquary with Christ in majesty from Limousin, France (late 12th century), Musée du Louvre, Paris.

Reliquary Income

Relics were big business. A church with a relic of high profile could bring pilgrims in droves, all seeking a blessing or a cure from sickness. The visiting pilgrim, often traveling thousands of miles, would be required to leave something of commiserate value for the church's benefit. If they did not leave a generous donation, they might be told by clerics that their arduous travel had been for naught! It was said that the relics were the "milk tooth" of the church, and that money received from pilgrims filled several baskets that had been placed upon the altars. It benefitted church coffers to hold the best relics.

In hope of a cure, or in honor of a cure, pilgrims often left wax or lead models of their troubled body parts as *ex-voto* offerings. A woman healed from an abscess on her nose once left a silver model of her nose. Iselda of Longueville was so appreciative at having her hearing restored that she made as an offering an actual piece of her ear, and Henry of Maldon left his long tapeworm hanging in the cathedral at Canterbury as a token of his appreciation.

The clergy kept mounds of *ex-voto* offerings for pilgrims to see, because miracles or claims of miracles were good for collecting offerings. Chains from prisoners who had been released in foreign lands were piled so high in some churches that railings had to be built in order to contain them. The writer of the *Guide for Pilgrims to Santiago* noted that chains of freed prisoners by the thousands could be seen at the church of Saint-Léonard-de-Noblat.[5]

STUMBLING STONES

Of course, there are two large problems with a dependence on relics.

First, the power of God is still available to any of us — right where we are sitting. God hears the prayers of His saints who are alive and well in our home towns, ready to pray on our behalf simply because Jesus loves us and His blood heals us. Multitudes are being healed through prayer in Jesus' name today. Any one of us would be excited to touch the very handkerchief of Paul, of course, but God loves us too, with or without relics to handle.

The second problem is a big one. Con artists might sell any item from their own graveyard as a precious relic, and who could tell the difference?

That's exactly what happened in the Middle Ages. The occasional miracles offered encouragement, causing multitudes to grasp at any random item that might carry with it divine power. Con artists hawked pieces of wood they claimed were shards of Christ's cross, shreds of cloth they claimed came from

---

5   Jonathan Sumption, *The Age of Pilgrimage: The Medieval Journey to God* (New Jersey: Hidden Spring, 2003) 226.

the apostles' clothing, fragments of bones that might have come from any grave. Relics offered hope to the hopeless, but there was no certainty the relics were genuine.

As new abbeys sprang up across Europe, the demand for relics increased. This presented the opportunity for relic "brokers" to make big money, which also resulted in the eventual practice of relic fraud. Those who had money were subject to unprincipled salesmen, and they bought what they were told were holy bits of bone, scraps of a garment, ancient hair or even the shriveled tongues of saints. Knights carried the ash residue of a saint corpse in their sword hilts, or the tooth of a saint in a small silver box that hung from their necks.

Just as heinous was the stealing of relics from one church to grace another. The Basilica of St. Mark in Venice, St. Foy at Conques, St. Nicholas of Bari and St. Benedict at Fleury all benefited from the theft of relics. In A.D. 385, several armed deacons in Jerusalem had to stand guard around what was said to be the True Cross. This was to keep pilgrims from kissing the wood and snatching away a splitter or two with their teeth.

Relics of Jesus were of course the most valued, which meant that fraudulent relics of Christ began to spread throughout Christendom. We all know about the search for the Holy Grail, but any remnant would do. An abbey at Soissons claimed to be conserving one of Christ's baby teeth, while the Sancta Sanctorum in Rome has held a wide variety of important relics, including the umbilical cord of Christ and the heads of several saints.

The *Annales Regni Francorum* for A.D. 804 describes how Charlemagne requested Pope Leo III to visit Mantua, Italy to determine whether rumors of Christ's blood being found there were true. According to legend, the soldier who pierced Christ's side was Longinus, said to be the centurion who declared in Mark 15:39 that Jesus was the Son of God. He supposedly scooped up some of the blood-soaked earth beneath Christ's cross and tucked it away in Mantua before his death. This relic was hidden again during the Hungarian invasion, and was rediscovered in A.D 1049. Pope Leo IX declared the blood as authentic four years later, and it is revered today at the Basilica of Sant'Andrea in Mantua as the *Preziosissimo Sangue di Cristo* ("Most Precious Blood of Christ"). Additional blood relics of Christ emerged throughout the 13th century.

Even more amazing, relics of the Virgin Mary — never before seen — began to pop up conveniently during the 11th century. Bishop Geoffrey de Montbray of Coutances (1048-1093) is said to have found one of Mary's hairs in the church's collection of relics. Geoffrey was instrumental in the cult of Mary veneration, and the '*Miracula Ecclesiæ Constantiensis*' is a collection of 32 stories that focus on miracles that took place during and after Geoffrey's episcopate at Coutances. According to legend, the presence of the hair of Mary eased the pain encountered in childbirth.

Mary's tunic was believed to be held in the Chartres Cathedral. Shawls belonging to Mary were claimed to have been found in both France and Germany. The Church of Santa Maria Maggiore in Rome alleged to have the crib of Jesus, as well as articles of Mary's clothing. A list from Munchsmunster includes the relic of milk from Mary's *breast*. Christ's swaddling garment was claimed to be held in a reliquary of gold in a shrine built by Charlemagne at Aix-la-chapelle.

Relics of the nativity were produced by various churches, including hay from the manger, baby hair from Jesus, a pap spoon from Jesus, and the cloak Joseph used to cover Jesus. Other churches held Joseph's girdle, his staff, and his hammer. There are even supposedly plows Joseph made with his hands as a carpenter.

True relics are tangible assets that evoke a visceral response and a cerebral connection with our human heritage. If an actual piece of the cross were found and verified as authentic, that fragment of wood would be cherished as a historical artifact but also as a symbol of the inestimable act which took place upon it. However, it's certain that a large number of relics contained in the reliquaries of Europe were hoaxes, and not even good ones.

Fakes and Frauds

One hundred years before the Protestant Reformation, Jan Hus sat on a tribunal to assess the validity of miraculous healings through relics. Archbishop Zbynek had ordered a committee to look into the alleged miracles at Wilsnack, and he ordered his sheep not to take pilgrimages there. The Wilsnack priests had claimed a certain boy was healed of a deformed foot, but when the committee investigated, it found that the foot was even worse than ever. There was also a report of a woman who was healed of her blindness, but it turned out she had never lost her sight in the first place. Jan Hus wrote a tract *De Omni Sanguine Christi Glorificati* (Of All the Blood of Jesus Glorified) in order to bring to light the fraudulent reports of miracles associated with relics.

This opposition earned Hus animosity from priests, who had depended on the miracle business for income. The enmity that developed eventually led to attacks on Hus as a heretic — and his death at the stake July 6, 1415 — 102 years before Luther produced his 95 Theses.

The shamelessness of some church priests was astonishing. The Rood of Grace at Boxley, a statue of the Lord Jesus on the cross, was found to have mechanical devices complete with wires and rods, which caused it to shed tears from rolling eyes, among other marvels.[6] Bishop John Buckingham of Lincoln in 1386 sought an investigation on a statue in Rippingdale, stating:

> Many of our subjects have made for themselves a certain pretended statue, vulgarly known as Jordan Cros, in the fields of Rippingdale. They have begun to adore it, and allege that miracles are occurring there. They preach, ring bells, and hold processions for the deception of the people and for their own gain. Indeed, laymen are said to be embezzling the offerings for their own use.[7]

---

[6] Groeneveld, Leanne, "A Theatrical Miracle: The Boxley Rood of Grace as Puppet." *Early Theatre* 10, no. 2 (2007): 11-50.
[7] As quoted in Sumption, *Age of Pilgrimage*, 390

THE TRUE CROSS

In the fourth century, Constantine's mother Helena was almost 80-years-old when she set off on her long journey to Jerusalem, determined to find the cross of Christ. When a regal dignitary like the emperor's mother makes a long, arduous journey, there's a good chance she will return with *something* relating to the cross.

Church historian Eusebius (A.D. 263-339) says nothing of this journey by Helena, though he lived during the reign of Constantine and recorded his life. He does say that the site of the Holy Sepulchre had been buried and a temple to Venus built on top, and Constantine had the temple destroyed and ordered

Figure 24: Empress Helena, Königsfelden Monastery Church, Switzerland.

Bishop of Jerusalem Macarius to build a church there. Eusebius writes nothing about Helena's discovery of the True Cross.

Socrates Scholasticus (A.D. 380-440) and Theodoret (A.D. 393-457) give the earliest accounts of the discovery of the True Cross. According to them, Helena found three crosses at the site of the Holy Sepulchre. In their version, she was the one who had it unburied and the shrine of Venus destroyed. She believed and officially declared that these very crosses were used to execute Jesus and the two thieves at Calvary. The titular — Pilate's wooden plaque — was also found, along with the nails.

Helena credited dreams and fantastic visions as the sources that guided her, but according to an A.D. 403 letter by Paulinus of Nola to his friend Sulpicius Severus in Primuliacum, Helena could not pinpoint the exact location and sought counsel in her search. She made it known far and wide that "the mother of the emperor" needed help to find the cross of Christ. She solicited Jewish scholars living in Jerusalem, but no one knew exactly where to dig. Eventually a Jew stepped out of the shadows of obscurity and pointed Helena to the precise spot where, sure enough, the three crosses were buried. Later tradition gave this Jew the name Jude or Judas, who converted to Christianity and took the name Kyriakos. When Helena returned with the crosses, no one argued with her. Who would?

Three fully formed, sturdy crosses were discovered stacked one upon each other. These items were found some 370 years after Christ's crucifixion, showing no signs of decay, and all neatly buried together. Convenient. It appears that nobody probed the authenticity of the find back then, but few would have had the gumption to question the mother of the Emperor of Rome.

Of course, after Helena legendarily found these items, the big question was which of the three crosses was *the* authentic cross of Christ. In Saint Ambrose's version, the titular on Christ's cross was sufficient to identify it. Various accounts offer another explanation. The story goes that Helena's attendants brought a woman who lay deathly sick (in Paulinus' letter, the individual is a man already dead). The three crosses were, in turn, presented at her bedside. They placed the first two crosses gently upon her and nothing happened. Then they placed the third cross on her and she was said to be miraculously healed at once. That was all that was needed to certify the third one as Christ's cross. These accounts of Helen's pilgrimage and discoveries were written nearly 200 years after the facts alleged.

The great historian Eusebius and the famed Bordeaux Pilgrim, both Helena's contemporaries, failed to mention Helena's discoveries in their detailed accounts. Both traveled to Palestine during this time frame on fact-finding missions, but there is not one word from either of them about any such find. It's also interesting to note that after the Bar Kochba Revolt, Jews were not allowed to live in Jerusalem or its surrounding environs for 200 years, from about A.D. 135 to the time of Constantine. Emperor Hadrian had Jerusalem plowed, and he built the pagan city Aelia Capitolina on top of it. Yet the particular Jew that Helena supposedly followed as a guide knew the exact location of the crosses? What's more, the Romans likely reused the crosses they had as valuable pieces of wood. Why would they have neatly buried all the implements of crucifixion for a criminal that was executed and hastily buried?

Whether the crosses were actually found by Helena, or the legend was created based on crosses produced later, it's most likely that the crosses and other materials found buried in Jerusalem were simply planted there by Judas, who took advantage of the naive. In his book, *Secrets of Golgotha*, Dr. Ernest Martin describes Judas in blunt terms: "People should realize that Judas Quiriacus was simply an opportunist and they should have dismissed his so-called 'discovery' of the cross of Christ. But that was an age of credulity — when dreams, visions and signs ruled the day."[8]

---

8   Ernest Martin, *Secrets of Golgotha* (ASK Publications, 1988), 134.

CHAPTER 27

CHARLEMAGNE

King Pepin the Short might have given the Papal States to Pope Stephen II based on the precedence of the Donation of Constantine. However, his son offered the light of education during his long, capable, industrious reign.

Pepin's wife Big-foot Bertha (I am not making this up) had the son who would become Charlemagne. Charles was a huge man for the time, with a height of about 6'4", and with him came a profound shift in power from the east to the west, and thus a new Europa was born.

Figure 25: "Coronation of Charlemagne" by Friedrich Kaulbach (1822-1903).

In 799, a weak pope named Leo III sat in Rome. He had enemies among the relatives of his predecessor Pope Adrian I, and during the procession of the Greater Litanies in April 799, he was attacked by a group of armed men. Seeking to make him unfit for the office, they attempted to cut out his tongue and slashed through his eyes. The attack left the pope injured and bleeding, but he was able to make a recovery of speech and sight. Leo III called upon Charlemagne to help put down the rebellion, and the King of the Franks did so with much force and success.

On Christmas Day the next year, A.D. 800, Charlemagne attended Mass at St. Peter's with Pope Leo III officiating. Leo crowned the king with a magnificent gold crown, announcing him to be the first Roman Emperor over the West in 300 years. The Holy Roman Empire thus received its first breaths of existence. It was a new beginning, when popes would start to make the claim they could rule the emperor, and through the emperor the world.

Charlemagne was a hard leader, but he was also industrious and actively involved in the lands he ruled. He willingly put people to death for small infractions — like breaking fast during Lent. His fervor for evangelism throughout the land was ambitious as well as shocking. For instance; upon conquering rebels in Saxony, he encouraged them to convert to Christianity. Those who refused his gracious suggestion to be baptized were met with a dire fate. In the infamous Massacre of Verden, Charlemagne had 4500 rebels beheaded in one day.

However, he was also thoroughly interested in improving his domains and especially the education of his subjects. He called on the few men of knowledge from around the realm to his Palace School to educate the children of the nobility. He encouraged monks to make copies of literature, both biblical and classical, and the lettering system we have today with both capital and lower-case letters had its start in the Carolingian miniscule of Charlemagne's monks.

Charlemagne saw himself as both the temporal and spiritual ruler of his subjects, and he oversaw the bishops and other clergy in his lands. In this sense, there were really two vicars of

Christ after that time. One was the king, who held the sword of a temporal world, but also the superior spiritual sword. Rome had given Charlemagne his title, and he ruled as a capable and intelligent king.

In the years after Charlemagne's death, the true seat of continuous power was found in the popes. By the end of the ninth century, however, things began to deteriorate rapidly. Six popes passed away between the beginning of 896 and January of 900. The years 904-963 have been called the "Rule of Harlots" with good reason. For instance, Pope John XI (931-935) — who took the Chair of Peter at the young age of 21 — was reported by the *Liber Pontificalis* to be the son of Pope Sergius III (904-911). This was made even more scandalous by the fact that John XI's mother Marozia, the most powerful woman in Rome, was married to Alberic I of Spoleto. The 200 years between Nicholas I (858-867) and Gregory VII (1073-1085) are called the Midnight of the Dark Ages, a time of trouble that included bloodshed, bribery, and corruption.

CHAPTER 28

THE CRUSADES

In 1095, Pope Urban II (1088–1099) famously declared at the Council of Clermont in France that the Muslims had taken over the city of Jerusalem. He provided the worst imaginable picture of the goings on in the Holy Land, and he urged the Franks to stop warring against each other and turn that energy on redeeming the Holy City — and so earn remission for their sins:

> A grave report has come from the lands around Jerusalem ... that a race absolutely alien to God... has invaded the land of the Christians...they have either razed the churches of God to the ground or enslaved them to their own rites.... They cut open the navels of those they choose to torment...drag them around and flog them before killing them as they lay on the ground with all their entrails out.... What can I say of the appalling violation of women? On whom does the task lie of avenging this, if not on you? Take the road to the Holy Sepulchre, rescue that land and rule over it yourselves, for that land, as scripture says, floweth with milk and honey.... Take this road for the remission of your sins, assured of the unfading glory of the kingdom of heaven.[1]

It has been argued that this report was grossly exaggerated, but it nevertheless garnered the intended response. The pope would bring together an army, but he needed this to be framed as a "just cause." He declared that those who made the pilgrimage

---
[1] Jonathan Phillips, *Holy Warriors: A Modern History of the Crusades* (New York: Random House, 2009), 3.

to regain the Holy Land would be making penance with the assurance of salvation.

Men by the thousands took up Pope Urban's offer to engage in a war that promised adventure in exotic faraway lands as well as absolution of all sins and immediate access to heaven. In the Middle Ages, this was a proposition better than any material riches. Not only knights and noblemen responded with glinting swords and shiny body amour, but the poor left their plows to join a cause much larger than their humble villages. Young, old, men, women and even the crippled answered the call of Pope Urban II. One witness described the gathering army as a locust hoard covering the ground. They came for many reasons, but all shared the desire to have their sins absolved forever.

The Crusaders were not many holy men and women. While some were filled with fervor to rescue Jerusalem from the unbelievers, Nivelo of Fréteval explained his own situation, which had started with his sins in Europe:

> Whenever the impulse of warlike fierceness roused me, I would gather about myself a band of mounted men and a crowd of followers. I would descend upon the village and freely give the goods of the men of St. Père of Chartres to my knights for food. Now, therefore, I am going as a pilgrim to Jerusalem, which is still in bondage with her sons, to secure the divine pardon that I seek for my misdeeds.[2]

It's ironic that followers of Mohammed used the same promise to sweep men into their armies. Those Muslims who died in battle were promised favor and salvation from Allah. Christians would earn the same benefits from God in their holy war. The Gospel of Christ was subverted, and Europeans were encouraged to adopt wanton violence as a merit of the Christian believer.

The Crusaders from the Rhineland began attacking unbelievers early, focusing their attention on the peaceful Jews who lived among them. They attempted to forcibly

---

[2] Phillips, *Holy Warriors*, 11.

convert Jewish populations in towns like Worms and Cologne. Chronicler Albert of Aachen describes the army of Count Emicho of Leiningen as particularly cruel in its brutal murder of men, woman, and children.

The disorganized army from the Rhineland was full of passion and left early. They reached Constantinople by the autumn of 1096, and their lack of disciple chagrined the emperor of Byzantium, Alexius I Comnenus. The Crusaders were impressed by the vast size of the great city of 350,000, but Alexius was impressed at the need to protect his city from this lawless group. Not waiting for the rest of the Crusaders, this "People's Crusade," led by one Peter the Hermit, crossed the Bosporus Strait into Asia Minor to go fight the Seljuk Turks. Alexius did little to offer them support and the People's Crusade was quickly destroyed. Albert of Aachen saw this as God's punishment for their slaughter of the Jews.

Figure 26: "Peter the Hermit Preaching the First Crusade" by James Archer in Cassell's History of England, Vol. I (1865).

The more formal and organized Crusaders set out in late 1096. Mothers tenderly kissed their sons' foreheads with hair soaked from trailing tears. The chronicler Fulcher of Chartres described husbands and wives lingering together for a last few moments, wives weeping and swooning as their beloved soldiers of the faith prepared to go — as though they had already lost them forever. The husbands and sons tried to comfort those they left behind and give them a time period for their return. After all, God's grace was upon all who defended the Holy Land. It was a landscape of fervor as the army marched with banners unfurled into a cloud of dust that would trail the 3000 miles from France to Jerusalem.

Poor and crippled pilgrims, both men and women, joined the crowd to free the Holy Land. They were ill-prepared for the journey, however, and many died along the way from disease, starvation, and thirst. Others had sold lands and found various ways to finance their trip, and the way to Constantinople was well known. They crossed the Bosporus with promises from Alexius for support and promises to Alexius to give him control over any lands they captured.

It was after Constantinople the real adventure began. The city of Nicaea was ruled by the Seljuk Turks at that time — about 90 miles into modern-day Turkey. The four armies of Crusaders that had met up in Constantinople hit Nicaea in May of 1097 and took it within a month.

The Crusaders were now traveling through unfamiliar enemy lands, and the 600-mile trip across Asia Minor was long and difficult. By the time they reached Antioch in Syria, the Crusaders had thinned considerably. Many proud knights were reduced to riding oxen because their fine horses had died and were eaten. Goats, dogs and sheep carried along bundles of supplies.

At Antioch

It was at Antioch that the Bible tells us the followers of Christ were first called "Christians," but the Muslims had overrun this proud ancient city. The Crusaders besieged Antioch, but it was a long, hard siege, and even when they took the city they had no food. Thistles, vines, and dried animal skins were boiled to survive. Some even ate the flesh of those persons they had killed. They were famished, hit by disease, and on the edge of complete collapse.

They were a demoralized force in Antioch, but most refused to turn around and go home. They desperately needed a miracle and it came by way of a man named Peter Bartholomew. Peter claimed to have received a holy vision from Saint Andrew, who told him where to find the spear that had pierced the side of Jesus! He reported that the holy lance was buried, and he took thirteen men to dig at the Church of Saint Peter in Antioch. Under the glow of torchlight; their spades hit a fragment of wood. It was the head of a spear. A man dropped to his knees and kissed the point of the spear still half-buried in the dirt.

The "miraculous" discovery of this holy spear was held in skepticism by some of the leaders, but it filled the soldiers with zealous hope and encouragement of God's blessing. Whether a trick or not, the discovery of the spear put a spark of holy fire in the belly of all the Crusaders. They took full control of Antioch, defeated their enemies, and despite disease and hunger, they headed south.

AT JERUSALEM

A full year later, on June 7, 1099, the worn travelers finally looked upon Jerusalem. They had reached the goal of their three years of anxious anticipation — to do God's bidding in a final, sacred battle. From the roughly 60,000 who had first set out, the Crusader force had declined to about 1,300 knights and 12,500 footmen. A trail of graves stretched several thousand miles behind them, but those who remained were chafing for the opportunity to take back the holy city for God and His church.

When they reached the city, however, an Egyptian garrison of skilled defenders was waiting behind a high and seemingly impenetrable stone wall.

A battle for the ages, a hinge in history, awaited as the army of the cross encircled the high, stone bastions. It was the height of summer and the land was parched. A six-mile walk

Figure 27: The attack of Jerusalem in 1099, from an unknown medieval manuscript.

was required for drinking water, and the water was full of leeches. The Crusaders also desperately needed wood for ladders, siege towers and catapults, and for a battering ram to bash away at the stone walls.

Solutions seem to come in the strangest ways. One of the leaders of the army, Tancred, stumbled across a hidden stash of timbers in a cave. He'd sought refuge in the cave, wanting privacy in order to relieve himself, and he found the cave stacked with piles of wood that had been hidden there by the Muslims. His distraught bowels may have been the most fortuitous bout of dysentery in all of history. The needed battle implements were constructed and the attack on the city walls was made.

At the start of the battle, the Muslims unleashed a horrifying defense. Arrows rained-down into tender flesh, impaling necks, arms and feet as men fell in choirs of gagging screams. Straw and mallets wrapped in pitch — along with burning tar — rained upon the men that assaulted the ramparts. The Crusaders used a metal-blunted battering ram to smash through the wall stonework. Fires raged all around them and searing smoke choked their lungs and burned their eyes. All day and all night the men fought on, trampling over heaps of dead as they pressed on to breach the defenses.

Eventually, warriors poured into the city. Slashing swords glinted in the cloudless sky, clashing with rabid swipes. The outnumbered defenders were soon hacked to death. Feet, heads and hands were scattered on the red-soaked ground. Babies were pulled from the clutches of their hysterical mothers and bashed against stone walls. Stomachs of prisoners were slit open in search of gold and valuables that may have been swallowed. Three years of pent-up rage was unleashed in an intense hellish vengeance.

Then, stained red with their enemies' blood, the Crusaders dropped to their knees and piously prayed to God. They would control Jerusalem for nearly a century.

More than 900 years have passed since the First Crusade, but the brutal memory of it lives on in the minds of Muslims and Christians alike. Both sides slaughtered their way into this city, and both sides have justified their actions as devotion to God. The Muslims had set their eyes on, not just the Holy Land, but the whole of Europe. They intended to conquer the entire world for Allah.

The resounding cry of the Christians was killing *for God*, killing for the pope, and killing for more land and treasure. It freed the bloodthirsty to slaughter their fellow humans, and the warriors felt it was a good death, because their soul's salvation had been *won*.

This was very little different than the Muslims, who believed they were following the mandate of Allah and his prophet Muhammad to win the world for Islam. Kill *for Allah*, kill for the prophet Muhammad, and kill for more land and treasure. Like the Crusaders, their salvation was assured by their valiant death.

Of course, both the Christian and Muslim warriors were sad cases, because the Bible does not teach that heaven is attained by shedding one's blood on the field of battle. It's a good motivator for winning wars, but it's a bad teaching, foolishly developed in contradiction to the mind of Christ. We might lay down our lives in the defense of our nation, our friends and families, out of love and courage. Military sacrifice is necessary to protect us from the would-be oppressors of the world. However, even this is not what saves our souls.

Jesus shed His own blood, but the battle He fought and *won* was a spiritual one. The eternal battle we fight is against sin. It is by the blood shed on the cross — and not blood extracted by the sword — that we earn eternal salvation.

TRADITION

I find it a great irony Pope Urban II never learned that the Crusaders had captured Jerusalem. He died in 1099, just two days before a courier brought the news of the victory.

Figure 28: "Taking of Jerusalem by the Crusaders, 15th July 1099" by Émile Signol (1847), The Bridgeman Art Library.

Chapter 29

The Third Crusade and After

The Crusaders held onto Jerusalem for nearly 100 years. A Seljuk general from Mosul successfully conquered the northern city of Edessa in 1144, spurring the Second Crusade, but Jerusalem remained safe for another half century. The Crusaders had failed repeatedly to take control of Egypt, and eventually Saladin's forces in Egypt invaded and began taking Crusader ground. On October 2, 1187, Balian of Ibelin surrendered Jerusalem to Saladin.

This was a travesty. King Philip II of France and King Richard I "the Lionheart" of England led armies to the Holy Land to retake the city. Marching the 3000 miles had proved devastating in the past, so the monarchs turned to the sea, hiring ships on the French and Italian coasts to transport them across the Mediterranean. After Richard arrived at the coastal city of Acre, it took one month of siege to conquer the city. When Saladin took too many weeks to negotiate a prisoner exchange, Richard decapitated 2,700 prisoners, including women and children. In response, Saladin slaughtered the Crusaders he had captured.

Richard then moved down the coast toward Jaffa, but was interrupted at Arsuf by an attack from Saladin's armies. In September of 1191, Saladin's forces at Arsuf fell to Richard, and the Crusaders headed south to capture Jaffa, and from Jaffa they headed east toward Jerusalem. However, Richard realized something important. He recognized that he did not have the forces to hold Jerusalem if he captured it, so he made a wise move. In June of 1192, Richard the Lionheart arranged the Treaty of Ramla as a peace treaty with Saladin. The Crusaders would leave Jerusalem in peace, and Saladin would allow Christian pilgrims to travel to holy shrines within the city.

INTERNATIONAL TRADE

One benefit arose from the crusades, and it came by way of exposure to contrasting cultures on both sides. Europe slowly began to emerge from its global isolation, and the heretofore ignorant citizenry came to realize that there was a world of non-Christians that had much to offer.

Camel caravans have been the Middle East's freight trucks since ancient times — slow, ponderous, yet steady and stout. The Crusaders met camels packed high with mysterious goods from the East: oriental rugs, multicolored spices, medicines, fine jewelry and exotic woods. From these caravans, the Crusaders found many new and wondrous items seldom seen by westerners.

In my mind, I can see a young English knight stopped at a caravan. This noble northerner is handed a yellow fruit he's never seen before — a lemon. The young warrior bites into the pulpy center and squeezes his eyes shut in shock. The merchant laughs at the knight's pursed lips, then hands down a slender glass vial containing drops of an exotic perfume. Its smell conjures thoughts of a hopeful reunion with his romantic love waiting far away at home.

Fear had insulated the Europeans from new ideas and new inventions, and Europeans were a culturally anemic lot. Those born in poverty were destined to serve as feudal slaves for life. Paternal decent of the privileged few made for long-lasting and unchanging dominance. Inventiveness was sluggish in Europe. Treatment by European physicians often caused more damage than cures. The blood of the ill was poured into bowls and examined for smell and greasiness. Medical charts dictated how to analyze urine for various maladies. Few treatments actually helped the ailing patient.

All this started to change after the crusades. Unique objects, the result of marvelous innovations from other lands, brought Europe out of lethargy and spurred the economy. Medical knowledge improved, and the new cures from abroad proved much more effective than medieval bloodletting. The Arabic numerals discovered during the crusades were found to be far more practical than Roman numerals in calculating sums. These written numbers found their way west, allowing merchants, bankers and scientists to decipher mathematical problems with much more efficiency and ease. Astronomical instruments used to determine time and direction, along with ground and polished glass eyewear, were all found to be miraculous advancements. Cane sugar, rice, garlic, olive oil and textiles were brought west and soon found their way to eager buyers in the ever-growing towns of Europe.

Large cargo ships had carried Crusaders to far-away battles. They were now used to transport lumber and wool from the west and bring back wonders from the east. As shipments grew in size, prices became more affordable for a burgeoning middle class in Europe. Even the poor could enjoy a modicum of luxury.

Since so many field workers had died during the crusades, land owners had to pay higher fees for laborers to tend their lands. Former serfs could buy their freedom, and some were even able to purchase land of their own. The pride of ownership resulted in increased yields from crops. Inventiveness and production rebounded. The bow drill that had been used since prehistoric times was replaced by the brace and bit. Industrial advances allowed for the eventual production of church bells, ink, paper, paint, and tanned leather goods. Detailed maps and harbor charts were crafted, and compasses from the orient were used by seafarers, making travel to distant shores more practical.

Once empty roads across Europe became well-traveled after the crusades, prolific with students and minstrels, postmen and drug merchants, tinkers and pilgrims who followed behind priests. They all trundled down earthen paths, sidestepping the dung deposited by the horses or pack-animals that had passed along before them.

From A.D. 900 to 1300 the population of Europe quadrupled in size, and shops sprouted as buyers became plentiful. Even some peasants were able to afford kitchen utensils and tallow candles for the first time.

It took time for the infrastructure of towns to catch up with the burgeoning growth. City sizes were limited by the perimeter of their protective rock walls. Water and sewer problems also served as challenges for growing towns. The maximum citizenry of the largest cities was 125,000, but there were uncountable hamlets and villages in rural settings, so that Europe held nearly 79 million people by the end of the 13th century.

Chapter 30

Torture

In most civilizations, execution is held as a last punitive resort, so it's remarkable how many people were put to death during the Middle Ages and into the Renaissance. From the Spanish Inquisition to Bloody Mary's brutal slaughter of Protestants, to the Salem Witch Trials, multitudes were put to death for heresy.

Torture Devices

The people of the Middle Ages were not known for their creativity. Even after Charlemagne urged an increase in education, the new books that were produced were mostly of the textbook variety. The time was not known for its art and invention. However, the Europeans of the Middle Ages did use a wide variety of different methods to torture people. Causing excruciating pain seems a hallmark of the millennium. The Romans and Persians had executed people in painful ways, but the folks of the Middle Ages didn't stop at impaling people on spikes or whipping them with shards of glass and bones. They had hooks, pincers, braziers with burning coals, racks for stretching the body until joints dislocated from their sockets, head crushers, slow strangulation devices, finger clamps, metal cages with spikes, iron maidens with spikes,

Figure 29: Depiction of Torture in the 16th century.

231

metal tongs to do things unmentionable, and cat paws to shred the flesh off the bone.

In 1692, Philipp van Limborch first published his book *History of the Inquisition*, in which he describes a simple but terrible variant of the strappado called *squassation*:

> Squassation, tis thus performed; The Prisoner hath his Hands bound behind his Back, and Weights tied to his Feet, and then he is drawn up on high, till his Head reaches the very Pully. He is kept hanging in this Manner for some time, that by the Greatness of the Weight hanging at his Feet, all his Joints and Limbs may be dreadfully stretched, and on a sudden he is let down with a Jirk, by the slacking the Rope, but kept from coming quite to the Ground, by which terrible Shake, his Arms and Legs are all disjointed, whereby he is put to the most exquisite Pain; the Shock which he receives by the sudden Stop of his Fall, and the Weight at his Feet stretching his whole Body more intensely and cruelly.[1]

This is not a particularly high-tech form of torture, but it does demonstrate a sadistic cruelty. Van Limborch notes that this was done to men and women alike, that women were stripped and bound just as men, regardless of whether they were virgins and chaste. This was all done to obtain a confession of guilt from somebody who might have been perfectly innocent. The crime of heresy did not require rejecting the basic tenets of Christianity, but simply believing anything other than what the official leadership dictated. As Bishop William Shaw Kerr noted:

> The most ghastly abomination of all was the system of torture. The accounts of its cold-blooded operations make one shudder at the capacity of human beings for cruelty. And it was decreed and regulated by the popes who claim to represent Christ on earth...[2]

---

1 Philipp Van Limborch and Samuel Chandler, *The History of the Inquisition* (London, 1731), 219.
2 William S. Kerr, *A Handbook of the Papacy* (London: Marshall Morgan and Scott, 1951), 239-40.

The Witches

There are real witches in the world, and there are people who serve Satan. In these days, however, we don't expect them to actually fly around on brooms.

The medieval years were a time of credulity. It was a time when people believed witches were prevalent and could change into any shape, fly far distances, and still cast their spells on the unsuspecting. Every village had its old women, and some had genetically deformed people. Being ugly, or old, or feeble-minded made innocent people more vulnerable to suspicion if anything went wrong in the village. Of course, things always went wrong, because this is the planet Earth. Anybody could be accused of witchcraft — and at any moment. We know the witches of movies, the ugly, warted and hook-nosed hags who performed magic using black kettles. In the Middle Ages, these women were feared, and pointed black hats were not required. The only thing necessary was an accuser.

Figure 30: The burning of alleged witches (14th century).

Of course, the residue of violence from the Middle Ages lingered through to the end of the Reformation period. The Puritans at Salem were no less guilty of murder than the priests of the Inquisition. Even newly formed denominations became so doctrinally rigid that people were often punished and even killed for criticizing their ecclesiastic leadership. These leaders of faith, one and all, appear to have ignored the words of Jesus in Matthew 5:44-45:

> *But I say to you, love your enemies, bless those who curse you, do good to those who hate you, and pray for those who spitefully use you and persecute you, that you may be sons of your Father in heaven; for He makes His sun rise on the evil and on the good, and sends rain on the just and on the unjust.*

God is kind to all, even the least deserving. While those in charge genuinely believed they were meting out punishments in the service of God, it was those persecuted souls who appeared best able to live out the love and mercy of Jesus Christ.

No Confidence Vote

In 1546, the Council of Trent decreed that tradition was equal to the Bible in its value, yet we see in the history of medieval Europe very little that gives us confidence in those traditions. We can trust that there were monks, nuns and village priests who devoted their lives to prayer and service, whose lives were dedicated to serving Christ in humility, but they were not the men in charge of the whole institution. The very people who *should* have been writing doctrine appear to have been eking by in poverty, while the wealthy and powerful used the church of God for their own self-aggrandizement — and then insisted that their words were beyond reproach.

Chapter 31

The Black Plague

The men returning from the crusades brought spices, silks and perfumes from the Middle East. Unfortunately, with the trade ships came pests — like rats. And on those rats were fleas, and in those fleas lived the deadly pathogen, *Yersinia pestis*. Nothing changed Europe so much as in October of 1347 when twelve wooden ships glided slowly into Messina, an Italian city on the northeast side of Sicily. These Genoese galleys held cargo believed to be from the Crimea, but they also carried a silent disease that would be known as the "Black Death."

Those who met the ships were filled with horror as they stepped aboard. The sailors on these galleys were all dead and dying, their ashen-grey bodies covered in dark sores and their tongues turned black. The first ship was ordered out to sea immediately, but the virulent disease spread fast, much like a match dropped onto a stack of parched straw. In the end, one out of two people in Europe would die from the disease. In some villages, every soul perished.

The effects of *Yersinia pestis* varied from person to person, but common symptoms were dark sores that covered the body, painfully swollen lymph glands, inflammation of the lungs and throat, unbearable pain, vomiting, spitting blood and horrific-smelling breath. Most of those inflicted died within three days, and only a handful of those infected survived. Some people awoke in the morning feeling fine but were dead by nightfall.

The plague was transmitted in various forms, but the airborne variety was the most easily spread. The disease jumped from town to town so fast, it seemed impossible to escape its deadly advance. The incubation period was short — just 2-6 days —

but it moved everywhere. Whole towns were quarantined, and whole towns died. Physicians could do nothing and priests were equally powerless. In fact, priests were terrified at the prospect of giving last rites lest they, too, became infected. It was like the end of the world, a terrifying apocalyptic event. It's estimated that 40-60% of Europe perished in the 14th century epidemic.

In Avignon, France, papal documents record that 1,500 died in just three days. Those numbers included five cardinals and 100 bishops. In sheer numbers, it was the worse catastrophe the western world has ever witnessed. People assumed it was a judgment from God for their sins, but they didn't know how to go about appeasing this angry God.

Was God's vengeance due to immorality? Was it due to corruption in the church? Was Providence enraged by the Crusaders' failures to drive the Muslims from the Holy Land? Surely, Europe was guilty of great sins, and a plethora of bizarre remedies surfaced.

In one movement, the Brothers of the Cross, known as "flagellants" traveled from town to town whipping their backs until the flesh tore off. The whips had leather strips with three nails tied at the ends, which made for a bloody display. Spectators lined up to watch the flagellants walk by. They delighted in dipping their own clothes in the holy, dripping blood of a flagellant. Women, children, and even knights joined the movement. If one joined the order, they committed themselves for 33 ½ days of absolute obedience to superiors. Two times a day, they marched in pairs to the church while singing hymns. After spending time praying, they formed a circle in the town square, bared their

Figure 31: Flagellants from a 15th-century woodcut.

backs, and whipped their skin to shreds. Another such service was performed in private, all the while kneeling and praying.

Strangely, those flogging themselves were given money to hear confessions. This took revenues from the clergy, and the pope soon put a stop to the movement by jailing or even executing the participants. The Brothers of the Cross disbanded as quickly as it had grown up.

Another response to the plague was anger. Who was to blame? Jews were the first scapegoats, because the faithful believed they had killed Christ. Jews were also accused of poisoning the water supplies. Their avoidances of unsanitary wells and rivers made them the prime targets of suspicion, because some Jewish neighborhoods had much lower death rates from the plague. The possibility that the Jews were helped by isolation in ghettoes might not have occurred to the angry mobs.

In Strasbourg, it is estimated that 800 Jews were rounded up and burned at the stake in a cemetery. Fanatical killings occurred in Poland, Austria, Spain, and France. The church authorities didn't incite or approve of slaughtering the Jews like this. Pope Clement VI issued two papal bulls in 1348 forbidding any more pogroms, yet the persecution continued. The Jews in Mainz, Germany fought to defend themselves, killing hundreds of Christians. In response, whole waves of Christians attacked Mainz, and on August 24, 1349 they killed 6,000 Jews.

Because so many died or feared for their lives, the pope lowered the age-limits for the clergy. Priests were ordained at twenty instead of twenty-five. Fifteen-year-olds could take monastic vows. The result was a much younger and much less *experienced* church leadership, with fewer mature mentors to offer wisdom and direction. This weakness in the church presented problems in the years to come, and the morning star of the Reformation slowly appeared in a very dark sky.

While big names like Martin Luther and William Tyndale are associated with the fires of the Reformation that raged across Europe, the spark for that fire smoldered because of the work of a professor named John Wycliffe.

Chapter 32

John Wycliffe

Figure 32: Statue of John Wycliffe in Worms, Germany.

In the still December morning, several men crunched across the frozen grass of the graveyard of St. Mary's church. They were carrying shovels. The men entered the chancel of the church and stopped over a section of floor covered in heavy stone pavers. John Wycliffe had been sealed under the church flooring for 43 years, and now the men began prying up the granite slabs. They dug into the shallow grave until they hit wood.

Wycliffe had died in 1384, and his body was buried there inside the church in Lutterworth, Leicestershire, England. Just over three decades later, the Council of Constance in 1415 ordered his remains to be removed from that holy ground, but it took until 1428 for the job to be completed. Wycliffe was deemed a heretic for translating the Bible into the English language. His bones were no longer welcome.

The remains of the great scholar were carried out to a gathered crowd. Some had heard of the great preacher, but most were too young to have ever seen him. They certainly all knew of this man, the most famous man to ever live in the village. The procession was somber, because the authorities were going to burn his bones, this priest who had been so brilliant in mind and superb in tongue. The Roman Catholic leadership had found Wycliffe dangerous and outrageous in his teachings, but the people had flocked to hear him preach, nonetheless. Some of the oldest adults in the procession had seen him. As little children, they had watched him preach, and the things he said were the same things the Lollards were still saying behind closed doors. He had obtained powerful friends in his life, which is why he was spared the fire till long after his death.

The crowd watched as the remains of John Wycliffe were desecrated in a waiting fire. After the skeleton was burned to ash, every granule that remained of him was tossed into the River Swift.

It's easy to forget that many of the original reformers were Roman Catholic priests. Wycliffe was included in this category. Wycliffe spent nearly 30 years at Oxford (from 1345-1374) as an esteemed Bible scholar, a theologian and philosopher. Despite the Black Death and other troubles during those years, he both taught and earned degrees, including his doctorate. He was already considered by some to be the most prominent theologian in England by the time he was sent to serve as parish rector at Lutterworth.

This time in history was ripe for Wycliffe's brand of Christianity. Poverty and the plague had done their damage to the country, as had England's "Hundred Years War" with France over the right of succession to the French throne. The world appeared to be ending, and it was easy to blame horrors on the clergy who were apathetic, lazy, and ignorant of God's Word.

John Wycliffe

The general moral decay was obvious (as it is in all times), and there were two rival popes both claiming Saint Peter's Chair.

This double-papacy was known as the Great Western Schism, and it lasted from 1378 to 1417. Rome had elected an Italian as pope in 1378 (Pope Urban VI), but the French Cardinals refused to accept Urban. They elected Clement VII instead, and he kept his papal throne at Avignon, France. The Roman Catholic Church was divided and, for 40 long years, each pope claimed rights as successor to Saint Peter. It was a salacious and embarrassing situation for the papacy, with several popes having been ensnared in scandal.

When he was given the rectory at Lutterworth, John Wycliffe began to write and speak in opposition to certain traditions of the church, and he possessed the theological credentials and backbone to advance his beliefs. Wycliffe felt the people needed a Bible in their own language — one that they could actually understand. Wycliffe criticized the French pope for his egregious misuse of church funds. The Oxford scholar coined the phrase "dominion of grace" to explain his strong belief that money given to the church should be used for doing the church's work of helping those in need, as well as teaching and spreading the word of God. Fleecing simple Christians for their money was wicked, and Wycliffe insisted that the church leaders should have nothing to do with worldly wealth.

In fact, English money gathered for religious purposes was being used to fund the war against England. Church leaders in France were taking money from the English in staggering sums — about half of what England produced — and giving it to the pope. Pope Clement would then hand over part of that English money to the King of France, who used it to equip his army to fight against the English. So, the English were, in essence, funding and equipping an army to fight against *themselves*.

Wycliffe was also troubled by what had happened as a result of the Fourth Lateran Council of 1215. The Council had been held in a grandiose setting with 71 patriarchs, 404 bishops, and 900 abbots and priors in attendance. Special envoys came from Emperor Frederick II and the Kings of France, England,

Aragon, Hungary, Cyprus and Jerusalem. They gathered in an extravagant and lavish setting, and the members of the council approved 70 canons under the leadership of Pope Innocent III (the same Innocent III who had approved of the slaughter of every townsperson in Béziers, France). While the first paragraphs of Canon 1 seem to be a statement of basic Christian faith, it is the third paragraph which Wycliffe considered an incorrect understanding of Scripture. The council had affirmed the doctrine of transubstantiation, but Wycliffe rejected the notion that the wine and bread of the Eucharist became the actual body and blood of Jesus Christ.

Wycliffe served God as a Roman Catholic priest, but he denounced the doctrine of transubstantiation, and by doing so he earned the obvious ire of the church leadership. That wasn't all, however. Wycliffe also preached against the practice of selling indulgences to free people from time in purgatory. He spoke against the need to confess sins to priests, and most notably, he began to have the Bible translated into English. The following were typical among the statements made by Wycliffe:

> But many think if they give a penny to a pardoner, they shall be forgiven the breaking of all the commandments of God, and therefore they take no heed how they keep them. But I say to you for certain, though you have priests and friars to sing for you, and though you each day hear many Masses, and found chantries and colleges, and go on pilgrimages all your life, and give all your goods to pardoners; all this shall not bring your soul to heaven…

> Trust wholly in Christ; rely altogether on His sufferings; beware of seeking to be justified in any other way than by His righteousness. Faith in our Lord Jesus Christ is sufficient for salvation…

> It is not confession to man but to God, who is the true Priest of souls, that is the great need of sinful man. Private confession and the whole system of medieval confession was not ordered by Christ and was not used by the Apostles, for of the three thousand who were turned to

Christ's Law on the Day of Pentecost, not one of them was confessed to a priest ... It is God who is the forgiver.[1]

A man who spoke against the church authorities might have easily been executed. However, Wycliffe was tremendously well-respected. He was initially supported by King Edward III's son John of Gaunt (1340–99), who had his own reasons for wanting the clergy to have less power.

John of Gaunt was the younger brother of Edward the Black Prince, who died a year before their father the king. When Edward III passed away, John of Gaunt helped rule the kingdom on behalf of his 10-year-old nephew, the new King Richard II, and thus Wycliffe received royal protection as long as he was in Gaunt's favor. Those who followed Wycliffe earned the name of Lollards, and there was more than one Lollard knight in the court of the young King Richard II.

Wycliffe encouraged evangelism to the people in the common language. He and his followers Nicholas Hereford and John Purvey created an English translation of the Bible. The official church regarded this work as casting pearls before swine.

In the end, Pope Gregory XI formally condemned Wycliffe and his teachings in 1382, but nobody followed the pope's order to arrest Wycliffe. Even after the Archbishop of Canterbury condemned Wycliffe and his writings later that year, nobody bothered him. The bold theologian continued to write until he died of a stroke in 1384 at the young age of 54. It took 31 years for Wycliffe to be condemned by the Council of Constance and even longer for Pope Martin V to approve the order to have Wycliffe's bones disinterred and burned to powdered ash.

He died well over a century before the Reformation, but John Wycliffe's influence certainly spread the ideals that were later carried by the reformers. He is thus called the Morning Star of the Reformation.

---

1 *Ibid.*

Chapter 33

The Lollards

Figure 33: Lollards being hanged and burned in the first year of King Henry V (1413).

The atmosphere that had protected Wycliffe did not last long. The young King Richard II had not been interested in burning people at the stake. After he turned 30, however, Richard did go on a rampage against his enemies from years before — aristocrats who at one point had seized the government. After two years of tyranny, Richard's cousin Henry arrived from France with a small army and crowned himself Henry IV. The defeated and deposed Richard died in prison the next year.

It took Henry IV no time at all to begin brutally opposing religious rebels in the kingdom. In 1401, he passed a statute that legalized the burning of heretics. Even before the law was official, however, the first Lollard martyr was burned at the stake. William Sawtrey was not a common layman. He was another priest who had followed the teachings of Wycliffe instead of those of the Catholic hierarchy, and they executed him for it.

The Lollards were among those most targeted. They supported positions that would now be recognized as thoroughly Protestant. They rejected the doctrine of transubstantiation, the veneration of saints and worship of their images, the swearing of oaths, confessions to priests for forgiveness, pilgrimages to relics, abstinence of nuns and priests and the granting of papal indulgences. They copied and passed around John Wycliffe's English Bible and read it in houses and villages outside the blessing of the church.

This was an outrage to the official church leadership, and in 1408 the Archbishop of Canterbury Thomas Arundel issued his *Constitutions against the Lollards,* in which he prohibited all preaching or teaching of the Bible — or translations of the Bible into English — without direct authorization by the official Roman Catholic Church. Arundel specifically targeted the writings of John Wycliffe, forbidding them from being read and taught upon pain of excommunication.

Henry IV wanted the Lollards all burned, but Wycliffe's teachings and his English Bible could not be stopped. The faithful had to move underground, but they continued to read God's Word together in homes and villages, and their words spread across England.

Figure 34: First verses of John's Gospel from a pocket Wycliffe English translation (late 14th century).

The Lollards

Someone might whisper around that a Lollard was coming to the village on a certain evening to read from the Bible. The man himself would arrive — in a barn or the woods or some other relatively private place — and find a totally packed crowd of people. Under a remote canopy of tree branches, with flames reflecting off the leaves overhead, the Lollard would stand in his bare feet and read straight from the Bible. Few of the people had ever heard God's Word read out loud — not in a way that made sense — and it amazed them to hear the words of Jesus himself. The Lollard might read from the book of Mark one night and then travel on to the next village. The following week another Lollard might appear and read the entire book of Romans. Many of these Lollards did this under great personal peril.

On occasion, one or two Lollards were caught and dragged before the local authorities. The law said they must be burned at the stake for their defiance. They were constantly at risk and were forced to hide in bogs, dells, forests, moss hedges and mountain caves. Both men and women memorized whole books of the Bible to share with others! The seeds of faith were tossed upon the fertile fields of well-plowed hearts and minds, and many converts soon sprouted.

John Wycliffe's close associate John Purvey, an ordained priest, was sentenced to death soon after Henry IV took the throne. At that time, Purvey recanted and escaped the flames, but guilt haunted him. In 1403, Purvey left his parish to serve as an itinerant preacher. He walked about from village to village carrying the English Bible he had helped translate. Just like his brothers, poor in wealth but rich in spirit, he hid in barns and homes as he journeyed from village to village. He is said to have died at Newgate prison in May of 1414,[1] but the ink which flowed from his pen has proved most indelible.

---

1 Anne Hudson, "Purvey, John," *Oxford Dictionary of National Biography* (Oxford University Press, 2008).

Chapter 34

Jan Hus

Although he died, and his bones were eventually consumed in flames, the teachings of John Wycliffe spread across England and even crossed the wind-tossed English Channel. Those who heard Wycliffe's ideas took them back to their homelands.

Numerous students from Bohemia had returned from England to Prague, where a young man named Jan Hus had chosen the priesthood. Hus worked and earned his Master's degree at the University of Prague, and in 1401 he was ordained as a priest. He began to serve as rector and dean of the philosophy faculty at the University of Prague. The next year, Hus became the preacher at Prague's Bethlehem Chapel, a popular and huge church that held 3,000 people. Bohemia was already more forward-minded than many other nations in Europe, and sermons were preached in the native Czech language of the people and not in Latin.

There were still two popes in Europe, and this schism contributed to a growing sense of disapproval of the Roman Catholic hierarchy. Simony, the selling of church positions for money, had threaded its poisonous way through the fabric of the Bohemian clergy. Church lands required the highest land taxes, and the poor — including poor priests — resented the wealth that flowed into the hands of the upper establishment. Those in the Bohemian reform movement had been reading Wycliffe's works, and Jan Hus was one of them. From his position as priest and teacher, Hus was able to become a loud and vocal proponent of church reform. Wycliffe's ideas grew in acceptance among the Czech masters at the university, while the German masters fought to maintain the status quo.

Hus quickly became a national figure, well-known and respected by the people. He drew ever close to the Bible himself. While he didn't disagree with transubstantiation the way that Wycliffe did, he spoke strongly against the abuses in the church.

The local clergy and the German leaders were angered by the things Hus preached, but he was temporarily protected by the Bohemian King Wenceslas. Archbishop Zbyněk had been relatively friendly toward Hus and his teachings at first, but eventually he bribed the new pope Alexander V to excommunicate Hus. Nothing came of it, and the king forced Zbyněk to declare his support for the great preacher.

However, Hus lost the king's favor when he began criticizing the anti-Pope John XXIII. In 1411, the anti-pope began selling indulgences, pulling money from the Czech peasantry to finance a war. King Wenceslas was taking his share from the proceeds, and that meant Jan Hus was stepping on the royal toes in opposing the sale of indulgences.

In June of 1412, Hus signed his own death warrant. He argued that no pope or priest could absolve a person from the penalty and guilt of sin, but that task lay with God alone. In time, Hus was hunted by both civil and church powers. He went into hiding, where he continued to write treatises against church corruption. Adoring supporters among the peasants gave Hus protection and care, but in the end, it wasn't enough.

In 1414, the Council of Constance convened — the same council that condemned the already dead John Wycliffe to burning. Hus was invited to come speak to the council and to present his arguments for open discussion, and he was guaranteed safe travel by the Holy Roman Emperor. While Hus was told he'd be allowed to address the attendees, the whole thing was a trap. When he appeared, Hus was arrested as a heretic. He was shackled in heavy chains and put through three sham trials, in which he was allowed to defend himself to little benefit. He was urged to recant, but he would not. He was therefore sentenced to death.

On July 6, 1415, Hus was taken to the cathedral and dressed in priestly clothing. These garments were soon ripped off his body to add shame to the whole sad affair. His head was shaved and then crowned with a pointed paper hat painted with demons. As Hus was led away to be executed, he was made to walk past a pile of his own books smoldering to ashes.

Hus was offered a chance to deny his faith when they tied him to the stake. He responded only with a loud prayer: "Lord Jesus, it is for thee that I patiently endure this cruel death. I pray thee to have mercy on my enemies." As the fire was lit at his feet, and the flames lapped his flesh, Jan Hus could be heard reciting the Psalms. The fires might have burned him, but they didn't burn his legacy.

And so, it came to pass, that two men who stood on principles they trusted were from God were hounded in life and reviled in death by a church that opposed anyone who dared teach straight from the Scriptures.

A century later, Martin Luther discovered a book of sermons by Jan Hus while looking through the stacks of a library. "I was overwhelmed with astonishment," Luther later wrote. "I could not understand for what cause they had burnt so great a man, who explained the Scriptures with so much gravity and skill."[1]

Figure 35: The likeness of Jan Hus in the Martinická Bible (1430).

---
1 From Introduction of Herbert Workman and R. Martin Pope, *The Letters of John Hus* (London: Hodder and Stoughton, 1904).

Chapter 35

Joan of Arc

Figure 36: "Joan of Arc in Armor before Orléans" by Jules E. Lenepveu (1889), Panthéon de Paris.

The Hundred Years' War brought a series of constant quarrels between England and France over large portions of France from 1337 to 1453. The English claimed title to the French throne as the nearest relatives of Charles IV, the last Capetian king who had died in 1328. During the decades of fighting, British armies captured much of the French coast with a focus on the duchy of Guyenne (Aquitaine) in southwestern France. While separated from home across the English Channel, the English had a well-disciplined 15,000-strong expeditionary force that proved difficult for the French to dislodge from their coasts. The English had developed the long-bow, which made them adversaries to be feared. They could shoot volleys of hissing arrows as far as three hundred yards, which proved to be a formidable advantage against the French crossbows.

Over the next sixty years, tactics changed to adapt to weaponry. Territories were exchanged back and forth as victories on both sides ebbed and flowed. The fighting was punctuated by intermittent stalemates at times. Following a victory at Agincourt in 1415, the English gained control of the majority of northern France, and it became apparent that England would soon conquer the French — thus bringing the two countries under one rule. It was a feared and repulsive scenario for the French citizenry. A miracle was needed...and soon.

During this time of English conquest, a most unlikely person emerged to inspire the impoverished French army. An illiterate farm girl named Joan was just 13 years of age when she received a message from voices she said belonged to Saint Michael, Saint Catherine, and Saint Margaret. Only Joan heard the voices, which she believed gave her instructions from God to free the French people from the English.

Perhaps the voices came from the imagination of a fanciful child living in the daily drudgery of a cow field. Perhaps they were real. We will never know, but they inspired a teenage girl to lead one of the greatest military victories in history. She made God a vow of chastity and at age 16 avoided the marriage her father had arranged for her. Through a series of wild events worthy of the best novel, this peasant girl from Arc found herself given an audience in early 1429, by the Dauphin Charles, the heir of King Charles VI of France. She promised him that she would see him crowned king and asked him for an army to march on Orléans to free it from the English siege.

Charles did not ignore the words of Joan of Arc. Astonishingly, he gave her the forces she requested despite the arguments of his advisors. He sent her off to Orléans in specially-made white armor and mounted on a white horse, and she led the French army to victory and ended the siege.

It was a much-needed morale boost which helped shift the tides of war: Joan was called the Maid of Orléans. Her grit and exuberance in the midst of gore-strewn battlefield belied the sensitivities of a teenager. She must have been sickened at the sight of mutilated men around her, but she shouted time after time for soldiers to fight in the name of God. She often stopped retreating soldiers and redirected them back into the fray. In one battle, an arrow pierced through her neck and stuck out of her back. Men carried her away from the fighting, where they clipped the arrow head from the shaft. Joan yanked out the arrow herself and later returned to the battle.

As promised, Joan saw King Charles VII crowned at Reims in July of 1429. The fame of Joan of Arc spread throughout all France. She was celebrated as a heroine, a national hero, a thorn in the side of the English. Everywhere she went — her battle banner snapping in the wind — crowds pressed around her, seeking to touch her glinting armor as she passed by. Not only was she a hero, she was a virgin, and in the eyes of the people that elevated her to the status of a living saint.

In May of 1430, the king sent Joan to battle against a Burgundian assault on the city of Compiégne. She was thrown from her horse and captured by the English, who took her to the English-occupied city of Rouen. The English resented Joan as much as the French adored her. She was tied to a horse with heavy ropes and pulled through the narrow streets of Rouen, to the castle tower where she was locked behind twelve-foot-thick stone walls. Shackled in chains, the 18-year-old young woman's only physical comfort was a sliver of light in the rock fortifications high above her.

At the trial that followed, Joan was subjected to brutal questioning. Bishop Cauchon hoped that his success in the trial would get him appointed Archbishop. Joan was given no defense lawyer and had to testify daily in unfair and grueling sessions that pounded away at her. She was charged with some 70 crimes — primarily of being a heretic and a witch, and of wearing men's clothing. The goal was to smear the name of this French heroine and to undermine the legitimacy of the rule of King Charles VII.

Over the next year, King Charles did nothing to negotiate the release of the woman who had seen him crowned. She remained in prison, and in May of 1431, she was brought into a torture chamber and threatened with brutal treatment unless she confessed that she hadn't heard from God. Standing there in that den of torture, staring at the hooks, pincers, braziers with burning coals, the rack and screws, she reportedly said, "Truly, if you were to tear me limb from limb, and separate soul from body, I will tell you nothing more."[1] She was spared brutality that day. Her stalwart attitude convinced her persecutors that torture would do nothing to move her.

Joan was questioned at trial one last time, and one final time she said:

> "What I have always said in the trial, and held, I wish still to say and maintain. If I were condemned, if I saw the torch lighted, the faggots prepared, and the executioner ready to kindle the fire, and if I myself were in the fire, I would not say otherwise, and would maintain to the death all that I have said."[2]

The next day, May 24, Joan was taken to a wooden platform at the cemetery behind the Church of Saint-Ouen. She was told that her mortal body would be burned to death there for her crimes. Joan had lost much weight and appeared now as a scrawny, forlorn girl. She had endured food poisoning and punishing questioning and harsh treatment. She was told that if she signed the scrap of paper, she would be placed on the mercy of the church. The young woman was illiterate and could not read what she was signing, and she scrawled her rudimentary signature on a confession.

---

[1] Lucy F. Madison, *Joan of Arc: The Warrior Maid* (Philadelphia: The Penn Publishing Company, 1918), 366.
[2] *Ibid*, 367.

Within a few days Joan retracted her confession, realizing she had been tricked. On May 30, 1431, at the age of 19, Joan of Arc was put to death in the most gruesome manner, burning in the fire she feared.

I have personally visited many locations in Europe where the events described in this book took place. A research team accompanied me, comprised of my brother Paul, researcher Bonnie Dawson, Dr. Frank Tarek and his sons Spencer and Austin.

The stone castle of Joan's imprisonment still stands in the medieval town of Rouen, France. The church of her trial is preserved, as is the spot in the Old Market where they took a brave teenage girl and killed her. Today, the Old Market is filled mostly with fish vendors and wine sellers. Opposite the Old Market stands a soaring cross, and just a few feet away is a cold, stone statue of Joan, shackles on her wrists, the flames creeping up her robes.

Gazing at that statue, I imagined it as a flesh and bone girl, hardly a woman by today's standards. I imagine the crowd waiting in morbid anticipation outside her prison. I imagine Joan hearing the shouts echo off the stone walls as she was taken from her cell. She wore on her shaved head a pointed hat that read "Heretic, relapsed, apostate, idolater." She was placed in a wooden cart and pushed down the cobbled street to the Old Market, escorted by eighty soldiers. Burgeoning crowns giddy with expectations of a public burning awaited her. The jeers became louder and louder as the stake drew nearer with each turn of the old wooden cart wheels. I imagine Joan gazing up at the bright blue sky above her. I imagine she rested her eyes on the May flowers that burst from patches of soil. She breathed a prayer, ignoring the straw and wood piled up at the base of the stake.

Figure 37: Joan at the stake, Rouen, France.

Above the stake, letters had been scrawled on a sign, but Joan could not read. She did not know the unjust words they spoke about her:

"Joan the Maid, liar, pernicious, seducer of the people, diviner, superstitious, blasphemer of God, presumptuous, misbelieving in the faith of Jesus Christ, idolater, cruel, dissolute invoker of devils, apostate, schismatic and heretic."[3]

When Joan reached the stake, she slipped to her knees and prayed to God. Ignoring the clamor of the crowd, she sought His forgiveness as she forgave all those that condemned her. One person tied two sticks together and offered Joan a makeshift cross. She pressed it tightly to her breast as she wept softly. It's hard to imagine that even those who had condemned her weren't moved by the sight of a frightened teenage girl being lashed to a stake. I imagine some sobbing in the crowd as the fire was lit.

The last thing that Joan's eyes saw before the smoke singed them to blindness was another cross that someone had brought from a nearby church. It was held up high so she could see it briefly through the growing flames. Her last trailing words were "Jesus...Jesus...Jesus..." as she slumped motionless into the fire, leaving only crackling blackness where pink skin had flushed just moments before. When the executioner was sure she was dead; embers were pushed away to show to all that the contorted, charred body was proof-positive the "witch" had floated away and escaped.

In the aftermath of that rigged trial, the chief prosecutor, d'Estivet, was found drowned in an open sewer, his body floating in excrement. The recantation letter that Joan signed was found in the official records to be a different letter than what Joan had originally signed. Twenty-five years after the execution, Pope Callixtus III examined the trial, pronounced Joan innocent and declared her a martyr. She is a saint and a national heroine of France today.

---

[3] Polly Schoyer Brooks, *Beyond the Myth: The Story of Joan of Arc* (Boston: Houghton Mifflin Company, 1990), 146.

Joan of Arc was one girl among thousands killed in the fires of political and religious hypocrisy during those harsh centuries. Many others had suffered similar fates. She was not killed because she was actually a witch or blasphemer. She clung to Jesus until the very end. She was killed because she dared oppose the forces who ruled in that day, and because she dared to claim direction from God outside the official church.

As we examine her death, we can see some interesting parallels between Joan's death and that of Jesus. There is obviously no comparing her death to the magnitude of the deed done by Christ at His crucifixion. Christ was the Son of God who paid an inestimable debt on our behalf. However, when considering the mindset of the killers, we see that history repeats itself when religious leaders execute those who threaten the status quo.

As in the case of Christ, it was politically expedient that Joan die in the name of God after a mock trial. The religious elitists pronounced the sentence and the civil authorities were left to carry out the deadly task. Soon after the death of the condemned, the accusers essentially heaped responsibility for the killing on the civil authorities who had carried it out. She had an object of shame placed on her head and so did Jesus. She had a sign put above her gallows and so did Jesus. She was affixed to a stake or wooden post in her execution and so was Jesus. Both died in public view as morbid examples, as warnings against making challenges to religious traditions, as visible warnings that others like them would be killed in the same gruesome way. Both had crowds that adored them, filled with people who merely wanted to touch them as they passed, but the fickle crowds were easily turned into jeering mobs by crafty, religious authorities.

We find a historical pattern by religious officials to self-justify the killing of others in the name of God. Human logic has always been pliable and adroitly blind to God's true intentions.

We can encounter statues of Joan of Arc across France today. Most of them reflect her as either defiant in her battle armor or standing demurely in a flowing dress, with chained wrists, tied to her execution stake.

Chapter 36

Opening the World

The Middle Ages was certainly a hideous era like no other, but three innovations helped give people a greater sense of power and the ability to protect themselves. The first of these inventions was gunpowder, which came by way of ancient China and eventually appeared on the fields of European warfare. Gunpowder offered a tangible means of protection from the threats of invading enemies. A gunpowder discharge projected ammunition at such a high velocity that it made a shredded decoration of the enemy's plated metal armor. The use of gunpowder stimulated advances in complex metal fabrication and also allowed kingdoms the needed confidence to shuffle the decks of power.

The Middle Ages faded away, not only in the light of the Renaissance, but in the opening of the world. Explorers sailed off to lands unknown, discovering the Americas for Europe and all manner of routes to India and the Far East. Adventurers supplied with gunpowder had an advantage; they were able to protect themselves in those great distances from home. Their explorations began to flourish, which brought about new opportunities in trade and commerce.

The second of these innovations was the magnetic compass, which gave surety of direction for those early explorers who sailed into the expanse of an endless horizon. Sailors had always had the stars, and the astrolabe had been used to determine latitude since the time of ancient Greece, but it was still easy to get disoriented without landmarks to follow. A teetering needle that pointed north became the metal stylist that etched the face of an ever-shrinking globe. Because of that needle,

Spain, England, France, Portugal, and the Netherlands subdued new lands for their countries, created new nation states, and produced staggering amounts of wealth.

The chemical components of gunpowder and the magnetic pull of the compass made external expansion possible for kingdoms. To me, though, the most important invention of all is the printing press. The printing press allowed for internal expansion of the mind.

About A.D. 1440, Johannes Gutenberg and his partners in Mainz, Germany produced a machine with removable type. By 1480, printers were working in 110 locations across Europe, and they revolutionized the Western world. This single invention opened an ignorant populace to a holy awakening like no invention before or since.

Prior to the printing press, copies of the Bible were done laboriously by hand in a monastery's room called a scriptorium. Interestingly, the scriptorium was the only room in the entire monastery which had a modicum of heat. The measure of warmth was not meant to comfort the scribe, but to keep the ink from freezing. It took scribes many long months or even years to finish a single Bible. Each volume represented ponderous numbers of ink strokes and the cramped hands of weary monks. Bibles were rare, expensive and hard to come by. Then came the printing press and, once the letters were set in place, dozens of copies of a page could be printed in perfect characters in minutes.

After the invention of the printing press, it became inevitable that Bibles and other books would find their way even into the dark recesses of the medieval world. People once floundering in ignorance suddenly gained new perspectives and, the most powerful of all commodities, knowledge!

Figure 38: "The Book Printer" by Johann Bernhard Basedow (c. 1770).

The powers in Rome did not trust the people to understand the Bible themselves. In 1234, the Council of Tarragona had ordered all vernacular translations of the Bible burned. Five years earlier, the Council of Toulouse had forbidden non-clergy to own a Bible, especially translated into the common languages. Those in charge were convinced that only the ecclesiastic leadership could understand the depths of such sacred and mysterious matters.

It is not surprising that Gutenberg decided the first major book he would print on his new press was the Bible. I don't know if the Roman Church disfavored this invention, but it quickly became a tool for those subversive to church traditions. Latin had been the chosen language for a unified church, and the printing press allowed Bible translations in the vernacular languages to multiply and spread. The printing press made it easier to obtain books, which made it easier for people to learn to read. Those who were literate could read the Bible to those who were illiterate. The flood of Bibles and other books could not be stopped by the church or the secular governments. The printing press slowly but powerfully unclenched the fist of power that had long clamped tight around the uneducated and ignorant multitudes. The people could finally judge church teachings against what the Bible actually said.

But even if we, or an angel from heaven, preach any other gospel to you than what we have preached to you, let him be accursed.

Galatians 1:8

CHAPTER 37

ST. PETER'S BASILICA

Ralph Waldo Emerson described St. Peter's Basilica in Rome as "an ornament of the earth…the sublime of the beautiful." I have walked through its glorious halls and gazed on the opulence that shines from every wall. I've stood mesmerized by its splendid sculptures. The eye cannot find a flaw, nor does the mind comprehend how the mortal hand of Michelangelo could chisel his masterful Pieta from a cold block of marble. The dead Jesus Christ held in the arms of his mother reflects a precious, touching moment. Lining the walls are the many stone-faced crypts that contain the remains of those who once held the papacy.

Many pilgrims walk about the cavernous basilica and snap pictures with their cameras, mumbling to themselves at its sheer magnificence. The Vatican is the largest and best-known religious site in the world, and a multitude of tourists feel they have made a sacred pilgrimage that began as a holy quest.

Emperor Constantine ordered the building of the original St. Peter's Basilica in Rome over the site of the Circus of Nero, and it was consecrated 30 years later in A.D. 360. For the next eleven centuries it stood, drawing countless pilgrims from across Christendom. In the early 1500s, Pope Julius II took charge of rebuilding the Basilica in even greater extravagance, and he began the process or replacing the old with the new. His successor Leo X readily continued the work on St. Peter's. Leo was known for his love of art and of all things fine and beautiful. He was also known for his ability to spend a lot of money very quickly.

On March 15, 1517, Leo X announced a special sale of indulgences, which would fund the immense building project. The pope announced that those who contributed could receive indulgences and thus earn time out of the fires of purgatory. In Germany, a Dominican named Johann Tetzel declared that these indulgences could cover purgatory time for sins that hadn't even been committed yet. Donors joyfully donated money for themselves as well as for their dearly departed. As soon as the coin hit the cup, the donors believed it had earned them complete absolution; they could fly to heaven on the wings of their indulgences. As a result of all that money flowing in, a magnificent church was built.

Of course, when Martin Luther encountered Johann Tetzel, he was outraged by these claims. Having been freed from his guilt and shame by faith in Christ, he could not bear the lie that Tetzel was perpetuating. It motivated Luther to write up his 95 Theses, the 27th of which declares:

> 27. They preach only human doctrines who say that as soon as the money clinks into the money chest, the soul flies out of purgatory.

Martin Luther's action set a flame to the Reformation, but it did not end plans to build the basilica. The massive dome of the new St. Peter's was finished by Pope Sixtus V. He had Caligula's Obelisk moved inch by tedious inch to St. Peter's Square with mules and hundreds of laborers, where it was erected it in its current resting place in the middle of the massive piazza.

The Naves in the Nave

St. Peter's Basilica is a magnificent structure, one which pilgrims can visit over and over and always notice something new. The entire church is a work of art. Yet, the popes who commissioned the beauty of its interior were not always pure in their own hearts.

Alexander VI (1492-1503) loved beautiful things, and he had Michelangelo draw up designs for the new St. Peter's Basilica.

Alexander also openly acknowledged that he had children by a variety of mistresses, and he is notorious for his political intrigue.

Pope Julius II (1503-1513) was the pope who ordered the new basilica be built, and the cornerstone for St. Peter's was set on April 18, 1506. Yet, this "warrior pope" had several mistresses, and his illegitimate daughter Felice della Rovere became one of the most powerful women of the Renaissance.

The 19th century historian Hesnaut lists cardinals who had contracted syphilis in the early 16th century, and he includes in his list Alexander VI's son Cesare Borgia and Julius II. Julius II is warmly credited as the *first* pope to contract syphilis, called the "French disease" because its appearance in Italy coincided with the French invasion of Naples in February 1495.[1] Hesnaut gives an anecdote about Julius II that has since been widely told (usually without citation):

> [L]e cardinal Julien de la Rovère, le futur Jules II, insigne débauché ... qui, devenu pape, ne quittera pas sa chaussure le vendredi saint, pour l'adoration de la croix, parce que son pied était rongé par le mal français;[2]

That is, "The future Julius II, a prominent debauchee who, after becoming pope, would not remove his shoe on Good Friday, for the adoration of the cross, because his foot was ravaged by the French disease."

It was Julius II who also commissioned Michelangelo to paint the ceiling of the Sistine Chapel. We have this strange counterbalance — popes who commissioned gorgeous buildings and amazing works of art by geniuses, yet their personal lives were filled with fornication and decadence.

Pope Leo X (1513-1521) continued the work of building the basilica. He frittered away the Vatican's money on opulent living, then sold indulgences to poor, desperate Europeans to pay for the incredibly beautiful structure. It was those indulgences that sparked Martin Luther to produce his 95 Theses.

---

[1] Peter Elmer, ed., *The Healing Arts: Health, Disease and Society in Europe 1500-1800* (Manchester University Press, 2004), 23.
[2] Louis Thuasne ("Hesnaut"), *Le Mal Français à l'Epoque de l'Expédition de Charles VIII en Italie : d'Après les Documents Originaux* (Paris:C. Marpon et E. Flammarion, 1886), 50.

The Catholic Church has not always been run by immoral men. Many of the popes were good men handed an exceptionally difficult job. In recent years, the Roman Catholic Church has become an institution of great humanitarian benevolence. It has provided and maintained hospitals and orphanages in areas once dominated by desert and wilderness. Roman Catholics have fought slavery when men were being sold like stockyard animals. They've helped the poverty-stricken and the destitute, and have brought spiritual comfort to millions upon millions.

When we consider the unborn, few have worked harder to advocate for their protection than the popes of the past four decades, setting a virtuous example for a secular world. I have personally witnessed Catholic aid-workers in the most impoverished lands of the world doing selfless work that eases pain. It has often humbled me to tears watching these dear souls tend to God's most needy.

Yet, we find in our religious history that the most beautiful sepulchers are filled with dead men's bones. St. Peter's Basilica is gorgeous and awe-inspiring, but the men who had it built were debauched and worldly. Thus, the building of St. Peter's cracked open rifts that had long fractured between those who sought to return to full dependence on the Bible as God's Word and those who clung to questionable church traditions. The original purpose of the Reformation was not to divide the church, but to cleanse and repair the errors that had crept into it. The Catholics regarded the Protestants as heretics who brought disunity and split the holy Church of God. The Protestants regarded the Catholic leaders as corrupt shepherds who deceived and abused the flock.

Chapter 38

John Colet and Erasmus of Rotterdam

John Colet (1467-1519) was an Oxford professor and Dean of St. Paul's Cathedral in London who started reading the Bible to his congregation as translated by himself from the Greek. The people were so hungry for the Word of God in their own language that they packed the massive Saint Paul's Cathedral to hear Colet preach. The bold voice of Colet sent forth what God said in His Word in clear English. The people loved it.

According to more than one council, Colet should have been dragged out of the pulpit for reading the Bible in any other language than Latin. He avoided being roasted at the stake for a fortuitous reason, however: his father was Sir Henry Colet, the Lord Mayor of London from 1486 to 1495.

Like many others who had gone before him, Colet began to openly censure the official church for its pattern of behaving like a money-making machine. It angered him that hungry peasants were pressured to give so much of their money to the Church of Rome when they were living in deep poverty. In 1502, a procurer-general of the parliament estimated that 75% of all the money in France was owned by those in the Church of Rome's hierarchy. Twenty-five years later, the Diet of Nuremburg estimated that 50% of the wealth of Germany belonged to the Catholic Church. The church profited greatly from the sale of indulgences, and Colet regarded this as pure robbery of Christ's flock.

Colet's firebrand sermons masterfully opposed traditional church teachings. The famous scholar Erasmus of Rotterdam came to England to hear Colet in 1499. Erasmus praised the preacher, later saying, "When I listen to my friend Colet I seem to be listening to Plato himself."

ERASMUS

It was the Golden Age of English Humanism and it was Colet who apparently inspired Erasmus to update the Latin Vulgate and to create a standard Greek text. The two men are said to have been the first to use the original Greek in order to discover what God really said in the Bible. They chose not to rely on the Latin translation which had many errors. The Vulgate had been in continual use for well over a thousand years, but it needed to be cleaned up. Erasmus put his new Latin translation on one half of a page while the Greek original was placed in a column on the other half — the original parallel Bible.

Figure 39: "Desiderius Erasmus" by Hans Holbein the Younger (1523), Kunstmuseum Basel.

Erasmus had a meticulous nature, but he worked at such a brisk pace in his translations that he did not catch certain mistakes before he sent them off to the printers. The entire New Testament was published in 1516 after less than six months of work. Erasmus embarrassingly admitted his work was not perfect and later editions were precipitously edited. Despite errors, his Greek New Testament was soon a best-seller. Five editions were published in 1516, 1519, 1522, 1527, and 1535, the year before Erasmus' death. Starting in the second edition, the text was called the *Novum Testamentum* — the New Testament.

Erasmus was an insomniac with particular ways and fastidious idiosyncrasies. He possessed a brilliant mind, and in spite of some earlier mistakes, many incontrovertible discoveries from The Greek translation of Erasmus would come to unlock the mighty, closed doors which had been bolted-shut and locked since the fourth century.

Erasmus never lost his adoration for the Mass, and he wanted to avoid the unpleasantness of conflict in that area. He wanted the church to reform, but he had no desire to split the church into pieces. Erasmus regarded himself as a faithful Roman Catholic, but he recognized that the official church of Christ had picked up some bad habits over the centuries. In 1511, Erasmus wrote his satirical essay, *The Praise and Folly*, which used sardonic wit to criticize the superstitions of the day and the superstitions present in Roman Catholic doctrine. In the essay, he openly mocked the clergy for their "cheat of pardons and indulgences" and expressed his belief that all the curative shrines and proclaimed miracles were nothing more than superstitious absurdities. He stated in his essay that they served, "as a profitable trade and [to] procure a comfortable income to such priests and friars as by this craft get their gain."

The friends of Erasmus were concerned that publishing this irreverent document would lead to his harm, and they warned him against making it public. However, to the surprise of Erasmus himself, it was a hug hit in Renaissance Europe. Even Pope Leo X was said to find it amusing. The pope might have read the sharp words of Erasmus with less humor if he could have seen the brutal swells of the Reformation rising on him from the horizon. While written as a satire with multiple levels of meaning, *The Praise of Folly* contributed to the growing impatience with Rome's ongoing abuses and was therefore one of the spurs to the Reformation.

The intellectual Erasmus was a man which had kings and nobles, scholars and priests longing to converse with him. He was considered to be the greatest Greek scholar in all of Europe. In a few short years, Martin Luther would have a change of heart and mind about the official church teachings, and the world would pivot on a new ecclesiastical axis.

Chapter 39

Martin Luther

It was late at night when I arrived in the old town of Erfurt, Germany with my research team. Snow was spitting down on snow that had already piled high. The cutting wind hurt my lungs just to breathe. The dark church looked cold and empty.

The monastery buildings around us dated from 1276-1340, and the monastery church had long been abandoned. On February 25, 1945, hissing British bombs rained from the sky and destroyed much of the city and monastery. Huddled in shaking terror beneath the library's cellars, 267 people were killed. Reconstruction work began again in 1946 and the new monastery was completed in 1957.

This was the monastery where Martin Luther spent so many years as a hermit monk. We walked to the church's front doors and gave a shove. A gusting wind at our backs aided us in pushing open the heavy doors. They creaked shut behind us as we made our way into a darkened chamber lit by a few struggling candles. The place exuded a medieval church ambiance that seemed to echo the chanting hymns of past monks.

Luther's childhood had not been particularly kind or gentle. His father thought that children were wicked, and Martin would later write about being lashed both at school and at home. His mother was pious and prayed often, but Luther would later say that she once caught him stealing a nut and whipped him until he bled.

As a young man, Luther studied dutifully and piously as a Roman Catholic monk. He ardently obeyed the authorities in Rome, and he lived an austere and severe life of his own free will. Throughout his full day of disciplined religious exercises, of reading and meditations, Luther did his best to be holy. Yet, he still felt his own dirt. He lived in mounting fear and anger toward a vengeful God and was often overcome by a tumbling cascade of depression. His confessions were so extreme, so ridiculously tedious about the smallest of infractions, his superior famously told him, "Look here, Brother Martin. If you're going to confess so much, why don't you go do something worth confessing? Kill your mother or father! Commit adultery! Stop coming in here with such flummery and fake sins!"[1]

In 1510, Luther climbed the Scala Sancta in Rome on his knees, repeating the Our Father on each step, an act which was said to have the power to redeem one from purgatory. When he reached the top of the 27 marble steps, however, he wondered if that was true. He did all he knew to do, but he remained in constant guilt.

Then, one day a fellow priest showed him a line in Habakkuk 2:4: *"but the just shall live by his faith."* That simple verse changed Martin Luther's life. In time, he would find that tormenting himself was unnecessary for salvation. Martin Luther would come to say:

Figure 40: Posthumous Portrait of Martin Luther as an Augustine Monk, from the workshop of Lucas Cranach the Elder (after 1546), Germanisches Nationalmuseum.

> I greatly longed to understand Paul's Epistle to the Romans and nothing stood in the way but that one expression, "the justice whereby God is just and deals justly in punishing the unjust." …Night and day I pondered until I saw the connection between the justice of God and the statement that "the just shall live by his faith." Then I grasped that the justice of God is that righteousness by which through grace and sheer mercy God justifies us through faith. Thereupon I felt myself to be reborn and

---

1 As quoted in Reeves, M. and Chester, T. (2016). *Why the Reformation Still Matters*. Crossway.

to have gone through open doors into paradise. The whole of Scripture took on a new meaning, and whereas before the "justice of God" had filled me with hate, now it became to me inexpressibly sweet in greater love.[2]

There was no need for more liturgies, more wafers in one's mouth, more cups of wine, more worship of church hierarchies and traditions made by dead men long before him. He had commissioned his soul to absolute obedience of the pope and the church for his hope of salvation. But the words in Habakkuk and Ephesians opened the very gates of paradise, and he learned that heaven was just a prayer away.

Luther had many faults, but he also had a dazzling intellect that astonished his peers. Luther was often an irrational mess, and his hyper intensity about everything he did comes through in his search for God's holiness. After he learned that "the just shall live by faith" however, we find in him an inner strength that proved stalwart when other men might have crumbled. Luther had discovered the loving God who had been so elusive to him, and he refused to bow before opposition.

Remember, like John Wycliffe and John Huss and John Colet and Erasmus, Martin Luther was a faithful Roman Catholic. These men all sought to serve God faithfully and heeded Solomon's words in Proverbs 4:7 to "get wisdom…get understanding." They were educated, intelligent men who saw problems that were being perpetuated by the leadership in Rome, and they sought to address real issues within the church.

Luther's own journey was one that took many years. In 1510 a dispute arose in the Augustinian order. Pope Julius II requested that two representatives travel to Rome to help settle the matter, and Martin Luther was one of those monks. It is said that when Luther crested the hill and saw Rome for the first time, he dropped to his knees and cried out, "O hail to thee, O holy Rome." The religious ecstasy of Martin Luther soon vaporized, however, when he found priests there who were indolent, lazy and seemingly deficient in spiritual sincerity. Their lack of

---

[2] As quoted in Bainton, R.H. (1978). *Here I Stand: A Life of Martin Luther.* Nashville: Abingdon Press, 49-50.

reverence, along with the many stories of sexual immorality, stunned the pious man from Northern Germany.

Soon after his return to Erfurt, Luther was transferred to Wittenburg, a small but prosperous town of about 2,500. The good waterways from the Elbe River allowed trade and ease of travel, and the ruler "Frederick the Wise" wanted Wittenburg to be the jewel of a university town. He brought in learned and competent educators, and Luther was called to be one of them. Frederick also wanted Wittenburg to be the Rome of Germany, and he placed many sacred relics inside the castle church. There were four hairs from Mary, seven from her veil which was splattered with the blood of Christ, three pieces of her cloak, and four from her girdle. There was said to be a thorn from the crown of Christ that had pierced his brow at the crucifixion, a scrap from his swaddling clothes, pieces of his crib, a strand of straw, a piece of gold and myrrh brought to him by the Magi, a hair of the Savior's beard, a crucifixion nail, a morsel of bread from the Last Supper, and a stone that was under Christ's feet when he ascended into heaven.

If these relic acquisitions were not sufficient, by 1520 the collection had swelled to include 19,013 sacred bones. On a certain designated day of the year, a person who gazed upon these relics and paid the right sum to the church would receive from the pope a whopping one million years from their time in purgatory. Since not even the pope knew the total time anyone spent in purgatory, it seemed an attractive offer for all who had the means to participate.

Chapter 40

Luther and the Pope

The popes in the 15th and 16th centuries lived in as much luxury as any Roman emperor. Revenue streams became rivers that overflowed with land acquisitions and wealth. Cardinals and even popes engaged in simony, the buying and selling of ecclesiastical offices and privileges. Wealthy fathers could buy their younger sons positions as archbishops, cardinals and bishops, ensuring they had plenty of wealth and power without dividing up too much of the family property. Once young men received their appointment, half of their first year's income went to Rome, followed by a tenth of their yearly income each year thereafter. When they died, all of their wealth went to Rome. Pope Leo X sold about 2,150 offices, which generated quite a bit of cash; it cost 30,000 ducats to buy the position of a cardinal.

Leo X came from the wealth and privilege of the Medici family as the son of "Lorenzo the Magnificent." He was made a cardinal at the young age of 13. As soon as the cardinals voted him as pope on March 11, 1513, Leo started spending money as if it were drawn from an endless well. The young Pope Leo X entered the pontificate with a great deal of money at his disposal, but he notably lived his life consumed with pleasures of art, hunting, and every manner of entertainment. He felt he could live a long life by avoiding any annoyances. He hired 683 courtiers to serve him personally and to care for the papal palace.

On March 12, 1514 Pope Leo X stood on a podium to receive the salutes of those making a parade march to the Castel San Angelo. The parade had a panther and two leopards along with an elephant supporting a silver castle on its back. The elephant made a great show by spraying the crowds with water from a bucket. On November 30, 1515, when Leo X entered his hometown Florence for the first time as pope, an even bigger extravaganza awaited him. A full 2,000 people had been hired to prepare for the event.[1] Pope Leo liked bullfights and feasts, extravagant parties, and hunts that lasted for weeks at a time.

This obvious display of wealth and opulence stood in tremendous contrast to another man who had entered Jerusalem fifteen hundred years prior. This other man rode an ass into the holy city with only the meager clothes on his back. The eager crowd reached out to him as well; not for any expected gold coins, but for a simple touch.

Despite Leo's vast income, it didn't take long for him to spend it all. The Vatican was forced to sell tapestries and furniture. It was when Pope Leo X found himself way over his head in debt that he decided to announce the special sale of indulgences that so infuriated Martin Luther.

Johann Tetzel was one man assigned by Pope Leo X to go out amongst the people and sell escape vouchers from purgatory. The Dominican friar was the greatest marketer of them all. He would travel from one town to the next with a big brass-hinged chest and a bag full of receipts to give out to people who gave him money. He carried a large cross that was draped with an official papal banner. As Tetzel entered a town, church bells would ring to alert the populace. The gathering crowd was met with flamboyant jugglers, candles, waving flags, and even relics of the saints. Tetzel would locate himself in the local church and open his bag, where he would call out:

> I have here the passports...to lead the human soul into Paradise. Inasmuch as for a single one of the mortal sins, several of which are committed every day after confession, seven years of expiation either on earth or in Purgatory are imposed — who, for the sake of a quarter of a florin would hesitate to secure one of these

---

[1] Robin S. Doak, *Pope Leo X: Opponent of the Reformation* (Minneapolis: Compass Point Books, 2006), 50.

letters which will admit your divine, immortal soul to the celestial joys of Paradise?"[2]

We can almost hear him hawking, "Passports! Come get your passports to heaven! Right here. Right here! Get your passports to heaven here!"

The people believed in purgatory as we believe in air. Tetzel easily surpassed his quota in Germany. He was offering a deal too good to pass-up. He said that his indulgences from Pope Leo X were so powerful, that if a youth had sexual intercourse with his own *mother*, that young man could put coins in the pontiff's bowl and receive immediate forgiveness. He made famous the saying, "As soon as the coin in the coffer rings, the soul from out the fire springs."[3] Forget genuine repentance or sorrow for sin.

The money poured in!

Tetzel made the biggest mistake of his (less-than-stellar) life when he chose to formally denounce Luther. It was one of the greater miscalculations in history. Soon Luther's thunder of discontent rumbled across all Europe. Luther had been freed from years of desperation and had come to know the love and forgiveness of God through Jesus Christ! He would not sit by while this evil extortion went on in Christ's name. All Germany heard of this ecclesiastical robbery of the people and cut-rate deals for the soul.

Yet, Luther initially kept his temper. The 95 Theses that Martin Luther nailed to the Wittenberg Castle Church door were intended to be matters of questions for debate, issues to discuss as intelligent men in a public forum. That was Luther's intention. He had little clue that those 95 discussion points would blast like an incendiary theological bomb on all of Europe.

Luther knew large crowds congregated at the Castle Church to see the relics on display, and that All Saint's Day — November 1st — was a particularly big day. Therefore, he chose to post his theses on October 31, 1517, with the title "Disputation for the Power of Indulgences." He sent a copy directly to Archbishop Albrecht, the very sponsor of Tetzel's money-raising crusade.

---
[2] As quoted in Eric R. Chamberlin, *The Bad Popes* (1969; reprint, New York, Barnes & Noble Books, 1993) 241.
[3] *Ibid.*

Tradition

The original paper on the church door was written in official Latin, but clever Luther also used a local printing press to make copies in German, and these were disseminated to church members.

The differences between penance and repentance had become very clear to Martin Luther, and his 95 Theses began with the following:

1. When our Lord and Master Jesus Christ said, "Repent" (Matthew 4:17), he willed the entire life of believers to be one of repentance.
2. This word cannot be understood as referring to the sacrament of penance, that is, confession and satisfaction, as administered by the clergy.

Figure 41: Luther's Ninety-Five Theses in Latin.

The 95 Theses were a salvo against a faulty church practice, but the words were tame in many aspects. Luther still believed that the pope held the keys of Peter. He assumed that he could promote a just cause to cleanse the greed and laziness and general corruption that had plagued the church. Instead, his action broke the dam of medieval discipline, and the tinder and dry wood that had been piled up by Wycliffe and Hus and Erasmus caught a spark that set it ablaze. The fire took a few years to build into a full roar, but it started that All Hallow's Eve in Wittenberg.

Chapter 41

The Popular Response

Pope Leo X at first regarded Luther as a troublesome, insignificant friar. The movement behind him shocked all of Europe with its ferocious pace and power. The common people began to see indulgences as a huckster scheme to raise money, one that had no power to free people from hell's shadow. All those in the ecclesiastic chain were thrown out of balance with the sudden rebellion. No one had seen anything like it before. The high clergy had been living on milk and honey while the people scraped by, and the collection of funds had been based on lies. The people rose up in anger. The pope called Luther a "wild boar loose in the vineyard," and he could not stop the movement that Luther had kicked off. On April 24, 1518, Luther was relieved of his duties as district vicar and, for all intents and purposes, the official Reformation began.

Europe fell into two camps. There were those who believed that the official Roman Catholic Church, with its history of papal bulls and council decrees, stood above the scrutiny of lesser men. These, especially those who benefitted from the decrees, insisted the church had no need to change. The other camp saw this as an opportunity to remove the shackles of religious tyranny. Many Germans voted with their feet and aligned with Luther in great crowds. Those in the Roman Church were forbidden to speak to Martin Luther, to listen to a word said by him, or to even look at him. Therefore, all who raced to join him were aligning themselves against the highest echelons of institutionalized Christendom.

All kings, noble, and princes were to consider Luther a fugitive of the law, and they had a moral duty to evict him from their lands or deliver him to Rome. However, the kings of Europe had long lived in a power struggle with the Vatican, and the rebellion against a corrupt papacy extended easily to the leaders of nations.

Luther's own position grew in its passion. As the Roman Catholic leadership opposed him and refused reasonably honest self-judgment, Luther started promoting a full rejection of the papacy. Loyal students of Luther showed their support of him by making a bonfire with books taken from library shelves. They cheered wildly one night as Luther stood in front of the dancing flames, a papal bull in his hand. Luther tossed the bull into the fire and declared in a loud voice, "Because you have corrupted God's truth, may God destroy you in this fire."

Discontent had long remained hidden in the inner sanctum of each man's hovel. Now, peasants from the field and merchants from the market were up-in-arms against the papacy. On June 11, 1518, Luther wrote, *"I have cast the die,"* and with that, the stage was set for one of the greatest stand-offs in all history.

Worms (pronounced "vorms") in Germany is a picturesque city on the west bank of the Rhine River. A monument erected in 1868 was placed in the park that was once the site of the town moat. Martin Luther stands at the center of the monument, flanked on either side by Frederick the Wise of Saxony and Philip of Hesse, the two powerful princes who were instrumental in the success of the Reformation. Behind Luther stand two Protestant scholars named Johannes Reuchlin and Philip Melanchthon, and seated at Luther's feet are Peter Waldo, John Wycliffe, Jan Hus and Girolamo Savonarola — all men who shaped the Reformation movement in different, yet intertwined ways. There is also a seated woman on the monument. She represents the first German cities to adopt Protestantism.

Close to the monument is the site where Martin Luther stood resolute in a great hall. Dressed in a simple, plain robe, he faced his stern accusers in what history calls Luther's trial — the "Diet of Worms."

THE DIET OF WORMS

The audience was packed with notables and clergy, as well as the upper-crust of society. These were dressed in richly-embroidered vestments, furred short jackets, sleeves and colorful britches with jeweled chains around their necks and drooping feathered caps on their heads. On the far right, Holy Roman Emperor Charles V held a scepter in his hand. Altogether, there were twenty-four dukes, six electors, eight margraves, thirty abbots and archbishops, seven ambassadors and many other members of the clergy, nobility, and royalty. They all crammed into the meeting hall to see what would happen to this German monk who dared question Rome.

Luther wore no hat, only his trademark tonsured, shaved head. His inquisitor, Johann von der Ecken, motioned towards a pile of books and documents. According to records of that day, von der Ecken asked if they were written by Luther. Those present had to lean in to hear Martin's calm, quiet answer.

"The books are all mine and I have written more," Luther stated.

Figure 42: Luther at the 1521 Diet of Worms in a woodcut (1556).

Von der Ecken bristled and pressed, "Do you defend them all or do you reject them in part?"

Luther, now reflective in his answer, said, "This touches God and his Word. This affects the salvation of souls. Of this Christ said, 'He who denies me before men, him will I deny before my Father.' To say too little or too much would be dangerous. I beg you, give me time to think it over."

Luther was granted a recess to construct an answer.

On the 18th of April 1521, at 6:00 p.m. the crowd had so swelled in size that a larger hall had to be selected. Luther appeared somewhat different this evening; a more resolute expression accompanied him into the proceedings. All through the night at his humble accommodations, Luther had received messages urging him to stand firm. That was easy for others to implore; their skin was not as close as Luther's to the flames — flames that had eaten the body of Jan Hus just a century earlier.

Van der Ecken asked Luther, "Do you wish to defend the books which are recognized as your work? Or to retract anything contained in them?"

Luther answered, "Your Imperial Majesty and Your Lordships: I ask you to observe that my books are not all of the same kind." He then went on to explain that some of his books were simply harmless Bible studies. Some were criticisms of the wicked abuses perpetrated by the papacy, and some were writings against private persons. In regard to his descriptions of papal errors, Luther testified:

> No one can either deny or conceal this, for universal experience and world-wide grievances are witnesses to the fact that through the Pope's laws and through man-made teachings the consciences of the faithful have been most pitifully ensnared, troubled, and racked in torment, and also that their goods and possessions have been devoured...If then I recant these, the only effect will be to add strength to such tyranny, to open not the windows but the main doors to such blasphemy, which

will thereupon stalk farther and more widely than it has hitherto dared...[1]

Luther concluded his statement by suggesting that if the things he had written could be shown faulty according to the Prophets or Gospels, he would be glad to throw his books in the fire.

Van der Ecken was not pleased by Luther's explanation and told him to stick to the point. With the full force of Rome behind his voice, the prosecutor asked whether Luther was prepared to recant or not! Luther answered for the benefit of all those in the room:

> Your Imperial Majesty and Your Lordships demand a simple answer. Here it is, plain and unvarnished. Unless I am convicted of error by the testimony of Scriptures (since I put no trust in the unsupported authority of Pope or of councils, since it is plain that they have often erred and often contradicted themselves) by manifest reasoning I stand convicted by the Scriptures to which I have appealed, and my conscience is taken captive by God's word, I cannot and will not recant anything, for to act against our conscience is neither safe for us, nor open to us. Here I stand I cannot do otherwise. God help me, Amen. [2]

Martin Luther stood there in that hall in Worms, the shadows of the valley of death falling grim and dark on his head. Remarkably, he lived through that night. Perhaps the church leaders realized that martyring this man would only incite the angry masses that stood behind him.

Martin Luther lived a long life. Within a few years, he married his beloved wife Katie and they produced a house filled with children. He translated the Bible into the German language and brought about the most effective and enduring elements of the Reformation.

---

[1] Henry Bettenson, Chris Maunder, eds., *Documents of the Christian Church, Fourth Ed.* (Oxford University Press, 2011), 213.
[2] *Ibid*, 214.

The God of Martin Luther was a God that spits lightning and peals thunderclaps from heaven. He was the God who moves mountains with a rumbling, tectonic force from the very bowels of the earth. He was an all-consuming deity of wrath, as well as a God of incalculable love, mercy and grace. In God, an infant born to a virgin among the hay and animals would heal the sick, feed the poor and with the wave of his hand, calm a writhing sea. Even in the hour of his savage death, Jesus remained all that is love, all that forgives and all that is holy. This was a Christ Jesus that too many bishops and cardinals had ceased to know.

Luther came to see the Lord as the only key to the gates of paradise. He took it upon himself to search the Scriptures, and he dared the angels to show him that there was any *other* way to attain salvation.

Chapter 42

Final Thoughts

I have stayed mostly within the bounds of the early church until the Reformation as I have written this book. However, it is obvious that traditions are found everywhere. They guide the thoughts and actions of those in many churches and religious constructs.

Traditions come naturally to us humans. It is easy for us to accept as self-evident those things we were taught by our parents and the people of our community. What's more, most traditions are not good or bad in themselves. All cultures have traditions that define the lives of the people that live within them. They help the people know how to live and abide in peace with those around them, and many traditions bring with them the comfort of familiarity, home and family.

There are traditions that the Bible itself started. The celebration of the Passover and other Jewish feasts were important for the Jews in maintaining their identity as the people of the Most High God. However, the Bible also makes it clear that man-made traditions should never be used to nullify the Word of God.

During the time of Christ, the High Priest of Judaism ruled over an esteemed body of men called the Sanhedrin. The Roman government gave these men, with some restrictions, supreme authority as a judicial body over the Jews. The men of the Sanhedrin were not completely unified in their views of the world. Just like any human body, there was division among them on how to interpret the Jewish law. Aristocratic leaders of the Sadducees refused to go beyond the written Torah. They had some issues, because they did not believe in angels or the resurrection of the dead, both of which are found in the Prophets of the Hebrew Scriptures. On the other hand, the Pharisees believed that Moses had passed down the Law on Mount Sinai in two ways. The first was the written Torah, and the second was the oral "unwritten" Torah. They combined these two together as the complete Torah.

Most Jews submitted to this blending of oral tradition with the written word without question. Jesus, however, was the exception. He stood like a wall against the co-mingling of Moses' written Law with man-made traditions.

Jesus had a confrontation with a group of scribes and Pharisees when they questioned Him about his followers. The disciples of Jesus were, of all things, eating with unwashed hands, which transgressed the rabbinic tradition. Eating with unwashed hands was not prohibited in the written Law of Moses, but the Pharisees treated their rabbinic rules as equal to Moses. What is particularly interesting here is washing hands is not a harmful regulation. It's a good thing to do. However, the Pharisees treated it as a legal requirement, and they demanded an answer from Jesus about why He allowed his disciples to ignore it.

Normally, the people would quickly conform to the Pharisees' rules, but Jesus did the opposite. When they confronted Him, He called the men "hypocrites" — because they knew full well that the Bible says absolutely nothing against eating without washing hands. The argument by the Pharisees was based on purely man-made rules — not on what God had said. Jesus criticized them for this, even though washing one's hands before eating is a good practice.

The Lord's primary issue was that the Pharisees habitually abided by these rabbinic regulations while ignoring the Word of God. They put their own decrees ahead of the words that God Himself had given Moses and the prophets.

The Primitive Baptists only sing in their congregations and don't play any kind of musical instrument. They teach their children to sing and read music, and the entire church is the choir of a Primitive Baptist church. It's beautiful to listen to a large congregation singing acapella with great skill. The precious Primitive Baptists are free to sing in the pure simplicity of human voices, according to the tradition of their congregation. However, these sorts of preferences should never be used to divide the Body of Christ. Church members should not divide in anger over the style of music played in worship.

Churches today can split apart at the seams over traditions that are as innocuous as changing the color of a church bulletin. That seems like an extreme example, but we see it. I have heard of Mennonite meetings called to decide whether the men would be allowed to wear belts instead of suspenders. It is absolutely ridiculous that man-made traditions established just a few lifetimes ago can be defended with as much passion as if they had been practiced by the twelve Apostles.

It seems oftentimes that traditions are set up as the idols of the church. Church members protect their traditions with more zeal than they protect their families. They dishonor the name of Jesus by casting love and mercy aside in the name of protecting some silly idea that great grandfather Morris dreamed up before the last world war.

Jesus accused the Pharisees in Mark 7:13 of *"making the word of God of no effect"* through their traditions. Jesus told them flat-out that they were making the very words of God null and void by stamping their manufactured traditions over the Scriptures, as if they were one in the same.

Our traditions must never be the cornerstone of our church constructs. God tells of a different cornerstone, the cornerstone of absolute truth. Where do we find it? In Jesus Christ. Our faith isn't built on good ideas. In Ephesians 2:20, Paul tells us we are members of the household of God, *"built on the foundation of the apostles and prophets, Jesus Christ Himself being the chief cornerstone."*

There will be no church doctrines, no liturgies or catechisms to save us when we are standing before the Throne of God. When we look to the left, there will be no pope, and when we look to our right there will be no preacher or evangelist. We will all stand there, mute, before the Most High God. The only Word we need, the only Person we can depend on is the One who died in our place and whose sacrifice paid for our punishment and cleanses us. When we stand before the Judge of all the earth, we want Jesus to claim us, and the angels to say, "He's written here!" or "She's written here!" We want to be found in the Lamb's Book of Life.

It all goes back to the Great Commandment. A lawyer, trying to trip up Jesus, asked Him what was the greatest of the commandments. Jesus didn't even hesitate. He said, *"You shall love the LORD your God with all your heart, with all your soul, and with all your mind."* [1]

How do we love Jesus? In John 14:23 Jesus tells us, *"If a man love me, he will keep my words: and my Father will love him, and we will come unto him, and make our abode with him."*

So, it is that many churches stumble along the path of intended righteousness, seeking to accomplish the will of God. We want God to make our paths straight, and we want to avoid those tangles and snares that can trip us up. We find we walk the straightest when we maneuver past all the idols of tradition, past the empty ceremonies, and focus directly on Christ. He speaks to us from his written Word. When we are born again in Him and walk in His Spirit, He will bear great fruit in us.

> *And now, little children, abide in him; that, when he shall appear, we may have confidence, and not be ashamed before him at his coming. If ye know that he is righteous, ye know that every one that doeth righteousness is born of him.*
>
> 1 John 2:29

> *Little children, keep yourselves from idols. Amen.*
>
> 1 John 5:21

---

[1] Matthew 22:37

ABOUT THE AUTHOR

BOB CORNUKE

A former police investigator and SWAT team member, Bob Cornuke is a Biblical investigator, international explorer, and author of nine books. He has participated in over sixty expeditions around the world searching for lost locations described in the Bible. These journeys include searching for Mount Sinai in Egypt and Saudi Arabia, looking for the remains of Noah's Ark in Turkey with astronaut Jim Irwin (the eighth man to walk on the moon) and researching ancient Assyrian and Babylonian flood accounts in Iran.

He has followed ancient accounts of the Ark of the Covenant from Israel to Egypt and across Ethiopian highlands, and, most recently, his research team found the probable location of Paul's shipwreck off the coast of Malta. This find has resulted in the accounting of what many are saying are all four anchors, as described in Acts 27. His most recent adventure is sparking international controversy. Chronicled in his new book *Temple*, Bob makes the assertion that the Temples of Solomon and Herod are located in the City of David and not on the traditional Temple Mount platform.

Bob has appeared on National Geographic Channel, CBS, NBC's Dateline, Good Morning America, CNN, MSNBC, Fox, ABC, History Channel and Ripley's Believe It or Not. He has authored six books and traveled across Afghanistan during U.S. bombing strikes on a video and photographic assignment. Bob is currently the President of the Bible Archaeology Search and Exploration (BASE) Institute located in Colorado Springs, CO. He also serves as special advisor for the National Council on Bible Curriculum in Public Schools and was invited by the President's staff to conduct a Bible study for White House personnel.

Bob has earned a Masters of Arts in Biblical Studies and a Ph.D. in Bible and Theology from Louisiana Baptist University, but his children believe that his most notable accomplishment, to date, is having his findings featured as a question on a Trivial Pursuit™ card.

While serving as a crime scene investigator assigned to major crime scenes, Bob gained invaluable training and experience in investigative and scientific research techniques. He has now turned his investigative skills toward Bible archaeology, using those skills and ingenuity to unlock the doors to sites that often go against traditional archaeological presuppositions. Bob is currently the host of the weekly Television show Gutsy Christianity on DirectTV on the National Religious Broadcasting Network (NRB).

Originally sought out by astronaut James Irwin (Apollo 15) as a security advisor, Bob was later recruited to join the expedition as they searched for the remains of Noah's Ark in Eastern Turkey.

His assignment was to provide protection for Irwin's team as they operated in the Kurdish-terrorist held region, but, upon completion of the Mount Ararat expedition, Cornuke and Irwin found themselves colleagues and close friends. Bob later became vice president of Irwin's "High Flight" Foundation, an exploration consortium dedicated to the search for lost Biblical locations and artifacts. Several years after Irwin's death, Cornuke founded BASE Institute to expand on the Mission of his mentor and friend. Bob also sits on the Academic Advisory Board for Koinonia Institute.

When not traveling the world, Bob lives in Colorado with his wife and children. From a majestic hillside near Pikes Peak, an expedition landmark for explorers from yesteryear, Bob directs the modern day efforts of the staff and volunteers of the Bible Archaeology, Research & Exploration Institute.